MEN AND PORK CHOPS

A History of the Ontario Pork Producers Marketing Board

by

Wilfred L. Bishop

With a foreword by
George Stuart Atkins

London, Canada:
Phelps Publishing Company
1977

Printed in Canada by
Petrolia Print & Litho Limited.
Petrolia, Ontario.

Typesetting by
The London Free Press Printing Company Limited
London, Ontario.

Binding by
Admiral Bookbinding Company
Point Edward, Ontario.

ISBN No. 0-920298-00-1

CONTENTS

Illustrations appear between pages 90 and 91.

Acknowledgments

Many persons have assisted the author in the writing of this book. Mention of all would be impossible, however, the major contributions of a few must not be overlooked.

Mr. George Stuart Atkins contributed valuable advice and wrote the Foreword.

Mr. R. Jerry Bluhm, Secretary of the Ontario Pork Producers' Marketing Board, provided considerable information, and wrote the Epilogue.

Hon. P. M. Dewan, of Ingersoll, former Minister of Agriculture; the late Paul Fisher of Burlington and the late Clayton Frey of Sarnia assisted with information at the start of this project.

Mr. John H. Lutman, of London, edited the text in consultation with Mr. Edward Phelps, also of London, my publisher.

The Ontario Pork Producers Marketing Board has taken a keen and benevolent interest in this, my own story of their life and labours in the cause of agriculture in Ontario; indeed, their support has made this volume a reality.

My family, who knew the personalities and events of this book at first hand, have also lived through the several drafts of the story over the last few years. For their patience I am grateful.

Wilfred Bishop

R.R. No. 3
Norwich, Ontario.

Foreword

Picture, if you will, an Ontario farmer in 1941 driving his market hogs up a loading ramp onto a truck and watching the truck disappear down the lane. It's all on faith, for sooner or later some money for those hogs will come back in a most unbusinesslike manner and in a way over which he has no control. Three decades later, however, that same farmer or perhaps his son or daughter now has a totally different feeling when the truck pulls out onto the road. Where it's going and how the hogs will be marketed are no longer shrouded in mystery. Now a democratically-controlled marketing board looks after all the details, selling the hogs for the highest possible price. In addition to that, payment will arrive promptly together with every pertinent detail of the transaction as a matter of record. How all that came about makes fascinating reading. Over 80,000,000 hogs were produced and marketed in Ontario during the three decades of history that are recorded in this book.

Although Hog Marketing is the central subject, the text is bound to interest a broad spectrum of readers as the author unfolds his story of the events he is writing about from the 1940's to the 1960's.

A casual observer of the orderly hog market which prevails in Ontario in the 1970's would require a vivid imagination indeed to conjure up such a set of circumstances as actually brought about the current state of tranquility. The stubborn determination of a small group of farmers made it happen. The author of this book was one of them, and thus has a thorough knowledge of the circumstances at every turn in the road. He's a farmer, he tells it like a farmer would, and as you read the story you'll be glad he was there for thirty years, even if only to be the one who would eventually put it all down on paper.

Every success story has its "ups and downs," its "skeletons in the closet," its "good guys and bad guys," its tragedy and humour, and this story is no exception.

One name stands out above all others, that of "Charlie" McInnis, who is responsible, more than any other person, for what is recounted in this book. Seldom does such a person appear among us. For two of the three decades he was both the driving force, and the driver, in this particular series of events. These events have made an inestimable impact on the development of producer-controlled marketing of farm products, not only in Ontario but in other provinces of Canada, and elsewhere. This man became a real folk hero from one end of Ontario to the other, and it's to the author's credit that he has recorded for posterity so much of what he knows of Charles McInnis.

The farm based movement to reorganize the marketing of hogs in Ontario was, of course, province wide and while some might fault the author for giving too much detail of what happened in and around his own county of Oxford, that, after all, is the area he knows best. What went on there is typical of similar activity in other parts of the province. It's first-hand information and I, for one, would rather read first-hand information any day than get it second or third hand. I'm sure you would too.

Looking down the road, there is no doubt in my mind that the subject of this book will be a significant segment in the history of Canadian agriculture. In addition, this particular work will, in its own right, become one of the important references on this period.

You're now about to read an interesting story told in an interesting way. I hope you'll enjoy it as much as I did.

George Stuart Atkins, P. AG.,

Senior Agricultural Commentator
Canadian Broadcasting Corporation.

"The Woodlands"
RR 2, Oakville, Ontario

January 1, 1977.

"I DEDICATE THIS BOOK TO ALL
MEMBERS OF THE ONTARIO PORK PRODUCERS
MARKETING BOARD, AND TO ALL COUNTY
ASSOCIATION OFFICERS, PAST AND PRESENT"

Wilfred Bishop

"CHARLIE" McINNIS

A founder and tireless worker since 1941, of orderly hog marketing in Ontario. Chairman of the first committee, 1941-1943; President of the Ontario Hog Producers Association, 1943-1960; President of the Ontario Hog Producers Co-operative Marketing Agency, 1955-1961; a Director of the Ontario Pork Producers Marketing Board, 1955-1960; President of Farmers Allied Meat Enterprises, 1960-1964.

viii

CHAPTER I

AN IDEA TAKES FORM

Should Ontario hog producers ever select a particular day for a gala commemoration it would certainly be April 21st, 1941. Cold cloudy April days often seem to deny the promise of bright spring sunshine. Such was April 21st in the grim war year of 1941. A few weeks earlier a letter from the Ontario Federation of Agriculture had gone out to county Federations of Agriculture and many Agricultural Representatives suggesting that a meeting be held in each county to plan the sending of delegates to Toronto to consider forming a new producer organization.

That April afternoon it required, not the Crystal Ballroom, but just a small room in Toronto's King Edward Hotel to accommodate the forty or fifty farmers and Government officials who met to consider whether or not Ontario hog producers should have some kind of an organization. Farmers recognized that milk producers for fluid, concentrated and cheese products were all organized. Why shouldn't hog producers be equally served? Government officials insisted that hog producers were too numerous and too scattered across Ontario to make an organization practical or workable. The job just could not be done.

While the issue rested, a white haired veteran of rural movements and politics rose to make his contribution. William Newman of Victoria County had been elected to the Ontario Legislature in 1926 as Liberal-Prohibitionist, later re-elected in 1929 and 1934 as a Liberal, and then in 1937 had lost his seat to Leslie Frost, the future premier. A lifelong participant in farm organizations, Mr. Newman had been appointed to the Farm Products Control Board and was so serving at this time. On this day Mr. Newman's message was clear and emphatic: "Don't think of me as a civil servant, just think of me as Bill Newman of Victoria County. This job of organizing the hog producers can be done and it must be done. Don't leave it to a committee of civil servants. Elect a committee of farmers and place on their shoulders the responsibility".

The atmosphere in that small room changed. It was agreed to elect a committee and to ask them to find an answer to how hog producers might be organized. Subsequently, seven farmers were elected, the Chairman of the day, Charles McInnis of Dundas County, a prominent member of the Board of Ontario Concentrated Milk Producers' League; Charles Milton, a former warden of Oxford and also a director of the Ontario Concentrated Milk Producers' Association; Arthur Wilson of Kent County; a member of the Board of Ontario Whole Milk Producers' League; Russell Templar of Brant County, well known Pure Bred Yorkshire Breeder and President of Ontario Swine Breeders at the time; Wellington Weber, a prominent farmer and Pure Bred Yorkshire Breeder of Waterloo county; Harry Hewitt, Clerk of and a former Reeve of Seneca Township, Haldimand County; and Wilfred Bishop, Oxford County farmer and, at that time, a part time extension lecturer on Co-operatives and Marketing for the Ontario Department of Agriculture. After the adjournment of the general meeting the committee met briefly and, with rural optimism, speculated hopefully that seeding might begin in a few days time and decided on a two day session in June.

The idea of organizing hog producers had not just taken form on April 21st. A few years earlier a short-lived attempt had been made. In 1932 Canada had entered an extensive trade agreement with U.K. in an effort to lessen the stranglehold of the Depression. Included was an opportunity to export substantial amounts of Canadian bacon to Britain. The price to Ontario producers had previously gone as low as $2.50 per cwt., live weight. Recognizing that at this time the quality of Canadian bacon was distinctly below that of Danish, a group of producers approached the Ontario Minister of Agriculture, Col. T. L. Kennedy, requesting help to develop an improvement programme. It was agreed that a producers organization be set up to handle this programme in co-operation with the Department of Agriculture. Mr. W. P. Watson, later Ontario Livestock Commissioner, then a fieldman for the Livestock Branch of the Ontario Department of Agriculture and a specialist in swine extension, was granted leave of absence from the Livestock Branch to head organizational work.

A number of county meetings were held at which producers offered their support. A constitution was set up. Plans were made to finance the association by means of a nominal levy per hog and a board was elected, including D. D. Gagnier of Paincourt, Jack Reid of Ripley, Bert Bradshaw of Stratford, Bert Warnica of Barrie, Walter Galbraith of Renfrew and F. M.

Chapman of Pickering. When Duncan Marshall became Liberal Minister of Agriculture in 1934 these directors called on him requesting moral and financial support. Meeting nothing but a violent tirade, they left discouraged. So ended the organizational efforts of the thirties. Knowledge of this experience certainly contributed to the pessimistic attitude of the majority of the Department of Agriculture personnel participating in the meeting of April 21st, 1941.

Other voices in the thirties were asking and thinking in terms of both organization and some type of marketing plan for hog producers. The April 1st, 1934, issue of the *Weekly Sun,* predecessor of the *Rural Co-operator* and *Farm and Country,* carried considerable material about the New Canada Movement, an active association of farm young people, pressing for a more just and sound economy. Under the heading "Tentative Program" and subheading "Hogs", the *Sun* proposed that the "Main problems of the Hog Industry could be solved through boards such as those visualized by the Marketing Act (Federal). Such Boards would influence prices by controlling Supply and Exports. Such responsible to producers, which involves producer organization".

Thus, the movement toward organization in 1941 didn't come as a sudden flash. There had been much thought and consideration before hand. From pioneer days, dairy by-products had been perhaps the most important source of protein supplements for hogs. Consequently, the majority of milk and cream producers in 1941 were also hog producers and very few hog producers were not milk or cream producers. Both in the Concentrated Milk Producers Association and in the Whole Milk Producers Association the idea was generating, "We are organized and have bargaining rights. Should we as hog producers not have similar rights?" Writing in May, 1940, to Russell Templar, President of Swine Breeders, Charles McInnis, related resolutions passed at the annual meeting of the Canadian Chamber of Agriculture, predecessor of the Canadian Federation of Agriculture, the annual meeting of the Ontario Concentrated Milk Producers Association and the Ontario Federation of Agriculture. These meetings called for an organization to represent hog producers. The letter states: "I am not aware of anyone else making an effort to organize the industy as I had hoped someone would. Do you think we should organize? If so we must decide separately or in conjunction with the growers of beef cattle and form a Livestock Association".

In December of the same year McInnis wrote again, explaining that the German invasion of France, which came so soon after his earlier letter, had resulted in the delaying of the idea. This letter continues, "Developments since have convinced me that we must look after the rights of the forgotten producer regardless of world conditions. The recent decision of the War Times Price Board to place a maximum price on butter, a product of the farm, while our friends in the city are enjoying economic security, as a result of minimum wage laws, proves conclusively that we, as farmers, have to press hard to get our rights".

A month later, Mr. Erle Kitchen, Secretary of the Ontario Concentrated Milk Producers Association, declared his board to be ready to help organize Swine Breeders and that Charles McInnis had been appointed by this board as a representative to this end.

These early moves bore fruit in March, 1941, when a committee representing the Ontario Concentrated Milk Producers, the Ontario Swine Breeders Association, the Ontario Whole Milk Producers League and the Ontario Federation of Agriculture convened in the office of the Ontario Whole Milk Producers League, 409 Huron Street, Toronto. Present at this meeting were Charles McInnis, Iroquois, Ontario Concentrated Milk Producers; Harry Scott, Norwich, President, Ontario Federation of Agriculture; R. A. Templar, Burford, President, Ontario Swine Breeders Association; A. D. Wilson, Chatham, Ontario Whole Milk Producers League; J. C. Weaver, Owen Sound, Ontario Whole Milk Producers League; C. B. Boynton, Gormley, President, Ontario Tamworth Swine Breeders Association; Stan Joss, Belleville, Secretary, Ontario Cheese Producers Association; Charles Milton, Princeton, Ontario Concentrated Milk Producer; and V. S. Milburn, 409 Huron St. Toronto, Secretary, Ontario Federation of Agriculture.

Subject matter discussed at this meeting was prophetic of the future. A committee of small packers, catering only to the domestic market and outside of the Meat Packers' Council, appeared before this informal committee asking farmers to take an interest in their problems. They feared lest they, as small processors, would be discriminated against in the application of various government programs. The main subjects discussed were:

1) Improved prices.
2) An intelligent educational program to familiarize farmers with quality and type required for the British and home markets.
3) Marketing conditions.
4) Rail grading.
5) Competitive markets.

The most important action of the day was the approval of a motion sponsored by A. Wilson and R. Templar asking the Federation of Agriculture to bring together a number of producers in each county to discuss marketing and production problems. It asked them, if interested, to select members to attend a meeting in Toronto to consider the advisability of a provincial organization of commercial hog producers. This early meeting discussed whether or not a hog scheme could be set up under the Farm Products Control Act. It even instructed McInnis and Milburn to interview

4

representatives of the government Marketing Board to this end. The committee appointed April 21st met briefly following the general meeting and decided to meet for a working session in June. It was decided to add a representative of the Cheese Producers, Mr. J. McAllister of Pendleton, Ontario.

When V. S. Milburn early in May sent out invitations, they went to the eight committee members, to the members of the early committee of the thirties and to a number of resource personnel. These were R. J. Scott, President of the United Farmers Co-operative; George Wilson, Director of the Marketing Branch of the Department of Agriculture; Harry Wilson, a respected and experienced leader of the livestock industry from Kent County; Ken Morrison, Manager of the First Co-operative Packers of Barrie; W. P. Watson, Assistant Livestock Commissioner of Ontario; Louis O'Neil, Livestock Commissioner of Ontario; and W. A. Amos, Clergyman turned farmer and veteran leader of the United Farmers of Ontario.

On the bright morning of June 2nd, there was confusion in a limited area of Toronto's King Edward Hotel. For some reason the scheduled room, 1690, didn't seem to be available. A telephone call from V. S. Milburn to the responsible desk solved the problem. "The desk clerk assured Milburn that room 1690 was reserved for a Wine Producers Meeting". An informal decision was reached at once that, if there was to be so much confusion between wine and swine, the name of the contemplated new arrival had better be Hog Producers' Association.

Individual hog producers had assured the committee, that "we are in favour of some kind of a producer organization. You find how best it can be done." There had to be democratic control; there had to be authority to act upon the part of producers; and there had to be adequate financing. The possibility of a market plan under current Ontario legislation was a popular solution to these prerequisites.

Before 1941 the idea of a marketing plan had been applied to fruits, vegetables, and cheese. Hogs offered a whole new set of problems. Perhaps here we should pause to consider the circumstances of Ontario Marketing Legislation. For two decades the idea had gradually been gaining support that farmers were entitled to have some government authority delegated to them as a democratic group whereby the majority might establish enforceable compulsory regulations and thus more efficiently market their common products. As early as 1922 the State of Queensland in Australia provided such legal opportunity to farmers. The United Kingdom followed with similar legislation and a number of so called "schemes" or plans for a variety of products were set up. In Canada the Depression brought such difficulty to agriculture that the Federal Government in 1934 enacted the Dominion Natural Products Marketing Act. This act gave wide power to a Dominion Marketing Board to regulate the marketing of natural or agricultural prod-

5

ucts. Soon a number of plans were set up in British Columbia and Ontario. However, there had been some question of the validity of the Act.

In June, 1936, the Supreme Court of Canada asked by the Government, confirmed these doubts and referred the matter to the Judicial Committee of the Privy Council. The Privy Council conferred the legal opinion that this legislation infringed upon provincial authority. Consequently, the Federal Parliament early in 1937 repealed the Act. British Columbia immediately enacted provincial legislation. In Ontario action came somewhat more slowly. Perhaps this was only a natural course of events. British Columbia farmers had been in the vanguard of those asking for marketing legislation. As early as 1929 and 1930 requests had come from B.C. fruit growers. The Canadian Horticultural Council had been established sometime before. It was the only national organization with an office in Ottawa. An early study had been made of the Hog and Potato Schemes in the U.K. The Horticultural Council had been the active body in making early representations to both parties in Ottawa. After 1930 had it worked with the Hon. Mr. Weir, Prime Minister R. B. Bennett's Minister of Agriculture, in drawing early drafts of legislation at a time when the economists and lawyers were opposing such innovations.

Implementation of new worthwhile ideas is always dependent upon the presence of the right man at the right time. Mr. Paul Fisher of Halton County was one such person. Dedicated to farm leadership, he graduated from the Ontario Agricultural College before the First World War, soon became one of the most prominent leaders of the Canadian Fruit Growers and served as an officer of the Canadian Horticulture Council from 1928 to 1937. He had also been an early proponent of the need for a Federation of Agriculture. No Canadian took a more active role in studying the beginnings of marketing legislation in Australia and the United Kingdom. He was particularly interested in the British Potato and Hog Schemes. In the case of the latter, registration of sows was required, monthly reports were given and permits issued to sell each litter and no buyer was allowed to purchase without the availability of this permit. If the efficiency of marketing farm products in U.K., Australia and New Zealand could be improved by the judicious use of delegated government authority, Mr. Fisher questioned why the same technique could not be used to provide Canadian farmers a more equitable share in the economy. William Lyon Mackenzie King, Prime Minister prior to the midsummer of 1930, was not interested. The Conservatives under R. B. Bennett promised support. The Hon. Mr. Weir, Minister of Agriculture from 1930 to 1935 under Bennett, was favourable to marketing legislation, but said he found the lawyers opposed. When the government finally accepted the principle, Mr. Fisher worked with Mr. Weir in drawing up the Natural Products Marketing Act.

One morning in 1936 Mr. Fisher's phone rang and the urgent and anxious voice of the Hon. Duncan Marshall, Minister of Agriculture in the Ontario Government of Mitchell Hepburn, came over his wires: "Paul! I am in trouble. There are seventy thousand cheese producers in Ontario and they seem to be all outside my office demanding action. Can you come to Toronto at once?" Mr. Fisher was not only a prominent farm leader, but also during the 1934-43 period of the Hepburn, Conant and Nixon Governments, he was a very influential Liberal, and played an important role in advising on matters of agricultural policy.

When he arrived in Toronto, Mr. Fisher found the requests of the cheese producers both practical and reasonable. They wished some authority by which a free competitive market might be established for the sale of cheese. Mr. Fisher was to discuss with both Premier Hepburn and his chief Lieutenant, Hon. Harry Nixon, the nature of the legislation which would be necessary to give producers of any given product the authority to accomplish this end. No opposition was offered by either government leader. Years later Hon. P. M. Dewan who had been destined to become Minister of Agriculture following the defeat of Duncan Marshall in the 1937 Provincial Election, recalled being invited to Harry Nixon's office for a discussion of this farmer request. The result was the passage of the Farm Products Control Act, patterned after British and Australian legislation. Details of this Act owe much to the experience and knowledge of Mr. Paul Fisher, who drew upon his years of experience in the fruit industry.

Almost immediately not only the cheese producers, but also producers of several fruit crops requested and obtained so called "schemes" under the Act. The term "scheme" was a copy of the terminology in use in the United Kingdom. When the hog producers first requested a "scheme", Department of Agriculture personnel insisted that the programme was more suitable for selling products such as fruit and cheese than any type of livestock. The original act of 1937 covered animals and meats as well as dairy products, fruits and vegetables, and gave the Governor-in-Council authority to designate products to come within the scope of the legislation. Authority was given to investigate, arbitrate, adjudicate, adjust or otherwise settle disputes between producers and processors. Also, authority was provided to investigate costs of production, distributing, transporting, prices and trade practices pertaining to farm products. Producer, or local, boards were set up for the purpose of carrying out the Act with powers which were delegated by the overall Government Board which was granted the authority to make the necessary regulations.

In the legislative session of 1938 under the new Minister of Agriculture, Hon. P. M. Dewan, amendments were made to make the legislation more practical and workable. Grains and seeds were added to possible products.

The nature of the producer, or local, board was clarified and "Regulated Products" was interpreted to mean any farm product and the term "scheme" to mean any plan in force. The composition of the Government Board was changed and made more realistic. Authority was given for price negotiating agencies. Provision was made for exemptions from various provisions of a plan or scheme and also for registration of producers and those engaged in the trade. Clearer provision was made for the delegation of authority from the Government Board to the local board and also for the termination of such authority.

Again, in the Session of 1939, further amendments were passed extending authority to include advertising. Under negotiating agencies authority was broadened to include prices for any grade of a regulated product and additional powers were provided to collect fair or minimum prices. Provisions were made for having a judge as the final court of appeal. The fledgling hog producer committee, not yet really an association, during the summer and autumn of 1941 still felt frustrated. The claim to speak for hog producers and the attempts to establish real recognition among government agencies and the trade seemed to meet solid resistance on all sides. In 1941 there were very few farmers relying solely on hog production for their livelihood. Almost all producers were dairy farmers with a hog side line or beef farmers milking a number of cows and separating the milk and using the skim milk as a source of hog feed protein. Nevertheless, substantial progress had been made in developing pure bred strains, particularly Yorkshires. In 1889 Joe Brethour of Burford had imported English Yorkshires or Large Whites and, with a continuing program of breeding, had made an important contribution to the improvement of Ontario's hogs. By the early part of the century, packers in Ontario were praising the vastly improved quality of Ontario hogs as a result of the blood lines of these imported Yorkshires.

Agriculture was still emerging from the great depression of the thirties. There as yet had not been any substantial reduction in farm population. World War II had now been under way for two years and only the lure of the factory and the call of the armed forces had brought any substantial reduction to the number of rural young people.

Farmers, however, were ready to speak loudly in their own behalf. Prices of feed and farm machinery were rising, as a result of the developing war economy, while prices of farm products remained low. It was essential, as it would be for the remaining war years, to make every effort to supply the maximum food for Britain's needs. Yet the farmer could not do it at the prices Britain was able to pay, as they were less than the Canadian domestic price. Under these circumstances, the Ontario Government was forced to make a radical departure from the policies of earlier years.

The Hon. P. M. Dewan, Ontario Minister of Agriculture, 1937-43 tells the story in his own words as to what happened:

"It was early in January, 1941. I happened to call at the Premier's office. At once he said, "I wanted to see you. Do you know, Mike, that the farmers are in a hell of a state of mind?" I said, "I do know and I wanted to talk to you about it." Well he said, "What can we do? What should we do?" I replied that I had been giving much thought to the matter for days and that I had a suggestion. I was almost afraid to mention my idea to him for I knew that he was violently opposed, as a matter of principle, to subsidies, as I myself would be in ordinary times. Anyway, I put forth my plan for a government subsidy on both cheese and hogs. Mitch accepted my suggestion thoughtfully. He said, "Don't say anything; let's think it over for a few days."

"Within about one week's time, as I recall it, we were in Ottawa to attend a Dominion Provincial conference. As I was leaving the Capital to return one evening since he was not coming back to Toronto until next day, he said, "Before I get back gather all the facts about your proposed subsidies, including what they would cost us. I said, "I can tell you now what they would cost." "Well, I think we should bring in legislation. We shall take it up as soon as I am back to Toronto."

"The result was that I introduced a Bill in the Legislature which was to have "effect from and after the first day of February, 1941". In support of this Bill and before introducing it, I pointed out to the Premier that circumstances of the times were altered by the war and that, even though he and I were inherently opposed to subsidies, they could be justified under the existing conditions. We were not operating freely under the laws of supply and demand. The British government wanted Canadian cheese and bacon in large quantities, but it had set maximum prices. Our farmers needed the market, but British prices were not good enough for our farmers. I followed the same reasoning in the Legislature. There was no opposition, except a feeble suggestion that we pay higher subsidies than we were planning.

"The provisions of the Act extended for only one year, but it was my privilege to bring forward an extension of the legislation in both the sessions of 1942 and 1943.

"In matters of this nature one sometimes get interesting reactions. In discussing the proposal of the subsidies informally with some members of the cabinet before the legislation was introduced, I found at least one farm oriented member critical. The subsidy on cheese would not help his area. On the other side I found lawyer members, as soon as they understood, very favourable. Tom McQuesten, Minister of Highways, was an example. He telephoned and requested to see me "to know what it was all about". When I briefly explained, he said "I am right with you." In spite of Tom's blustery ways, especially when receiving delegations (I am sure some of them must

9

have thought him a boor), I always found Tom a true gentleman.

"There was one annoying outcome of the legislation. It was always my contention that raising the value of cheese would tend to advance the values of other milk products. Not all branches of the industry took it this way, or at least they pretended not to, which made it embarrassing for me and the government. Certain delegations came but frankly I had very little tolerance for their approach.

"This legislation, I must say, was passed without any political notice. The aim was primarily to give farmers assistance to which they were entitled. But no one can deny that it had political repercussions. The Liberal government of Ontario became very popular in late 1941. As that year advanced I was riding on the train with a Federal member who later went on to higher positions. He said "your government is riding on top of the world right now; ours is not."

"Had Mitch Hepburn decided to appeal to the electorate in 1941 his party would have swept the province. Harry Nixon so believed and it was one time he was right. It was four years since the previous election; an appeal to the electorate would have been following the usual course. But for some reason best known to himself, Mitch kept avoiding an election. Meantime his criticism of Mackenzie King and jousts for Party Leadership in Ontario critically weakened the government in the public eye and brought about its defeat in 1943. Had an election been held in 1941 the course of Ontario political history in the last quarter of a century would have been very different."

On December 2nd, 1941, the hog producers committee met in the Board Room of the Ontario Federation of Agriculture. Present were Chas. McInnis (Chairman), Art. Wilson, W. Bishop, R. Templer, Chas. Milton, W. Weber, Harry Hewitt, V. S. Milburn, (Secretary) and Harry Scott. R. J. Scott attended in the afternoon.

Mr. Milburn reported that a limited amount of work had been done since the June meeting. A draft of a constitution was approved after discussion. Approval was also given to an outline of principles planned to serve as both a basis of policy and a foundation for a "Scheme" under the Farm Products Control Act.

From the minutes it was recommended that a scheme be prepared by the Farm Products Control Board which would include the following principles and permit the implementation of them:

1. That a strong organization of Commercial Hog Producers be effected so that producers may be represented in negotiations on Bacon contracts etc.
2. That it is essential a correct ratio be maintained between food costs, food reserves, freight rates, etc. and hog prices, in order that the industry may

10

be placed on a sound, long-time basis and be assured of continuity of supply.

3. That every effort should be made for the standardization of type with high killing qualities in relation to market requirements.

4. Re-adjustment of the industry after the war, which may require increased or curtailment in production; this to be brought about by adjustment in prices and possibly quotas.

5. To negotiate fair or minimum prices and to establish fair, rather than arbitrary discounts in respect to the different grades.

6. To set up a check grading system in order to establish confidence in the minds of producers.

7. To establish the hog producing industry on a long-time permanent basis in so far as possible.

8. To encourage an educational programme that will make possible all the above principles.

In order to implement the formation of an organization and to regulate and finance this part of the industry it was recommended also that all buyers and processors be licensed at a nominal fee and that proof of their financial responsibility and interest in the industry be established in granting a license; further, that a collection of 5¢ on each hog marketed be collected by the processor and turned over to the Treasurer of the Provincial Association, the moneys so acquired to be administered by the Board of Directors to be appointed under the attached drafted constitution.

A committee was appointed to meet the Farm Products Control (later Marketing) Board to present the proposed Constitution and principles of the scheme. They were to request that a Commercial Hog Producers' Scheme for Ontario be approved and presented to the hog producers for their consideration. The members of the committee were Charles McInnis, Wilfred Bishop, Russell Templar and R. J. Scott. In December 1941 Russell Templar resigned from the committee to join the armed forces. The committee was also instructed to interview Mr. W. R. Reek, Deputy Minister of Agriculture, Hon. R. M. Dewan, Minister of Agriculture, and others, seeking their support. The President was instructed to arrange for appointments with the above mentioned parties.

It was agreed that a draft of the minutes of this meeting, along with copy of the Constitution and the principles of the Scheme, be sent to all members of the original committee. It was also recommended that a copy of the Constitution, the principles of the Scheme, a draft of the minutes and a covering letter be sent to all County units of the Ontario Federation of Agriculture.

Two meetings of the committee were held in February and by the time of the second of these, held on February 24th, 1942, the committee and the sub-committee had made sufficient progress for the agenda to include a meeting with the Farm Products Control Board and with the Hon. P. M. Dewan on that same day. As a climax to these discussions, a very significant proposal was voiced by Mr. Louis O'Neil, Livestock Commissioner for the Ontario Department of Agriculture. The Department of Agriculture would be willing to make available $500.00 to the Hog Producers Committee for the purpose of holding a series of meetings in a group of approved counties. Farmers' opinion would be tested as to whether they really wanted a Hog Producers Association and a marketing plan. The producers committee readily approved this suggestion. The next question concerned what counties should be selected as the test area. The first selected list of counties included Huron, but the President of the County Federation of Agriculture, Nick (Wilfred) White, objected strongly. Since it was planned to use the help of each Federation of Agriculture, Huron County was dropped from the list and the final selection of counties included Bruce, Grey, Waterloo, Brant and Oxford. Beginning March 9th, at Glen Christie in Waterloo, and concluding at Dundalk in Grey County on April 10th, forty-four meetings were held in all.

A special presentation of the reasons explaining why hog producers should be organized was made to the Waterloo Seed Fair and here only one farmer raised objections. All other meetings were unanimous in agreeing that organization had brought advantages to milk producers and others and that hog producers might expect similar advantages. The chairman of the committee, Mr. Charles McInnis, spoke over Wingham radio. "Tommy" Cooper, Agricultural Representative for Grey County, discussed the material in his weekly broadcast from Owen Sound. Mr. William Ritchie of the National Film Board distributed producer material, while showing the film "Bacon for Britain". Material was placed before the Farm Radio Forums of Ontario.

At this time, the Forums, which were local community groups, met each Monday evening to listen to special national farm broadcasts. These broadcasts were sponsored jointly by the Canadian Broadcasting Corporation, the Canadian Association for Adult Education, and the Canadian Federation of Agriculture. Questions proposed by the broadcasts were discussed and opinions were reported to provincial officers. These groups were then in their hey day of strength and influence. Substantial material promoting a hog producers organization was sent to each Ontario group.

The final report of the provincial officers made to Hon. Mr. Dewan in April, 1942, which illustrated the unanimous support of the community groups. It concluded with the following summary:

County	No. Meetings	Attendance
Grey	11	244

Bruce	12	416
Brant	5	108
Oxford	9	250
Waterloo	8	695
		1,713
Provincial Meetings		200
Radio Forums estimated attendance of hog producers		600
Estimated personal contracts definitely reported		60
TOTAL representative producers giving support		2,573

A further summary appeared in the *Radio Forum Notes* of May 21st, 1942, under the heading of Forum Findings:

"Question 'two' asked if the local forums were in favour of the proposal for a Hog Producers Association. "Sixty-three spread over 25 counties expressed themselves as unanimously in favor; some were very enthusiastic to get such an association started. Three forums voted over 90% in favor. Six forums were opposed to participating in an association; four of these were in Huron, one in Middlesex, and one in Algoma. One in York was doubtful; one in Prince Edward and one in Renfrew felt they had not sufficient information to pass judgement. The Algoma Forum, opposing, felt the district was too remote from Southern Ontario to be well served by the Association. Two opposing forums in Huron believed the hog job should be done directly by the Federation without a separate association".

As a result of these meetings, the Ontario Minister of Agriculture, Mr. Dewan, accepted the new organization as the spokesman for Ontario hog producers. The first great battle thus had been won.

Changes soon occurred in the executive of the organization. V. S. Milburn, Secretary of the Ontario Federation of Agriculture, had turned an increasing amount of the organizational work, particularly in Western Ontario, over to committee member Wilfred Bishop, Field Secretary, and soon acting Secretary. At the annual meeting held on April 7th endorsement of the progress already made was given and George Wilkinson of Alliston took the place of Russell Templar as representative of the pure bred breeders. Mr. R. J. Scott of Belgrave, President of the United Farmers Co-op, became more actively involved.

A few county organizations had already been set up. Prior to the first general meeting in April, 1941, two counties had already organized. On April 5th of that year Lincoln County had organized a county association and four days later Oxford had done the same while planning a delegation to the projected provincial meeting. Following the provincial meeting of April,

1942, and continuing through 1943 and beyond, a determined effort was made to develop a local organization in each county. In some instances it was a county Hog Producer Association. In others it took the form of a Hog Producers Committee of the Federation of Agriculture. In the Eastern half of the province, county organizational work was largely handled by the President, Charles McInnis. In the Western half of Ontario the task was in the hands of Wilfred Bishop who had gradually taken over the functions of secretary originally handled by V. S. Milburn, Secretary of the Ontario Federation of Agriculture. He became first Acting Secretary and, at the annual meeting of 1943, Secretary-Treasurer.

Most county records go back little further than 1946. There were no funds available earlier than that and few formal minute books were obtained any earlier. County Federations of Agriculture were a constant source of help in the development of grass roots machinery all over the province. The following letter from W. A. Stewart, who became later the Conservative Minister of Agriculture in Ontario, provides an excellent illustration.

Denfield, Ont.
Nov. 27, 1943.

Mr. Wilfred Bishop,
Norwich, Ontario.

Dear Wilfred:
At our annual meeting of the Federation of Agriculture in Middlesex County on Dec. 8 & 9th we are having a short discussion on the hog situation. We would appreciate very much if you could forward us any information on this subject.

There has been a strong feeling for a higher price for bacon in this county and we feel there should be some explanation given why this price was not forthcoming and why the bacon quota was reduced. Farmers are being asked if there is plenty of feed grain available in the west to carry them through until another crop can be harvested.

As the hog situation is a very controversial subject, we would like to have as many facts on it as possible and to have any information which your committee can forward us.

Yours truly,
Wm. A. Stewart. (Signed)

Through 1942, following the annual meeting, the Board met more frequently. It continued contacts to encourage local organization and maintained pressure through discussion with both the Minister of Agriculture and the Farm Products Control Board. Department officials, however, con-

14

stantly voiced the opinion that it would be too difficult to operate any marketing plan that would handle livestock and cover the whole of Southern Ontario.

The close association of the youthful hog producer organization with the Federation of Agriculture sometimes resulted in confusion of terminology. Board members spoke of the Hog Producers' Association, but sometimes the term Hog Producers' section of the Federation was used.

Stenographic work was done at the Federation of Agriculture office, 409 Huron Street, Toronto. Small grants were being made by the Department of Agriculture through the good offices of the Hon. Mr. Dewan. Five dollars per diem and basic out of pocket expenses to officers and board members was the format of remuneration.

In December, 1939, the Bacon Board was set up as an agency to handle the export of bacon and other pork products to the United Kingdom. Some years later the name was changed to the Meat Board. Under this name, until some years after the end of the war, it continued to handle the export of meat products to the U.K. where they were so urgently required during the war years. For nearly a decade prices established by the Bacon or Meat Board determined prices received by Canadian producers. During this period the domestic market paid more than the export price, but supplies permitted on the domestic market were limited to ensure that Britain obtained her requirements. Consequently, increased Canadian production allowed a greater percentage for the domestic market with the result that the greater our production, the higher the price to the Canadian farmer.

So important was the function of this Government board that the Order in Council of May 5th, 1941, setting out amendments to the original provisions establishing the Board, seems worthy of reproducing here because of the effect upon producer price, supply, volume and, in fact, the whole of the new producer organization.

P.C. 2978

AT THE GOVERNMENT HOUSE IN OTTAWA

MONDAY, the 5th day of May, 1941.

PRESENT: HIS EXCELLENCY THE GOVERNOR GENERAL IN COUNCIL:

Whereas by Order in Council dated the 13th day of December, 1939, P.C.4076 as amended by Orders in Council dated the 20th day of December, 1939, P.C.4248, and the 27th day of December, 1939, P.C.4353, regulations were established setting up the Bacon Board with authority, inter alia, to control the marketing of bacon and other pork products exported to the United Kingdom Ministry of Food;

And whereas the Minister of Agriculture reports that since March 27th,

1941 the United Kingdom Ministry of Food has forwarded two separate requests for additional quantities of bacon, totalling 55,000,000 pounds for delivery during the next five months:

That there has been a marked increase in domestic consumption of bacon and other pork products because domestic prices based upon the export bacon prices are low in comparison with prices of other meats; and

That it now being evident that the bacon requirements of the United Kingdom for the immediate future and during the third year of the war, will be substantially greater than previously anticipated, it may be necessary to regulate the quantity of pork that may be distributed in the domestic market;

Therefore, His Excellency, the Governor General in Council, on the recommendation of the Minister of Agriculture and under the authority of the War Measures Act, is pleased to amend the regulations established by Order in Council dated the 13th day of December 1939, P.C.4076 and they are hereby further amended as follows:

1. Paragraphs a) c) d) e) g) h) and i) of Clause 4 (1) are repealed and the following substituted therefore (amendments italicized)

   a) to regulate the export of bacon and other pork products to Great Britain pursuant to the agreement made between the Governments of Canada and the United Kingdom and to that end to arrange with or require any packer *or other person* to ship and deliver bacon or other pork products of the quantity and quality specified in such arrangement to the United Kingdom Ministry of Food at seaboard ports in Canada.

The Honourable The Minister of Agriculture shall have authority:

   c) to determine the prices which shall be paid to packers *or other persons* for bacon and other pork products delivered in accordance with requirements of the Board: Provided that in the case of pork stored in accordance with the requirements of the Board the price to be paid for bacon made from such pork shall not exceed the price of bacon at the time the pork was taken into store plus carrying and storage charges approved by the Board; and provided further that in determining the prices which shall be paid for bacon and other pork products delivered as required by the Board and in requiring packers to store pork and in exercising all or any of its other powers it shall be the duty and responsibility of the Board to have regard to the present future conditions of the bacon market and the undertakings and needs of the Government of the United Kingdom under its agreement with the Government of Canada.

   d) in determining the prices to be paid packers of *other persons* as hereinbefore provided to establish differentials in prices that will be

16

paid for official grades, selections and weights of bacon and other pork products.

e) to requisition cheques to be drawn against the Fund, hereinafter referred to, for the payment of bacon and other pork products and *all other charges and liabilities in respect to such bacon or other pork products* delivered pursuant to the requirements of the Board.

g) to require any packer or other person to give priority to the processing and delivery of bacon and other pork products to be delivered pursuant to a requirement of the Board.

h) to fix the minimum price to be paid by packers *or other persons* for hogs.

i) to order that packers *or any other persons who slaughter hogs or process bacon* shall obtain licences from the Board and to issue licences to such persons upon such terms and conditions to be fixed by the Board and to fix fees payable on account of such licence shall not be deemed to affect the liability of such persons to obtain a licence as required by any other statute or law of Canada or any province thereof.

2. The following is added to Clause 4(1) as Paragraph (o)

"(o) *to regulate the quantity of pork that may be distributed in the domestic market or the number of hogs that may be slaughtered for distribution in the domestic market by any packers or any other person when such action is required to secure the necessary quantities of bacon and other pork products for export to the United Kingdom, and, to that end, to limit the number of hogs that may be slaughtered for distribution in the domestic market or the quantity of pork that may be distributed in the domestic market".*

3. Sub-clause (3) of Clause 4 is repealed and the following substituted therefor:

(3) Upon receipt of a requirement of the Board to deliver bacon as hereinbefore provided, a packer *or other person* shall comply such requirement according to the terms thereof, and *upon delivery of such bacon properly processed in accordance with the standards of workmanship and condition as prescribed by the Board,* shall be paid therefore at the price or prices determined by the Board in accordance with these regulations.

4. Sub-clause (2) of Clause 5 is repealed and the following substituted therefor:

"(2) The Minister of Finance may, subject to the provisions of these regulations, on the requisition of the Board, pay out of the Fund to the extent only of the Fund sums necessary to compensate packers and *other persons* for bacon and other persons for bacon and other pork products *and all other charges and liabilities in respect of such*

17

bacon and other pork products delivered by them pursuant to the requirements of the Board, but no other payment shall be made a charge on the Fund".

"A.D.P. Heeney, Clerk of the Privy Council"

The influence of Bacon Board policy and program upon producer activities is shown by the suggestions offered to local groups by the provincial organization in October 1942.

Suggested Hog Production Programme for 1942 - 1943

A small committee, consisting of Messrs. Chas. McInnis, Wilfred Bishop, R. J. Scott and V. S. Milburn were appointed by the Hog Producer section of the Ontario Federation to prepare a programme of Hog Producer activities. The committee reported that plans should be made to increase Ontario hog production by 25% for the next twelve months. In order to implement the recommendation for increased hog production as a definite part of our immediate war effort the following programme as to general principles was set forth:

"Can Ontario increase its hog production by 25% in the next twelve months? Before answering this question one must take into consideration:

(a) Effectively organizing such a programme by an Ontario Federation of Agriculture (County and Township Federation.)

(b) Concurrence and support of the provincial government and Agricultural Representatives.

(c) Concurrence and support of the Federal Department of Agriculture.

Production in Ontario of grains in 1943 will likely be markedly below 1942 in the number of acres cropped, and quite possibly in the yield per acre.

An adequate supply of grain should be made available from Western Canada under the Freight Assistance Policy so that every farmer could be assured of sufficient grain to carry out his increased programme of hog production.

In quite a number of instances it will be found necessary to make short-term credits available to the farmer for the purchase of grains necessary to such a programme, although the majority of farmers can probably finance an expansion of 25% in hog production.

The availability of concentrates necessary in the production of high quality bacon, at minimum costs, should be organized, and the fullest information regarding the usage of same made available to the farmer.

Literature, possibly in the form of pamphlets and placards which rendered valuable service some years ago, should be made available for distribution by government authorities and farm organizations, setting forth the

18

most up to date feeding information in a form readily understood and easily put into practice by the hog producer.

Labour saving equipment should be described, possibly in diagram form, for distribution by the above agencies, for we firmly believe many labour saving innovations could be introduced into the field of hog production. Some of these might include a design of a hog range area, giving the approximate size for a given number of hogs, cuts drawn to scale of weatherproof range feeders, low cost hog sun shelters, and approved type of water container for range, etc.

The lower cost of producing hogs on range in the summer months has not been fully appreciated by many Ontario hog producers and could well be discussed and information prepared regarding it. A very substantial increase in hog production, by the range method, should be possible in Ontario at a minimum labour expenditure.

The securing of good quality breeding stock could be greatly encouraged by a dynamic programme of all agencies co-operating together. Litters born in April and May should have six or seven months of summer range conditions when they could be produced with a minimum of labour on range.

Radio Forums, if a definite hog programme was undertaken, could provide a basis for discussion by many hundreds of groups of farm people over Canada, where information could be widely disseminated and followed up by local initiative.

Britain and Canada will need all the bacon we can produce, and in our opinion it would add to the dignity and prestige of the Federation of Agriculture if they were to initiate, and with the co-operation of governments, carry on such an essential programme at this time."

The committee agreed that in order to implement the above principles several steps in organization should take place:

1. A meeting with provincial government authorities, seeking their full support in the plan. (This meeting will take place on October 14th.)
2. The support of provincial government authorities should be sought in calling a meeting which will include federal government authorities.
3. Approval of the Executive of the Ontario Federation of Agriculture should be secured.
4. A general Hog Producer conferences should be called and provincial and federal authorities should be invited to attend.
5. Four Forum meetings should be planned on the Farm Radio Forum project programme on hog production and Hog Producer organization as follows:

FIRST PROGRAMME
Outline of plan to increase production, approval of increased produc-

19

tion, appreciation of government's action to increase hog production by increasing price by 10% – hog production requirements and necessity for beginning such action.

SECOND PROGRAMME:
Outlining principles and needs for hog Producer Association through which we may implement the hog production programme, stating briefly how the machinery of the Federation may be used to promote same.

THIRD PROGRAMME:
Giving details as to production programme such as improved feeding methods, encouraging range feeding, feeding formula, inexpensive housing and labour saving devices.

FOURTH PROGRAMME:
Further needs for hog producer organization, including grading, marketing, production and post war adjustment of the industry.

6. A detailed outline of the use of the township, county, provincial and national Federations of Agriculture in this project.

7. Preparation with the co-operation of the provincial Federation of Agriculture and all those who have made a study on feeding of details with regard to a production programme which would include shelters, feeding formula, printed material and labour saving devices.

The plan proposed by the sub committee appears to have considerable value since it sets forth the principles of an objective and then proposed to create the machinery to do this work, suggesting that the organization plan the detail and put the policy into operation.

This proposal should add stimulus to organization, secure the respect of provincial and federal governmental agencies as well as the support and respect of the packers, Feed Producers and the public generally. It also provides a constructive lead for an important part of Agriculture's wartime programme, recognizing that the people of this country, together with those in the armed forces and those in allied countries must be fed at all cost.

Respectfully submitted,
The Hog Producer Committee, appointed by
the Hog Producer Section of the
Ontario Federation of Agriculture

In December, 1942, a special Ontario Department of Agriculture Bulletin was issued supporting hog production expansion and making practical suggestions to this end. In order that contracts be made with as many farmers as possible a request was made to the head offices of all chartered banks operating in Ontario that literature, including the Government Bulletin and a letter from the Hog Producers Association, be placed in each branch. The reaction was favourable. However, one chartered bank replied

20

that they didn't want to have anything to do with "a bunch of farmers."

Another issue receiving considerable attention from farmers concerned the soundness of Condemnation Insurance. It was funded in the form of deductions made from livestock settlements and was used to compensate packers for animals and parts of carcasses condemned by government veterinarians as being unfit for human food. There seemed to be a resentment by the trade and government officials alike that farmers should delve into such problems and ask questions. Hon. P. M. Dewan, Minister of Agriculture, loaning a copy of a study which had just been made by Dr. Pine, a recently retired Government veterinarian, wrote as follows:

"For your information I am enclosing a copy of the official report on Condemnation Insurance. This is my own copy and I am sending it to you in a confidential way. You need not say anything about receiving it from me. I would prefer that you take from it what information you require and return it at the earliest convenient date".

A request for condemnation information, directed to the office of the Veterinary Director General, brought an evasive reply from the Secretary of the Bacon Board. On the other hand, Mr. Roy Grant, Manager of Maritime Cooperative Services of Moncton, New Brunswick, freely supplied the Association with condemnation figures, concerning their experience in marketing Maritime hogs. Mr. W. B. Somerset, one of the elder statesmen of marketing in Ontario, obtained detailed experience figures from the Canadian Fowler Company.

Farmers' personal experience with condemnation insurance was often unsatisfactory. A producer in Dereham Township, Oxford County, had been feeding a barn full of hogs. There was heavy condemnation for Avian T.B. from the first shipment of hogs going out. Word spread, and no packer would accept hogs from this farm. The Ontario Hog Producer's Association was not satisfied, as this meant that there was no real insurance as far as the farmer was concerned. A man who had paid deductions for years had no protection when he was in trouble.

When discussions were held with the packers, smooth talking, shrewd Sam Todd, Manager of the Industrial Development Council of Canadian Meat Packers, eloquently explained that the present system had been operating for years and should be taken to have all the effect of common law. Farmer representatives went away wondering if Mr. Todd took them to be 'dumb hay seeds' who would fall for a common law story if it were told well enough and often enough. Mr. Todd commanded a great deal of respect for his shrewd and penetrating mind and his ability to sign up problems as they came along. The comment was often heard: "I wish he were on our side".

Progress in obtaining a Marketing Scheme seemed frustrating and slow.

21

While government assistance kept the organization alive, the lack of funds limited the scope of service that could be rendered. The Concentrated Milk Producers Association had been operating for some years under a voluntary agreement with the processors. A small deduction was made for each cwt. of milk and this was used to finance the producers association, including its locals around each plant. Could something similar be worked out between the Hog Producers Association and the Meat Packers?

Ontario Hog Producers decided to try to find the answer. Charles McInnis, Art Wilson and Wilfred Bishop were appointed to meet representatives of the major packers. It was a friendly discussion held March 19th, 1943 in Toronto. But the packers were adamant. They declared that a deduction of so much per hog just couldn't be done on a voluntary basis. It would be thoroughly illegal. Later on the sidewalk of St. Clair Avenue three farmers looked at one another. "We tried our best. We could debate equally but there wasn't power behind our words." "How much was each of those men paid for this afternoon compared to our five dollars per diem if there is ever enough money to actually pay us?" The Packers Council years later listed this meeting as a significant milestone along the road towards a marketing plan.

The annual meeting in the Spring of 1943 (April 6th) was again a step forward with more counties organized and a larger provincial gathering. The letterhead which appeared on all stationery displayed the clear designation of the Association.

Ontario Hog Producers' Association

President	Vice-President	Secretary-Treasurer
Chas. W. McInnis,	A. D. Wilson	Wilfred L. Bishop
Iroquois, Ont.	Chatham, Ont.	Norwich, Ont.

Executive Members

Chas. Milton,	R. J. Scott,	John MacDonald	Wellington Weber,
Princeton, Ont.	Belgrave, Ont.	Harriston's Corners, Ont.	Elmira, Ont.
Geo. A. Wilkinson,		Address All Correspondence	
Alliston, Ont.		Norwich, Ont.	
		Telephone 84-R-4	

Up until mid-summer of 1943, through the assistance of the Hon. P. M. Dewan, a total of 2,500 dollars had been made available by the Department of Agriculture. This along with stenographic services provided by the Federation of Agriculture and a great deal of voluntary effort, provided the impetus to carry forward.

Early in May a letter from W. R. Reek, Deputy Minister of Agriculture, stated that Mr. Hay, Departmental Solicitor, would be forwarding a rough draft of a Marketing Scheme. A few days later Mr. Hay stated that so far copies of the plan were only rough drafts and would require a great deal of additional work.

In July, with an election campaign already under way and voting scheduled for August, Chas. McInnis and Wilfred Bishop were delegated to meet Hon. Mr. Dewan to plead the farmer's case for a Marketing Scheme at the earliest possible time. On this occasion Mr. Dewan made a very significant statement: "As soon as this election is over I am prepared to give you a Marketing Plan in spite of the officials of my Department".

The following month however, the Government of the Hon. Harry Nixon, who had followed Gordon Conant and Mitchell Hepburn as Premier of Ontario, was defeated at the polls. Hog Producers owe a debt of gratitude to P. M. Dewan. Without his sympathetic attitude and assistance the new organization might never have been able to get off the ground in its first two years.

Perhaps his own early struggles gave him insight as to what could be done. Early in life he determined that he must have a better education. He obtained his B.A. degree from St. Francis Xavier and his B.S.A. from the Ontario Agriculture College. He served on the staff of the Kemptville Agricultural School. When an opportunity came to take the management of two weak co-operatives at Woodstock, one marketing eggs and one handling farm supplies, he had no hesitation in leaving the security of a government position in order to serve farmers in his own community. In 1934 he was elected to the Ontario Legislature and three years later became Ontario Minister of Agriculture. He had practical ideas of what could be done to help farmers. He was a man all too rare among cabinet ministers.

The spring of 1943 had been late and very wet causing such difficulty in seeding across Ontario that the province's oat and barley crops were among the poorest on record. At this time spring grains provided the bulk of the feed for Ontario hogs. By harvest time it was evident that Ontario hog production could only be maintained by bringing increased quantities of grain from the west. Thus, the Association became engaged in a major battle to convince the powers in Ottawa that the farmer could only stay in business if grain prices were eased or hog prices raised. This would enable him to pay for increased amounts of Western grain.

In spite of the gathering clouds of a feed and price crisis, the Association found time to provide leadership in co-operation with H. H. Hannam and the Canadian Federation of Agriculture. It planned and promoted the first national meeting of Canadian hog producers. During the second week of September, 1943, Ontario producers were joined by delegations from the Maritimes and the West, meeting in Ottawa to discuss for the first time national policies and programmes. The meetings, subsequently held at the time of the annual meetings of the Canadian Federation of Agriculture, were a continuance of this initial gathering.

On September 1st, 1943, a letter, which follows, was dispatched to all the active supporters of the Association across the province inviting their opinions.

Norwich, Ont.
September 1, 1943.

Fellow Hog Producers of Ontario –

We have just been passing through a few months when our organizational activities have been at a slightly lower ebb than normal, in as much as pressure of farm work has limited what it has been possible to do.

However, the provincial executive has met May 27, July 8, and August 26, consistently working towards a practical basis for the completion of the development of our machinery in the province.

The next ten or twelve months may well prove to be the most critical in the whole history of our hog industry. As an executive, we feel prospects of obtaining improved prices that are fair and that it is sound practice to stay in the hog business using grain from the west. In this connection, your executive would ask hog producers to co-operate fully with the county units of the Federation of Agriculture in organizing the purchase of adequate quantities of western grain. We are much indebted to V. S. Milburn and the Ontario Federation of Agriculture for organizing the current campaign for purchasing of western grain.

On September 14, hog producers from all across the Dominion are to meet in Ottawa under the auspices of the Canadian Federation of Agriculture to plan unified national action re price, marketing problems, etc. Inasmuch as Ontario is somewhat in advance of most of the other provinces in the development of a provincial organization, we are preparing a brief re the present hog situation.

As a means to this end, please send to the secretary by return mail answers to the following questions:-

1. To what extent are farmers in your district going out of the hog business?
2. How much of an increase in price would be necessary to induce you and your neighbours to maintain hog production?
3. What would constitute a satisfactory hog production policy for the current year?

Your executive needs this information urgently and at once so that your secretary may tabulate the answer prior to September 14.

Most sincerely,
Wilfred Bishop, Secretary
Ontario Hog Producers.

Letters poured in with unanimous verdict. Farmers would be unable to maintain hog production no matter how patriotic they might be without an increased price.

Mr. Erskine Johnson, the first president of Carleton County Hog Producers and afterwards for many years Conservative member of the Legislature, wrote as follows:

Secretary, Ontario Hog Producers.

Dear Sir:

Yours rec'd today, might say your letter was a bit too late coming to enable me to get a true feeling of the hog producers in Carleton County. However, I am answering these questions myself in a hurry with the hope it may be of some assistance to you in preparing your brief.

#1. I would say 25% of the sows have been sold in the last two months and young pigs are for sale in general all over our district.

#2. I believe we should have a basic price of $20. per hundred dressed weight and should be guaranteed us for at least a year.

#3. I believe the price is the biggest factor to consider as well as letting the farmers know definitely that this western grain will be available and at a set price. Most people are afraid to stay in the business due to labour, feed, and lack of confidence in the whole set up.

Yours truly,
W. Erskine Johnston,
Carp, Ontario.

P.S.
If I knew more of this meeting, where it is being held etc. I would make an effort to be present at it.

The well known purebred breeder, William New of Simcoe County, replied as follows:

Craigvale, Ontario.

Mr. Wilfred Bishop,
Norwich,
Ont.

Dear Sir:

In reply to your questions I believe hog production is being cut at least 25% in this district.

In order to entice farmers, who have already marketed their sows to go out and buy gilts and considering the higher price of grain (western) and the difficulty in securing it; I do not think that a price of $20. per cwt. dressed weight would be any more than ample to ensure our hog production being high enough to meet export demands.

As soon as the authorities know the new price it should be announced immediately (I am taking it for granted that it will be higher than at present) in order to stem the present marketing of sows as quickly as possible.

Yours truly,
Wm. T. New.

The volume of the response established the case for farmer support and resulted in a slight raise in the price that the British Ministry of Food was willing to pay. However, the producers were still dissatisfied, and their dissatisfaction was indicated in a telegram to the new federal Minister of Agriculture, the Hon. J. G. Gardiner:

Toronto, October 28, 1943.

Hon. J. G. Gardiner,
Minister of Agriculture,
Parliament Buildings, Ottawa.

The Executive of the Ontario Hog Producers Association meeting today in Toronto wish to draw to your attention the complete inadequacy of the present price to maintain our hog production in Ontario. The recently announced price increase will not be sufficient to meet the additional costs farmers are facing this year and if further increases or adjustments are not immediately made the hog industry in Ontario will be seriously handicapped with the result that the industry will decline to dangerously low levels. Producers are anxious to meet all requirements even under the most difficult circumstances. They also recognize that in our present economy it requires price to secure the needs for production.

Wilfred Bishop,
Secretary Ontario Hog
Producers Association.

The Producers' decision was to continue to press the farmers' case. The following letter was sent to federal M.P.s from rural ridings.

November 26th, 1943.

Members of the House of Commons from Rural Ridings.
Gentlemen:

The Ontario Hog Producers Association is convening representatives of hog producers from across the province.

The meeting will be held on Tuesday, December 7, 1943, in the Yellow Room of the King Edward Hotel, Toronto, beginning at 10:00 a.m.

The critical situation in which our Ontario hog producers find themselves makes it imperative that further representation be made to the authorities in Ottawa lest the Ontario industry be hopelessly crippled and unable to carry on and play an integral part in our future agricultural economy.

26

As a member of a rural riding you are very cordially invited to be present at this meeting.

Yours very truly,
Wilfred L. Bishop, Sgnd.
Secretary.

The special meeting was well attended by producer representatives including a fair number of Members of Parliament. There the Hog Producers explained their case. One farmer was emphatic in telling how his son had been able to make between five and six dollars profit per hog. Suddenly a well known voice from Grey boomed out, "Sit down, I don't believe a damn word you are saying." The meeting brought all the simmering discontent into the open. In addition, every member of the cabinet received a letter from the Hog Producers, setting forth the farmers' position. The Hon. Mr. Gardiner, Federal Minister of Agriculture, responded:

Dear Mr. Bishop:

I have your letter of January 1st, stating that you have written to each of the other Members of the Cabinet setting forth the views of your organization with regard to hog prices.

I may say that the possibility of a longer time contract than the present one looks encouraging from the discussions which we have had with the British representatives, and the question of further returns is under consideration.

Yours sincerely,
James G. Gardiner. Sgnd.

CHAPTER II

THE STRUGGLE FOR
A MARKETING PLAN

With the change of Government in Ontario it seemed that a new start had
to be made to win government support. In October the Association Directors had met the new Minister of Agriculture, the Hon. Thomas L. Kennedy,
who returned to the agricultural portfolio after an absence of nine years. He
had been Minister before, prior to 1934. On November 1st, Hon. Mr. Kennedy wrote to the Association:

> "I have your letter of September 30th about a loan of $5,000 to carry on
> your work. We can give grants but we cannot make loans without
> special authority of the Legislature or unless they come under a special
> Act.
>
> Up to the present I notice that you have received a grant each year. In
> 1942 you received $1500 and in 1943 – $500. And by the report I hear
> you have done some splendid work and have had a number of meetings
> in the Province. I want to keep your group organized and I wonder if
> the first time Mr. McInnis or someone from your Association is in
> Toronto, he would come in and have a talk about it. Do not make a spe-
> cial trip, but if you are in on any other business we could go into it."

About the same time, the Minister promised the Association adequate
funds after the 1st of April if it went ahead and completed local organization.

During the winter, activities increased. More committee and board meetings were held. When the annual meeting was held on March 16th, 1944, a new face appeared among the directors, that of W. E. Tummon, who was destined to make a major contribution in the next decade.

Mr. W. E. Tummon of Foxboro in Hastings County brought to the Association a new dimension of experience. From 1925 to 1935 he was a Conservative Member of the House of Commons. He had spent a period managing a business firm and was a prominent breeder of Ayrshire cattle. He was also an influential layman of the United Church of Canada. The measure of his character was shown when he was elected chairman of the Belleville Presbytery of the United Church. This honour gave him more satisfaction than any other he had ever received.

The year 1944 was one of frustrations. Work and responsibilities had increased but there were no funds. Promised financial support from the Department of Agriculture had never materialized. W. E. Tummon went to see Col. Kennedy, the Minister to enquire. "Why, haven't you people received any cheque? I authorized a payment of $1,000", said the Minister of Agriculture. "No, we have received nothing", replied Mr. Tummon. Col. Kennedy picked up his phone and called Mr. Reek the Deputy Minister of Agriculture, "Bill, what happened to that thousand dollar cheque for the Hog Producers?" The reply came through clearly, "I have it here in my desk; it has never been sent to them." The cheque arrived very soon afterwards and helped to make partial payment on the outstanding debts.

The directors of the Hog Producers knew perfectly well that neither the officials of the Department of Agriculture nor the leaders of the trade were enthusiastic about seeing farm representatives installed in any position of strength in the industry. However, they were reminded of the words of the former Minister, Hon. P. M. Dewan, who had said the year previous, "I am prepared to give you a marketing plan in spite of the officials of my department, as soon as this election is over."

Another peculiar fact made for pessimistic thinking. Mr. Todd, the Manager of the Industrial and Development Council of the Canadian Meat Packers, and Mr. William Reek, the Deputy Minister, had both graduated in 1910 from the Ontario Agricultural College where they had not only been close friends but also roommates. Was it possible that each of them had equally serious misgivings and doubts about the advisability of farmers themselves assuming more authority? Did they instead believe that everything should be left to the technical men of the trade and to the agricultural departments? Could Mr. Todd have influenced his old friend Mr. Reek to proceed slowly and to hold back as much as possible? Perhaps they concluded that these farmers would get tired of coming to Toronto and paying their own expenses, and would finally stay at home and at their work instead. The skill in dealing and carrying out managerial functions possessed by Mr. Todd makes this seem a reasonable conjecture. Nevertheless, both men were probably sincere and honest in seeing their respective duties.

Troubles didn't end. Progress was desperately slow towards a "Marketing Scheme." Without funds to pay the $5.00 per diem or travelling expenses, directors were reluctant to take time away from work to come to Toronto for meetings held in the Board Room of the Ontario Federation of Agriculture.

Vivian S. Milburn, Secretary of the Federation of Agriculture throughout this period, was almost the founder of the Federation. He was a man of attractive personality, immense vigour and thorough dedication to the struggle of achieving economic equality for Ontario farm people. Because of increasing pressure of other farm problems he had become less active in the administration of the struggling infant hog producer organization.

However, party politics played an active role in farm organizations during this period. It was a maxim that he who held office in farm organizations certainly got much further if he had a record of active participation in the affairs of the particular party that happened to control the government at the time. Therefore, as a Conservative, Mr. Milburn was much better able to approach the Drew Government with the Col. the Hon. T. L. Kennedy as Minister of Agriculture than were most of the officers of the Hog Producers Association. Consequently, Mr. Milburn carried back an unofficial message that the Government had no confidence in the President or Secretary of the Hog Producers Association, but would be prepared to grant a "Marketing Scheme" for hogs if these men were both replaced.

Shortly afterwards a special Board Meeting was held in the Federation of Agriculture Board Room to discuss this unofficial message and develop a policy to cope with it. Lack of funds and little prospect of receiving even any out-of-pocket expenses resulted in board members not attending meetings. They were ready to give up. The financial position of the Association was reflected in the amounts owed to the executive at the rate of $5.00 per diem and 5¢ per mile. The secretary was in excess of eight hundred dollars behind, the president was over five hundred dollars in the red, and smaller losses had been sustained by other executive members.

At this meeting Charles McInnis, President, Charles Milton, W. E. Tummon and the Secretary, Wilfred Bishop, were present. It was agreed that more important than anything else was the continuity of the organization. Hog producers must have a strong commodity group to serve them. It was agreed that an annual meeting should be held early in the new year of 1945 to effect changes in personnel. It was agreed that W. E. Tummon should become President and that Charles Milton should become Secretary-Treasurer. W. E. Tummon had been a Conservative M. P. for ten years. Charles Milton had been Conservative candidate in Oxford in the Federal election of 1940. He had been Warden of Oxford a few years earlier, held executive

30

office in a wide range of municipal and farm organizations in Oxford, and, like Charles McInnis, was a member of the Board of the Ontario Concentrated Milk Producers. Would the Government continue to object if any Liberals should be elected to the Provincial board at the next annual meeting? Milburn replied that there would be no objections to Liberals serving on the board.

Another aspect of the situation required attention. The Drew Government was in a minority position in the Ontario Legislature after the C.C.F. had elected enough members in 1943 to create three substantial parties. A new election was contemplated in 1945. A further complication was that Hon. Mitchell Hepburn, the dynamic former Liberal Premier, had come out of retirement and had again taken over the leadership of the Liberal opposition. There was the possibility that another election might return him to office. There was a danger that this political atmosphere of the nineteen-forties might bring difficulties to an organization that had geared itself to work with the Conservative Administration. To meet this problem head on, Wilfred Bishop offered to stand ready in this eventuality to go to whomever Mr. Hepburn might ask to assume the agricultural portfolio and urge that the Hog Producers should not be made a political football, but that the new officers should be kept in office and should receive Government confidence and co-operation. However, this never became necessary, as the Liberals were not returned to power. Needless to say, this whole arrangement had to be kept secret or its purpose would be defeated.

A decision was made to revise the constitution. A President and Vice-President were to be elected from the floor of the convention. The province was divided into seven zones, delegates from each electing a director. The proposed grouping of counties into zones as proposed by the retiring secretary must have been very satisfactory, for the zones were continued in almost the exact form for a quarter of a century, and were copied by other commodity groups.

The annual meeting of 1945 occurred in January. Delegates arrived from all the counties in greater numbers than ever before and more determined than ever that hog producers should have a properly financed organization to take care of their interests. The financial report drew a bleak picture. No funds existed to pay directors their out-of-pocket expenses and no one who had done anything for the association had been reimbursed. William Newman who, back in 1941, had swept away doubts and persuaded the farmers at the first meeting to stand firm and set up a provincial committee again came to the rescue and proposed that everyone toss in 50¢ for every hog he had marketed in the past year. The response was instantaneous. Hats were passed and in minutes a pile of bills had accumulated on the table at the front of the hall. Bills rolled in balls came flying through the air. One of the veteran participants in early meetings, Arnold Burnside of Dufferin County, reminisces that he contributed $12.00. However, he kept enough to be sure that he could get home. Almost everyone at the meeting responded.

When the time for elections came, Charles McInnis' proposal that he retire as President was swept aside and he was returned for another term. Charles Milton was elected Vice-President. He succeeded Wellington Weber who had briefly followed Art Wilson in this office. Mr. Weber had sold his farm and was going into the milk distribution business. Wilfred Bishop told the meeting that he wished to retire as Secretary-Treasurer in order to have more freedom of action and to give more time to his farm and municipal affairs. Mr. W. E. Tummon was elected as his successor.

Several new names that were to appear often in the years ahead joined the Executive at this time: Alva Rintoul in District 1, Norman MacLeod in District 5, and George Johnson in District 6. In District 7, Southwestern Ontario, Tom Robson of Middlesex County was first elected, but since he lacked confidence in the prospects for the Association, he declined to act and was succeeded by Cecil Stubbs of Essex County. Mr. W. E. Tummon was elected in District 2 as was Geo. Wilkinson in District 3. Wilfred Bishop, the former Secretary-Treasurer, was elected to the Executive from District 4. Mr. Milton, the new Vice-President was also made Treasurer following the annual meeting.

The Association seemed little nearer to the achievement of a marketing plan. Men active in the Hog Producers Association, both provincial and local, who were also prominent Conservatives, insisted that the Government allow producers to vote on a marketing scheme. Mr. James Matches of Grey County, active among hog producers and in municipal affairs, was one of the most prominent of these. Feeling in Grey County was so strongly in favour of a marketing scheme that Dr. Phillips, Member for Grey North and Minister of Health, was threatened with the loss of his party nomination if he did not support his constituents in this drive.

The Federal and Provincial elections of June, 1945, fought almost simultaneously, resulted in emphatic victory for the Conservatives in Toronto and for the Liberals in Ottawa. In the atmosphere of the strong party feelings that prevailed in the forties, both Governments were more inclined to listen to farm organization men who belonged to their party and whom they felt they could trust. Consequently, a pattern developed. Men of both parties worked closely together on the hog producers' board and other boards. They displayed confidence in one another. However, one group went to Queen's Park and the other to Ottawa to seek support.

As the decade unfolded Charles McInnis emerged more and more as the most dynamic and colourful leader on the Ontario farm front. He served on the Concentrated Milk Producers Board and on the Executive of the Federation of Agriculture, as well as being President of the Ontario Hog Producers Association. To everyone who knew him he was a unique personality. He was absolutely sincere, totally dedicated, honest, unselfish and eloquent. He was willing to go anywhere, work long hours, and fight any battle he thought would improve the position of the farmer. He might not always tolerate those who sometimes disagreed with him, even though they were equally sincere and dedicated. This sometimes lead to factional differences on the board, the lines of opinion being drawn differently on varying issues. However, in spite of those clashes of opinion, the Hog Producers' Association would never have acquired the status and prominence it did without Charles McInnis.

In 1945 it was more and more definite that in Ontario the Hon. Col. Kennedy was prepared to give hog producers an opportunity to vote on a marketing scheme. During the early part of 1945, a petition was circulated among farmers requesting a vote to enable the establishment of a hog marketing scheme. Five thousand signatures from the counties of Southern Ontario appeared on this petition. This did the trick, for at a special producers meeting on Oct. 16th, Col. Kennedy announced that a vote would be taken.

Financial forecasting on the part of the Hog Producers' Association had always led to the opinion that a levy later to be known as a "license fee" of four cents per hog would be the minimum upon which a worthwhile program of service could be built. So when the Government proposed a scheme with only a two cent deduction there was, for a time, serious consideration as to whether or not to reject the holding of a vote on this basis. The final decision was to proceed and hope that the inadequacy of resources would clearly show itself, creating an environment such that an increase could be obtained. The vote was called for November, 1945. The agricultural representative in each county allowed a great deal of leeway as to how voting details should be developed. With the co-operation of county associations, county committees and local Federations of Agriculture, producer information meetings were organized in every corner of Southern Ontario. The Districts of Northern Ontario were specifically exempt from the proposed scheme. Speakers often emphasized that here was an opportunity for hog producers for the first time to have authority within their own industry and to have a few dollars to spend on behalf of producers. Provisions were made for negotiating authority with both the packers and the truckers.

The Association suffered a severe loss in the middle of the campaign. Mr. Milton, the Vice-President, suffered serious illness resulting from a gash in his knee while moving some sows. Infection set in and made it impossible for him to take any further part in the campaign or the initial board activities following the vote.

Department of Agriculture representatives were returning officers with broad authority to arrange for the vote in any manner and over a period of a week or ten days. G. R. Green, Agricultural Representative in Oxford County, arranged for one ballot box to be always in the office, one to be with him, either in his car or at any meeting he might attend, and for his assistant, George Bell, to do likewise. To further encourage producers to vote, Mr. Bell drove one half day in each township with a local hog producer director calling on producers and urging each to register and then to vote. The regulations stated that the presence of a department official with a ballot box constituted a legal polling booth.

A total of 31,796 hog producers registered. Of these, 29,757 cast ballots with 29,353 voting in favour and 205 voting against; 199 contributed spoiled ballots. Producers now had authority for the election of a seven man local board with power to control all marketing of hogs in Ontario and regulate their sale in accordance with the provisions of the Farm Products Control Act. The local board also had the authority to stimulate, increase and improve the marketing of Ontario hogs and to use the proceeds of licence fees for this purpose. While the original scheme gave authority for even an agency program, under which the local board would have full power to sell every market hog in Ontario, nobody was suggesting such a procedure at this time. Regulations set up for the actual operation provided, as a major tool of operation, a negotiating committee composed of three representatives of the Packers and three of the local board. Less formally at first, efforts were likewise made to negotiate with the representatives of transporters of hogs.

When the vote was past, all attention began to be directed towards the implementation of the new scheme. With future revenue assured, the Department of Agriculture advanced five thousand dollars, allowing some payment on old debts and some funds to use from day to day. The old Prince George Hotel on the corner of King and York street, in Toronto, where Secretary W. E. Tummon stayed while in the city, became the hub of activities. In 1946 the annual meeting was held on March 1st. Still there were no funds to pay delegates expenses, luncheons, or to provide for more than a one day meeting.

At the time of the elections of directors, Mr. Cecil Stubbs, who had taken little real interest in the organization, was replaced by Mr. Clayton Frey of Sarnia, destined to be one of the real founding fathers. Bald, slight of stature, with a keen, penetrating mind and a rugged determination, Clayton Frey made a place for himself on the board of directors which could have been filled by no one else. He was born in Waterloo County, graduated from the O.A.C. with his B.S.A. Degree in 1921, served as Agricultural Representative in Haldimand County, then left the Department of Agriculture to farm in Lambton County. Here he grew asparagus and had one of the early commercial hog farms of Ontario. Another change was the replacement of George Wilkinson by Heber McCague, eldest of the well known McCague family which for the next couple of decades left a real imprint on agricultural life in Ontario.

More and more time was required on the part of Mr. Tummon to prepare for the operation of the board. Fortunately, it was possible to obtain the services of Miss Jean Issacs (later Mrs. Wright) as office secretary. She had been employed in the office of the Ontario Federation of Agriculture and came with an excellent background in farm organization knowledge. Office space was obtained on the second floor of the Prince George Hotel. Years later, Mrs. Wright recalls the thrill that she felt on the morning of April 6th as she went with the key in her hand to open for the first time the first office of the Ontario Hog Producers Association. Mr. Tummon was a few steps behind her.

CHAPTER III

THE NEW BOARD
IN ACTION

On May 1st, 1946, the Marketing Scheme came into effect with a seven member board. The members were as follows: District 1, Alva Rintoul; District 2, W. E. Tummon; District 3, Heber McCague; District 4, Wilfred Bishop; District 5,Norman McLeod; District 6, George Johnson; and District 7, Clayton Frey.

When the board met to organize on May 7th, Norman McLeod was elected as the first Chairman; Charles McInnis, President of the Association, was not an actual member of the Board, but sat in on its meetings. Mr. W. E. Tummon became both Secretary of the Board and of the Association. Mr. Charles Hilton as Vice-President of the Association also attended meetings until 1947 when he left to become full time Secretary-Treasurer of the Ontario Concentrated Milk Producers' Association.

Meeting for a second time June 13th, 1946, the Board set the per diem rate for board members at $7.00. Car allowance was 7¢ per mile, maximum allowance for a hotel room, was $3.50, and the maximum allowance per day for meals was set at $2.50. At the same time Mr. Tummon was placed on an annual salary of $3,000 plus a car allowance of $1,000. The office sharing arrangements and the location in the Prince George Hotel both quickly proved to be inadequate and a new office was found late in the year in an old building, next to the King Edward Hotel at 95 King Street East. The two cents per hog was at last providing a little trickle of revenue.

The first major aim of the directors was to establish adequate prices for the producers. Some of the difficulties were expressed in a letter sent to W. E. Tummon, dated May, 1946, from L. W. Pearsall, who had now become Secretary Manager of the Meat Board, (formerly the Bacon Board), and which contained an explanation and defense of the price structure of the day:

a) I have for acknowledgement your letter of April 26th, requesting information with regard to the position of the producer in connection with the recent increase in price for export bacon.

b) There appears to be a general conclusion among producers that since there is a set price for export bacon, this should in turn provide a uniform and set value for hogs. This is not necessarily the case, and the reason should be clearly understood by the producer in endeavouring to relate export price of bacon to the price of hogs.

c) The Meat Board pays all packers the same price, quality considered, for bacon at Canadian seaboard. This provides what is considered a floor price in the various areas, depending on freight costs based on distance to seaboard. There is also a ceiling price on domestic pork products which somewhat higher than the export value. For some time past, the Meat Board have been requisitioning bacon for export, thereby shortening domestic supply to the point where it is reasonable to assume that all domestic product can be sold at the ceiling price. Hog prices may, therefore, fluctuate between the floor and the ceiling, and the average price will depend on the percentage going into export and the percentage left for distribution in the domestic market. For example, if only one out of every ten hogs is exported and the packer received domestic ceiling prices for nine and export price for one, the total value would be greater than if nine hogs were sold at export price and one in the domestic market.

The following tables show the export prices being paid for bacon at Canadian seaboard prior to the price increase on April 1st, and also the price schedule now in effect:

Table II

Price Schedule for Wiltshire Sides from Hogs *slaughtered on and after January 2nd, 1945.*

	50-55 lbs.	55-65 lbs.	65-70 lbs.	70-75 lbs.
d)				
A-1	$22.25	$22.75	$22.25	$20.20
A-2	21.75	22.25	21.75	19.70
B-1	21.65	22.15	21.65	19.60
B-2	21.05	21.45	21.05	19.00

Table III

Price Schedule for Wiltshire Sides from Hogs *slaughtered on and after April 1st, 1946.*

	50-55 lbs.	55-65 lbs.	65-70 lbs.	70-75 lbs.
A-1	$24.95	$25.20	$24.45	$22.45
A-2	24.55	24.80	24.05	22.05
A-3		24.20	23.45	
B-1	24.35	24.60	23.85	21.85
B-2	23.95	24.20	23.45	21.45
B-3		23.60	22.85	

c) On April 1st, the price for "A" Grade No. 1 Sizeable Wiltshire sides (55-65) was increased from $22.75 to $25.20. This increased the export value of a hog, from which is produced "A" Grade Sizeable Wiltshire sides, from $26.45 to $29.30 Canadian seaboard, or a total increase of $2.85 per hog. In terms of hog price, warm dressed weight, this is equivalent to an increase of $1.90 per hundred pounds, warm dressed carcass weight $(\frac{285}{150} \times 100)$. In other words, all other factors being equal, the increase in price of bacon on the export portion of the hog is equivalent to $1.90 per hundred pounds, warm dressed weight, or $2.85 on a 150 pound carcass. At the same time that the export bacon prices were increased, the Wartime Prices and Trade Board increased domestic ceiling prices on pork which, in turn, increased the value for a portion of the by-products of an export hog. Some of the items such as bone, scrap and tankage material were not affected. It was estimated that this increase would be equivalent to at least 10 cents a hundred pounds, which should make the total increase on an export hog $2.00 a hundred, made up of $1.90 on the export portion and 10 cents on the domestic portion of the carcass. The total increase in the hog price of $2.00 a hundred on a 150 pound carcass would, therefore, be $3.00 per hog. At the same time the premium was reduced from $3.00 a hog to $2.00 a hog, and it was on this basis the announcement was made that the average increase to the producer would be equivalent to about $2.00 per hog.

Hog quality was very early a question of importance. On July 5th, 1946, a special meeting was held by the board with representatives of both the Federal and Provincial Departments of Agriculture. Many hogs from Eastern Ontario were going to the Montreal Market. With no licencing possible for packers outside of the province, the question of whether a marketing agency was feasible as a means of controlling the hogs from Eastern Ontario first arose. Methods of selling hogs differed tremendously across Ontario. In Western Ontario closer proximity of packing plants and greater concentration of hog numbers gave a degree of competition which provided settlement forms in many cases quite satisfactory to the farmer. These showed weight, grade and deductions. In much of the rest of the province this was not the case. Deterioration of settlement forms continued to the point where some farmers received nothing more than a statement of so many dollars for so many pigs written out on a piece of brown paper.

Twice during the summer of 1946 the negotiating committee, composed of representatives of the board and the packers, met and began to straighten out this problem and other issues in the industry.

By March 1, 1947, significant results had been achieved:

Rules respecting the sale of hogs in Ontario have been unamimously approved by the Negotiating Committee composed of the official representatives of the hog producers and hog processors of the Province. These Rules have been approved by order of the Farm Products Marketing Board, are now in effect, and must be adhered to.

1. All hogs slaughtered by a licensed processor, where Dominion Government hog grading facilities are available, shall be graded in accordance with the standards for grades set forth in "Regulations with Respect to Hog Carcass Grading, being P.C. 2064, dated July 27th 1939, as amended by P.C. 2197, dated March 30, 1944, made under the Dominion Government Live Stock and Live Stock Products Act, 1939" and amendments thereto.

2. All hogs purchased by a licensed processor, where Dominion Government hog grading facilities are available, shall be paid for on the basis of the grade as shown on the grading certificate issued by a grader under the Hog Carcass Grading Regulations under the Live Stock and Live Stock Products Act, 1939, and amendments thereto, with price differential between grades.

3. All hogs purchased by a licensed "buyer" for resale to a licensed processor where Dominion Government hog grading facilities are available shall be paid for to the producer by the Licensed buyer on the basis of the grade as shown on the grading certificate issued by a grader under the Hog Carcass Grading Regulations under the Live Stock and Live Stock Products Act, 1939, and amendments thereto, with price differential between grades.

4. No grading certificate shall be used as a basis of settlement for any hog carcasses other than those for which it was issued.

5. Every "buyer" producer's agent or processor's agent, (or processor in case of purchases direct from producers), shall place, or cause to be placed, a distinct and specific tattoo mark of identity, or other mark of equal value approved by the producer, on each hog of each farmer's lot before they are allowed to mix with other hogs.

6. When hogs are processed where Dominion Government facilities are available prices quoted for hogs and all transactions, including final settlement to the producer, shall be on a warm dressed Grade A basis, with price differentials for other grades.

7. Every processor, "buyer" producer's agent and Processor's agent shall make out and sign a receipt on a prescribed form, or on a form approved by the local board, showing the producer's name, address, number of hogs, their mark of identity and shall cause same to be delivered to the producer at the time the hogs are received by the processor, "buyer" or agent.

8. Every producer's agent, or in case of direct sale every processor, shall make out, or cause to be made out, and furnish to the producer at the time of final settlement, a statement showing for each producer's lot of hogs:

A. which have been sold to a processor where Dominion grading services are available:

a) name and address of the producer,
b) name and address of processor,
c) date received by processor,
d) date of slaughter,
e) total number of carcasses,
f) identification mark,
g) warm weight of each carcass,
h) number of carcasses in each grade,
i) grade of each carcass,
j) the price paid per pound for each grade or the differential between grades,
k) gross amount paid, delivered to processor's plant, condemnation, insurance deducted.
l) amount of all deductions, including transportation, agent's commission, and other charges,
m) net amount to the producer, and

B. which have been sold to a processor where Dominion grading facilities are not available clauses (h), (i) and (j) of Section (A) may be omitted.

9. Every "buyer" or processor's agent shall make out, or cause to be made out, and furnish to the producer at the time of final settlement, a statement which shall show.

a) name and address of the producer
b) name and address of the processor
c) date received by processor
d) date of slaughter
e) total number of carcasses
f) identification mark
g) warm weight of each carcass

40

h) number of carcasses in each grade

i) grade of each carcass

j) the price paid per pound for each grade or differential between grades

k) net amount to producer

Except that in case of sale to a processor where grading facilities are not available clauses h), i), and j) of this section may be omitted.

10. A producer's agent shall not receive a commission for any remuneration of any kind whatsoever from other than producers; and a processor's agent shall not receive a commission or any remuneration of any kind whatsoever from other than processors.

11. In the case any regulations included in the Hog Grading Regulations under the Live Stock and Live Stock Products Act, 1939, and amendments thereto, have not been included, amended or varied by these rules the same shall be deemed to be in force in Ontario.

March 1st, 1947

These meetings represented one of the earliest efforts to bring all branches of the industry, producers, packers and government officials together in the sponsorship of a quality program. In August these representatives met and set up an ambitious program which included barn meetings and carcass demonstrations. The proposed programme that recommended a series of Barn Meetings should be held in the Counties under the sponsorship of the County Hog Producers' Associations or County Hog Producers' Committees, as the case may be, and in co-operation with Department officials and representatives of other interested groups. These meetings were to provide a means for reaching not only quality conscious farmers, but also many others not so interested.

In so far as possible, these were to be followed up by Hog Carcass Demonstration Meetings. The County Hog Producers' Associations were to seek the co-operation of the Agricultural Representatives to help with publicity, securing of proper halls, etc. The number of meetings to be held over the province and dates for same to be worked out at a later date.

The holding of Hog Demonstration meetings required the co-operation of the Dominion Department of Agriculture in the supplying of staff, equipment, cost of freight of materials, etc., the packers, in processing material and arranging for shipping, the Ontario Department of Agriculture through Agricultural Representatives, and the County Hog Producers' Associations, for all local arrangements such as advertising, creating local interest, arranging for halls and cost of halls, etc.

The Tentative Schedule for 1946 and 1947 was:

Dec. 1-15. 1946   (8 meetings),

January, 1947   (20 meetings),

41

February, 1947   (15 meetings),
March, 1947   (8 meetings).

3. Breeding Stock

Percentages of hogs that go into the Regular Market Grades:
3% belong to C and D
1.8% belong to Lights, Heavies and Extra Heavies
6% belong to B2 and B3 Grades
44.9% belong to B1 Grade
44.3% belong to A Grade

It was felt there should be some plan worked out with regard to breeding which would help to improve the quality of hogs and put the largest percentage produced in the "A" Grade. The real test for any boar is how he breeds, not how he looks. A boar will influence the type and quality of perhaps 200 to 300 pigs in a year, whereas, a sow may influence only 20 pigs in a year. Hence, it is felt the quickest way to show improvement in Ontario's hogs is to do something about more testing boars. Perhaps the reason for the start of opposition from truckers and shippers in Western Ontario was that they were inclined to feel directed to themselves the very severe criticisms levelled at the lack of proper forms farther East in the province.

At a board meeting held on September 10th, 1946, the question of uniform settlement forms came up for study and consideration. The minutes of November 12th contain a discussion of the inadequacy of the two cent levy per hog and the question of how the Minister of Agriculture might be persuaded to raise the levy to four cents per hog. Clayton Frey of Sarnia, a Board member from Southwestern Ontario for fifteen years, summed up the objectives of the Association and Board at this time years later: "The main objective was to establish a genuine competition in pricing all hogs in Ontario and to bring the market place within the reach of all producers, a competitive market within geographical reach of every producer . . . Processors wished a supply to keep their plants going and to this end had manipulated everything except a competitive pricing system . . . Perhaps producers were harsh in asking processors to correct the system".

The first annual meeting with the marketing scheme, or plan, in effect was held on March 26th, 1947. Mr. Milton had retired to become the full-time Secretary of the Ontario Concentrated Milk Producers' Association. Mr. Tummon now became Secretary-Treasurer. Again proposals were made that the fee be raised in order to better serve producers.

The Hon. Col. Kennedy was interviewed by the Board and suggested that, first, greater efforts should be made to collect on all hogs. This included those from the smaller processors and from hogs going out of the province.

Some small processors were declining to make the collections and packers outside the province considered themselves under no legal authority to make the collection. In the post war economy farmers costs were going up. The situation in 1947 was made more serious by a cold wet spring. Farmers were unable to finish seeding oats and barley until well into June. In July it was evident that there would be a serious shortage of home grown grain in the province. The Board felt that an increase of $2.00 per cwt. was the very least that would enable producers to provide the volume which Britain needed almost as much in the immediate post war period as during the time of hostilities.

With the current of party politics running strongly as it did in the forties W. E. Tummon would say at Board meetings: "I will handle everything at Queen's Park, but I won't talk to Gardiner". Almost in the same breath, he would move that McLeod and Bishop be sent to Ottawa. So at this time these two Liberals were again dispatched to Ottawa to see "Jimmy" Gardiner, the Federal Minister. With the support of Canadian producers and an understanding of their difficulties, Mr. Gardiner was ultimately to obtain an increase in the amount to be paid for Canadian pork being shipped to Britain.

Political connections were a natural tool to be used on behalf of farmers. Board members worked together and agreed on what must be done on behalf of the farmer. They used every possible means to persuade governments to implement farmer proposals. On one occasion, when the whole board was in the office of Col. Kennedy, he turned to Mr. Tummon and, having alluded to some particular proposal under discussion, asked: "Ernie, how will this help us get more Tory votes?" Col. Kennedy was a very good friend of the farmer who understood well the problems and concerns of the man on the back concessions. But he was compelled to balance his own opinions with Government inclinations to go slowly or to stall completely.

Frequent talks with Mr. Gardiner either by a committee or by the majority of the board paid off and the Meat Board obtained successive increases in the price paid by the British Ministry of Food for Canadian Wiltshire sides. In the later years the Canadian Government added some subsidy to help meet producer costs. Rt. Hon. James G. Gardiner, Minister of Agriculture for Canada, in the King and St. Laurent Governments from 1935-1957, was one of the most colourful political personalities of his era. Born on a Huron County farm he had gone to Saskatchewan as a young man to teach school. He went on to University, obtained his degree in economics, bought land and went into politics. Before going to Ottawa to join the King Government he had been Premier of Saskatchewan.

Mr. Gardiner was a strong political partisan as well as a realist. At the same time those who knew him were always impressed by his ready understanding of the farmer's problems and his practical down to earth approach. On one of his annual visits to the Canadian Federation of Agriculture his train was late and the announcement had been made that his address would be delayed. In came the Minister, kicked off his rubbers, threw his coat and hat on a chair, marched to the rostrum, reviewed policy and conditions and fenced questions in abundance without a note. In discussing farm conditions in Ontario with a small group of supporters of the Government during the late forties, Mr. Gardiner remarked "You can travel across Ontario, look at the farm houses, see by their architecture when they were built and notice almost all were built during war periods — the only time the farmer ever had enough money to build a house." During the 1957 federal election, Mr. Gardiner was introduced on one political platform in Ontario as, "A great agriculturalist, a great statesman and a great Canadian." However, Mr. Tummon's constant discussions with the Hon. Col. Kennedy continued to assist the hog producer programme. At the Board meeting held on August 28th, 1947, provision was made to clear off the old debts to directors, to the counties and to the Federation of Agriculture. In all, seven thousand dollars was so allotted.

By September, 1947, there was no doubt that farmers would be short of home grown feed as a result of a poor season and increases in cost of production would occur. Organized labour in the meat processing industry, with their usual disregard for the fate of the farmer, picked the Autumn of 1947 for a major strike. The small processors remained in operation, but all the large packers were closed by the strike. There was a very real danger that hog prices would drop to disastrous levels. The reaction of the Marketing Board was that, since they had a marketing plan with authority to negotiate with the packers on such matters as minimum price, this was the time to use such authority. To the producers' surprise there was no difficulty arriving at the figure of $23.00 per cwt., dressed, as the minimum price. In actual practice large numbers of the men on strike went out and worked extra shifts in the smaller plants and the fall runs of hogs were handled without any really serious bottle necks. Without this minimum price, it was generally conceded that the price would have dropped to about $19.00 per cwt., or perhaps even lower.

The office space at 95 King Street had not proved adequate. Early in the Autumn of 1947 a search for better accommodation lead to more adequate facilities at 77 York Street south of the Prince George Hotel. Here was space for the Secretary, for office staff and for a board room. Seventy-seven York Street was headquarters until the late nineteen-fifties.

Another instance of the growing legal strength and prestige of the hog producers' organization was soon evident. While progress had been made in improving methods of sale and settlement forms, there were still many cases of the shipper or drover collecting payment from the packer and distributing cash or cheques to farmers. One of these drovers had delivered hogs to a packer and received payment which he deposited in his own account, pending the issue of cheques to the farmers in question. In the meantime, the bank forced him into bankruptcy and took possession of his assets including the monies he had deposited in receipt of hogs shipped. The Ontario Hog Producers' Marketing Board challenged the right of the Bank of Toronto to take over monies that were in reality the property of the farmers who had supplied the hogs and were in the process of being transferred to the farmer. W. E. Tummon and Clayton Frey, representing the zone in which the farmers involved were resident, spent considerable time and effort working with solicitors employed by the Marketing Board to argue the producer case against the bank. The court ruled that the monies representing payment to the farmers were not a part of the assets of the drover and that the Bank of Toronto must turn such funds over to the individual hog producers involved.

Hog purchasers had long questioned the fairness of the way they were charged to cover insurance on their hogs while in transit to various packing plants. The bulk of this insurance was in the hands of an American based company which charged excess rates. In many cases the amount of the insurance was charged back directly on the settlement form where such was in use. This was an Association matter rather than a Marketing Board concern. The action of the Hog Producers' Association was to approach the newly organized co-operations Insurance Association, recently set up with Federation of Agriculture for assistance. Co-operators Insurance agreed to enter the field of transit insurance. Although it did not sell a great many policies, competition was provided that resulted in substantial savings to Ontario farmers.

Gradually, live buying of hogs had been disappearing. By the early months of 1948 it was almost a thing of the past. In the year 1948 post war bacon contracts still influenced producer price and increases achieved were still inadequate. The increase in 1948 was only 25¢ per cwt. At the Board meeting of April 27th, 1948, W. E. Tummon was commended by his colleagues for his work in setting out the prices position of hog producers in a brief for presentation to the Royal Commission investigating prices.

The grass roots strength of the Association had been increasing. More credit in this field was due to "Charlie" McInnis than to anyone else. He had become "Charlie" to thousands of Ontario farm people. It may well be that no one farm leader either before or since has wielded quite the same degree of influence. In addition to being President of the Hog Producers, he served on several executives. He was a member of the executive of the Concentrated Milk Producers' Association, a member of the executive of the

Ontario Federation of Agriculture, and served for a time as a director of United Co-operatives. "Charlie" could always be counted on to bring out a crowd to a farm meeting. Never at a loss for words, he combined sincerity with constant humour, attacking interests that exploited farm people with all the rhetoric and fervor of an old fashioned evangelist. He was always in demand at rural meetings from Windsor to the Ottawa River. On the platform he would plead for his hearers to remember that. "It was our forebearers who cleared the land and built this country. Why should we be second class citizens?" McInnis became a common sight hurrying through the rushing throngs in Toronto's Union Station to his home away from home, his book filled permanent room 202 on the second floor in the north-east of the Old Walker House Hotel just west of the Union Station. If it was a Monday morning his clothes would be crumpled by an all night ride in a day coach from his Eastern Ontario home in Dundas County. His hat would be shoved back on his head displaying the bald dome he liked to joke about on the platform. Any friend in the throng might be assured of a friendly greeting as Charlie strode to his hotel.

As the years went by "Charlie" spent more and more of his time in Toronto or travelling across the province. He never received any salary; just the per diem allowance that happened to be current at the time and expenses for meals, lodging and travel. The Walker House, where he stayed, was one of Toronto's older hotels and it had seen better days. Each room boasted running water only. As room 202 gained recognition as "Charlie's" personal abode, it became lined with books dealing with marketing, economics and organization. McInnis educated himself. His extensive reading added year by year to his basic high school education.

The feeling of frustration in dealing with governments, packers and drovers created both the substance and the style of McInnis's homespun oratory. There was developed a very strong grass roots depth of interest and support for the struggles of the board and association across rural Ontario. Arnold Burnside of Dufferin County, a participant in the Association for many years, had this to say of McInnis:

"I used to enjoy Charlie's addresses. He could really hold an audience. I used to say he would make a good evangelist. He put his all into that association and he believed in his idea of the farmer controlling his product. I thought he was a good man and I still do. He was sincere and devoted to his dreams".

But for "Charlie", the Marketing Board would not be what it is today. He had help from other leaders, but he was the spark that assured the eternal flame. The full and varied effect of McInnis' speeches and personal contacts can never be completely evaluated. Mr. Everett Biggs, later Deputy Minister of Agriculture in Ontario, has said that listening to "Charlie" McInnis address a meeting of Middlesex County Hog Producers, where Biggs was assistant agriculture representative in that county, inspired him to go on to take post graduate work in agricultural economics.

It is only fair to say that "Charlie's" weakest spot was his belief that those who disagreed with him, whether they were opponents in industry, in government or among his colleagues, must be completely wrong. There was early on evidence of a growing confrontation between "Charlie" McInnis and "Ernie" Tummon traceable to basic personality differences between the two men. They had many things in common. Both were particularly active laymen in the United Church, both were members of the same fraternal order, but they were almost exact opposites in their administrative views and in their attitudes towards the role of government.

"Charlie" McInnis became more and more critical of W. E. Tummon's approach to negotiations with both processors and government officials. "Charlie" felt Mr. Tummon was much too inclined to compromise with both groups and to back away from an unyielding stand for the farmer viewpoint. He was inclined to blame Tummon when progress was not as rapid as might have been desired. One member of the board approached each of them suggesting a compromise between their conflicting philosophies, he was turned down by both.

County associations were now playing a more active part in supporting the provincial Board. Lincoln County, for example was co-operating with the local board representative in checking on local small processors in order to ensure bringing them within the "Scheme".

In 1947 "night letters" had been dispatched by county association to the Prime Minister, Minister of Agriculture and local members, urging enhanced prices to enable continuance of the desired volume of pork for Britain. In the same year a local boar bonusing programme was instituted to encourage improved quality of product. Local directors were meeting regularly and the local member of the provincial board often was present to report on the programmes and policies being developed through the Toronto office. There was a social aspect to these Lincoln County meetings as time after time wives of some of the local directors served a bountiful lunch at about midnight to conclude the deliberations of the evening.

From the start of the Marketing Scheme a constant problem was the movement of Ontario hogs to the Montreal market. As a result of representations to the Federal Government, an act entitled "An Act to provide for the Marketing of Agricultural Products in Interprovincial and Export Trade" was introduced March 14th, 1949, and subsequently enacted. The significant authority was spelled out as follows:-

1) The Governor in Council may by or order grant authority to any

board or agency authorized under the law of any province to exercise powers of regulation in locally within the province, to regulate the marketing of such agricultural product outside the province in inter-provincial and export trade and for such purposes to exercise all or any powers like the powers exercisable by such board or agency in relation to the marketing of such agricultural product locally within the province.

In May of the same year L. W. Pearsall of the Meat Board in correspondence with Secretary W. E. Tummon spoke as follows referring to this legislation: "Its intent is to authorize provincial boards with respect to out of province movement, to exercise all or any powers like those exercisable by such Board in relation to marketings within the province."

The question arose in 1949 as to whether federal carcass grading regulations were really enforceable. Would it be of assistance if they were incorporated as a part of the regulations under the provincial plan? The result was that these grading specifications of 1947 were included in the regulations under the provincial scheme and the federal graders were given provincial status as well. Rules governing sales remained a problem and required further modifications as exemplified by the Rules of April 14th, 1949.

Rules

1. When hogs are processed where Government Grading facilities are available prices quoted for hogs and all transactions shall be on a warm dressed Grade A basis, with price differentials for other grades.
2. Every buyer, producer's agent or processor's agent, (or processor in case of purchases direct from producers), shall place, or cause to be placed, a distinct and specific tattoo mark of identity on each hog of each farmer's lot before they are allowed to mix with other hogs.
3. Every processor, buyer, producer's agent and processor's agent shall make out and sign a receipt on a prescribed form, or on a form approved by the local board, showing the producer's name, address, number of hogs, their mark of identity and shall cause same to be delivered to the producer at the time the hogs are received by the processor, buyer or agent.
4. Every producer's agent, or in case of direct sale every processor, shall furnish to the producer on the statement as required under Sections 8 & 9 of the Grades and Sales Act, and in addition thereto, the following:-
   a) Gross amount paid, delivered to processor's plant, condemnation insurance (if any) deducted.

   b) Amount of all deductions, including transportation, agent's commission etc.

   c) Net amount to the producer.

5. Every buyer, or processor's agent shall furnish to the producer on the statement as required under Sections 8 & 9 of the Grades and Sales Act, and in addition thereto, the following:-
   a) Net amount to the producer.
6. A producer's agent shall not receive a commission or any remuneration of any kind whatsoever other than that shown on the producer's statement; and a processor's agent shall not receive a commission or any remuneration of any kind whatsoever from other than processors.

There continued to be difficulties in persuading shippers to take out licenses as shown by this note from W. E. Tummon to Mr. Frank Perkin – Chairman of the Farm Products Marketing Board. "Enclosed is a copy of Notice we have sent out to all shippers who were licensed in 1948 but have failed to make application again this year, according to the reports we have received from your Department. The notice in question was as follows:-

Notice to "Shippers" of Hogs

If you already have your license as "shipper" for the period beginning April 1st, 1949, and ending March 31st, 1950, or have made application for same, this notice does not apply to you. *It does apply to those who have not made application for a license.*
Under the recently amended Hog Producers' Marketing Scheme a "shipper" is defined as follows: "Shipper" means a person who,-

   i) Receives hogs as agent for a processor; or
   ii) Assembles, ships and transports by any means of transportation and offers for sale hogs to a processor as agent for a producer.

Therefore, if you are engaged in the assembling, shipping or transporting of hogs, other than your own production, for processing, you are required to obtain a license. Application should be made immediately to *THE FARM PRODUCTS MARKETING BOARD, PARLIAMENT BUILDINGS, TORONTO,* which is a branch of the Ontario Department of Agriculture. Any person whose application has not been received by September 30th and continues to act as a "shipper" will be reported to the Board at the Parliament Buildings and legal action requested. Trusting we may have your co-operation."

But there were other problems and efforts to improve the regulations under the marketing plan as witnessed by the following letter from W. E. Tummon to Mr. Perkin:

In regard to the Hog Producers' Marketing Scheme, our Board respectfully suggests:

1. That under the Regulations the interpretation of "shipper" as in the Ontario Hog Carcass Grading regulations be adopted. That definition is

as follows:- "Shipper" means a person who-

i) assembles, ships, transports, or offers for sale hogs to a packer as agent for a producer: or

ii) assembles, ships and transports hogs as agent for a packer.

We believe it would be better to have the definitions in the Hog Carcass Grading Regulations and the Scheme the same and our Board prefers the definition in the Hog Carcass Grading Regulations.

2. That a clause be inserted in the Regulations of the Scheme requiring that "shipper" to protect the producer's hogs while they are in transit from the producer's premises to the processing plant.

Quite a number of shippers in the past have carried their own insurance i.e. they provided for any loss in transit in the commission they charged for marketing. Our observations are that those who assumed the responsibility for losses in this manner proved more satisfactory than those who carried Transit Insurance. Therefore, we do not favour a regulation stating simply that the shipper carry Transit Insurance but that he protect the producer's hogs either by Insurance or otherwise.

Trusting these suggestions will meet with your approval, I remain.

Two months later additional correspondence tells a story in itself:-

Dear Mr. Perkin:

Relative to the proposed additions and amendments to the Regulations of the Hog Marketing Scheme and with particular reference to the subject matter dealt with in Section 4, Sub-section 2, of the Grading Regulations, which reads:

"A packer shall prepare, in quadruplicate, for presentation to a producer the statement of account portion of the certificate in respect of the hog-carcasses of the producer."

1. At present 60% or more of all settlements for hogs are made by packers direct to producers. Producers are demanding that all hogs going direct from their premises to the processor shall be settled for by the packer that the processor is the purchaser of our hogs and therefore we have a right to expect from them a statement of account at time of settlement. The packers object for they feel this sub-section, as it is, places upon them the responsibility of policing the shippers who are agent for the producers, or in other words, telling the shippers what they should do. They claim they are willing to make out the statements of settlement if requested by as they say, our agents, the shippers.

We were requested to try and arrive at an arrangement that would meet the wishes of both sides. We think a regulation something like the following might be satisfactory:

"That when delivery of hogs by a shipper is direct to a processor the

50

shipper shall authorize the processor to prepare and complete the presentation to the producer the statement of account in respect to the hogs of the producer."

2. Hogs that do not go direct to the establishments of the processors go on the Stock Yards to be offered for sale by the Commission Merchants. Often these hogs are sold to small slaughterers who, nevertheless, are designated as "Processors" under our Scheme. We believe that, when the shipper delivers the hogs to a commission merchant, the shipper should authorize the commission merchant to make out the settlement statement of account.

3. If it is found that it is difficult to show a form of settlement in the regulations, since the present combined Grading and Settlement Form is supplied by the Dominion Government free of charge, then it would seem that the alternative would be to make a regulation that would enumerate the items required to be on the Form.

4. May I mention a point that is giving me concern: Our entire Scheme is built up on "hogs" whereas all purchases and settlements by the larger processors are on a carcass basis. A hog carcass is no longer a hog. It is true that butchers and small processors, where grading facilities are not available, may purchase on a hog basis, but 90% is sold and purchases on a carcass basis. It would perhaps be advisable to have a look at the Scheme and Regulations with this point in mind.

No. 1 is the only point we anticipate having any trouble with in getting the approval of the Negotiating Committee and we would be glad to have a draft to submit to the Committee at the earliest possible date.

If it is found necessary or advisable to define "carcass", it would need to be something like this:

"carcass" means the warm carcass of a hog, with viscera removed, head and feet on, and leaf lard and kidneys in."

British Bacon Contracts were gradually being phased out towards the end of 1949. The Ministry of Food in the U. K. claimed it was financially impossible to maintain the prevailing price for Wiltshire sides but finally agreed to a price of $29.00 at Seaboard, a decline of $7.00 cwt. The Canadian Government added $3.50 per cwt. late in 1950, while The Meat Board added another $1.25 later in the year. After September 1st, 1947, limitations on the amount of pork products available for the domestic market were lifted. So called "contracts" were merely an expression of the amount that the British Ministry of Food would take. The following document clarifies the relationship between Bacon Contract Price and domestic price of warm dressed carcasses:

Re: United Kingdom Bacon Agreement and Price

The question is asked, why are the Packers paying $28.50 for hogs when the price was supposed to go up $7.00 per hundred. The increase of $7.00 per 100 lbs. is the price of Wiltshire sides F.O.B. Seaboard, and net on the Warm Dressed Carcass weight. A hog weighing 200 lbs. live weight will produce approximately a 150 lb. warm dressed weight carcass but there are only 116 lbs. of Wiltshire in that carcass. The balance is head, feet, and trimmings, which amounts to 34 lbs. The 7c increase per lb. is on the 116 lbs. making a total increase of $8.12.

The packer thus has the 34 lbs. of head, feet and trimmings which at the old price had a value of about 12c a lb. or $4.34. The $7.00 increase from $29.00 to $36.00 is an increase of 24%. An increase of 24% on $4.34 is $1.04 thus, the $7.00 increase on 116 lbs. Wiltshire — $8.12 — 24% increase on 34 lbs. head, and etc. — $1.04. A total increase on the 150 lbs. carcass — $9.16 or about $6.00 per 100 lb. carcass weight. Add $6.00 per hundred to $23.00 the old minimum price makes it $29.00 F.O.B. Toronto.

Our feeling at the moment is that the new price will settle somewhere around that figure. Just now no one knows whether the consumer will pay an increased price for the head cheese, hocks etc. which must be sold on the same market. You must also remember the price quoted now of $28.50 is F.O.B. Toronto, and the drovers charges all come off that.

The growing realization that the British market was gradually becoming less dependable and the continuing failure of the Negotiating Committee to find agreement with the packers in the establishment of a minimum price led the Board to think more and more about new means of ensuring producers a fair price.

The first thought of Central Selling, that is, taking control of the hogs and selling them as an agent of the producer, was thought to be particularly relevant to the problems of Eastern Ontario hogs being shipped to Montreal. The first man to exress confidence in a Central Selling Agency was George Johnston of Grey County who had joined the Board in 1945. At first, other Board Members were sceptical about whether the idea could be developed into a practical mechanism. The first effort to make a serious study of central selling possibilities was the appointment of a special committee consisting of McInnis, Johnson, Rintoul, Frey and Bishop at the Board meeting of July 26th, 1949. At this time the idea was to set up an agency for a given area and to be sure that the consent of the producers in the particular area was obtained for the experiment. This committee continued its study during the autumn, and, in December, went to Ottawa to discuss the possibilities with Mr. A. M. Shaw, former Dean of Agriculture at the University of Saskatchewan. Mr. Gardiner had brought Mr. Shaw to Ottawa as one of his major aides. They also met with Mr. Alex Turner, one of the chief economists of the Federal Department of Agriculture. The main outcome of these discussions was the assurance by Government officials that the product might be controlled, but the persons in the trade could not be.

Mr. Johnson was on record proposing that as much speed as possible be used so that a report of their findings might be ready by the time of the coming annual meeting.

Since 1941 there had always been marked differences of opinion as to the sharing of authority between hog producer leaders and the processors in the industry. Mr. Arkell, retired former head of the Livestock Services of the Federal Department of Agriculture, had in the mid 1940's been employed as a consultant. In 1949 the Board felt it wise to obtain a comprehensive study of the whole swine industry in order that some authoritative guide posts might be set up to meet forthcoming problems. Dr. J. E. Lattimer seemed to be the right man for the job. As a young man, he gave up farming in Brant County, improved his education and became one of Canada's best known agricultural economists. Now in 1949 he has recently retired as head of the Economics Department of MacDonald College, the agricultural college of McGill University, Montreal. Dr. Lattimer made an extensive study which was presented to the annual meeting in March, 1950.

The substance of the report encouraged the Board to go forward in developing new policies. On March 3rd, 1950, the Board sought advice from Leonard Mitchell, a Bay St. lawyer who served a number of co-operative organizations. Mr. Mitchell advised seeking changes in the Farm Products Marketing Act to establish a more definite base for a central selling agency. Producers definitely were not satisfied with how hogs were picked up at the farm. Too often they were taken wherever the trucker wished. The continuing discussion of these difficulties led to the Economics Division of the Canadian Department of Agriculture early in 1950 appointing Mr. J. S. Rackham to make a study of how hogs in Grey County were actually marketed. The time selected was a four week period between March 2 and April 22, 1950. The findings were indicative of marketing methods across Ontario. Here are some excerpts from the report finally published in 1952:

Producers' Participation in Marketing Process

The producer's principal means of participating in the marketing of hogs was in his choice of trucker or method of shipment. While only 12 per cent of all producers specified where their hogs were to go, at least 47 per cent knew their destinations and many of these may have determined the destination by the selection of trucker or shipper. On the other hand, 46 per cent of the producers stated that they did not know at the time the hogs left their farms where, or to whom, they would eventually be sold.

Many producers had no information as to prices in effect at the time of shipment of their hogs, 64 per cent reporting that they had no specific information in this regard.

Another important factor in this regard is that prices on the Toronto market are usually unsettled in the early part of the week and it is usually Tuesday or early Wednesday before relatively stable prices are established on this market.

When a producer ships hogs to the stockyards or a packing plant, final settlement is not made until after the hog is slaughtered and the carcass is weighed and graded. Then the producer is normally paid by a cheque accompanied by a settlement statement. The price quoted per 100 pounds on these settlement statements will be termed throughout this report as the "gross price".

A common form of settlement statement showed a price at the packing plant, deduction for haulage from the farm, the assessment for the Ontario Hog Producers' Association and condemnation insurance. Another common type showed only the latter two deductions on the statement, the haulage charge having already been deducted from the gross price.

Since the settlement statements showed a gross price which in some cases was F.O.B. plant, in others F.O.B. farm, and in still others some intermediate point of the marketing process, it is difficult to compare gross prices received by producers during the survey period. The only item on the statements which is quoted in a uniform way is the gross price.

These excerpts show the confused market situation prevailing in the province.

During the annual meeting sessions of March 1st and 2nd, Central selling figured prominently in the discussions.

The year 1950 was one of growing tension in the association. W. E. Tummon, looking at the issues with a conservative eye, was rather sceptical of the possibilities of Central selling. There was a generation gap between him and the majority of Board as he was a couple of decades older. This naturally made some difference in his thinking. This Board majority was largely representative of producer feeling across the province. The British market was disappearing and there seemed no authority by which the producer might be assured of a fair price. The minutes of a Zone Four meeting called during the year cast interesting light on the conditions prevailing on the board:

A meeting of Zone Hog Producers was held, with members present from Brant, Oxford, Haldimand and Wentworth counties. There were 39 present. The meeting agreed that Mr. Earl Hopkins should be Chairman and Kenneth Best, acting Secretary. The minutes of the meeting are as follows:-

"The Chairman called upon Wilfred Bishop to explain the purpose of the meeting. Mr. Bishop explained that a crisis had arisen in the Provincial Executive. The main difficulty had arisen due to the actions and feelings of the Secretary of that Organization and the Marketing Board. Mr. Bishop also explained that a majority of the members of the Board had agreed informally that they felt the Secretary of the Board should resign.

The case was further explained with several illustrations. He stated that the Board has been attempting to get negotiations for minimum prices on hogs. He felt that the case is as strong or stronger than is the case with milk. When a motion concerning the above was passed at a meeting of the Board, the Secretary said that he would not act. Due to this situation Mr. Bishop felt that a meeting of the counties in the zone was necessary. During the period of low hog prices in September, Mr. Bishop said that the Secretary of the Board had been asked to call a meeting and this he claimed was not done and he further stated that it had been impossible to contact the Secretary during this critical period.

To further explain the lack of confidence in the Secretary, Mr. Bishop referred to minutes of a board meeting in which any criticism of the Secretary had been deleted and personal opinion of the Secretary had been given a prominent part. At this point Mr. Bishop tabled his resignation in the capacity of zone representative so that the meeting might deal freely with the matter.

The Chairman at this point commented that at the last Annual Meeting of the Provincial organization, he had been approached to speak for the zone, for a more suitable secretary-treasurer. He stressed the fact that it was essential that unity in the organization be preserved and had, therefore, let the matter rest for the time being.

Mr. Hopkins further stated that with due regard to Mr. Tummon, he felt that he could not fully represent the producers. Mr. Hopkins next called on Norman McLeod of Galt, Chairman of the Board, to present his feelings about matters.

Mr. McLeod added that Mr. Tummon had been instructed several times to meet with commission firms at the Stock Yards on behalf of the Central Marketing Agency. This request he explained, had been ignored. Mr. McLeod further explained difficulties which members of the board had encountered at the time of low prices during the second week in September.

Mr. McLeod also explained the matter of the motion of the board at the time it attempted to set up negotiations. He felt that the Secretary had not said that he wouldn't act, but rather that he personally did not wish to act on this matter, with the implication that someone else perhaps more capable should act in this capacity. Mr. McLeod assured the meeting that the board and its Secretary got a "run around" at Queen's Park. He agreed that it is time for a showdown.

Mr. Hopkins, at this point, opened the meeting for a frank discussion. Mr. Pearson of Brant County, suggested a vote of confidence in the Zone Representative. Mr. Lockwood, of Oxford, expressed the opinion that if the Board is not co-operative it is time for house cleaning or else the Board should be dissolved. Mr. Lockwood commended aggressiveness in a search for protection.

A Norfolk representative assured confidence in Wilfred Bishop. A member from Haldimand asked if the Board has a right to ask the Secretary to resign and received a reply that the Secretary is hired by the Board, upon which a member expressed the opinion that house cleaning was in order.

Several questions followed concerning the hiring and firing of a Secretary. At which point it was explained that the Board consists of seven zone members. The Executive consists of the President of the Hog Producers in addition to this Board. It was further explained that the Board hires the Secretary and that it happens that he is also Secretary of the Executive.

It was stated that Mr. McInnis, Provincial President, was experiencing a very similar difficulty. It was cited for example that an invitation had been sent from the Bruce County Local to speak at one of their meetings and the Secretary had taken it upon himself to answer the call.

Mr. Gushart, of Wentworth, commended Mr. Bishop for calling the meeting and suggested that the meeting lend support to the Provincial Executive. It was moved by Andy Gushart, seconded by Russel Smith that this meeting support the action of Mr. Bishop on the Provincial Executive. Motion was carried unanimously.

It was moved by Mr. Pearson, seconded by Harry Lockwood, that we also send a copy of the resolution to the Chairman of the Marketing Board, to read before the Board, that the meeting strongly endorses the action of Mr. Bishop, our Representative on the Board. Motion was carried unanimously.

Mr. Hopkins at this point, expressed the confidence of the meeting, to Mr. Bishop and asked that he carry on as Zone representative. Mr. Bishop thanked the group and offered assistance at any local meetings, including reports of developments."

Mrs. Jean Wright, after four years of service to the Hog Producers', left to rejoin the office staff of the Ontario Federation of Agriculture. Her position was filled by Miss Orma Clarke who was to serve for an equal number of years.

CHAPTER IV

A SIDE VENTURE HAMILTON CO-OPERATIVE PACKERS

Canadian farmers have continually used co-operative action as a weapon in the struggle for economic betterment. The frustration experienced by Hog Producers in 1950 directed the thoughts of some leaders in the movement towards the possibility of co-operative processing of meats. In District No. 4 action was taken in April, 1950, when a committee was set up to investigate possibilities in this field. During the summer and autumn a careful and cautious study was made. Rumors of the plant of John Duff and Sons being for sale lead to a meeting with officials of this company in December, 1950.

During the period of British Bacon Contracts a number of the middle sized plants neglected domestic sales, failing to maintain sales staff and concentrating on the export of Wiltshire sides to Britain. When exports declined, these plants found it difficult to operate profitably. The Duff plant was one in this position. Following the initial talks with the Duff Bros., who currently operated the business, there were discussions with Mr. K. N. Morrison, manager of First Co-op Packers, Barrie, and other leaders of the co-operative movement in Ontario. With Mr. Morrison's assistance, on March 15th, 1951, a tentative price for the plant, equipment and real estate was worked out. Real estate consisted of a whole city block in the industrial area of Hamilton. The tentative price was $535,000 of which at least one hundred thousand was to be paid in cash. A mortgage was to be held on the remainder. Goods on hand were to be priced at cost or at the market value, which ever was the lower, and were to be settled for on a cash basis.

The sum of the proposals involving this purchase were taken to the farmers, first in county meetings and then to a general meeting held at Kohler in Haldimand County. After a complete discussion and review of the studies that had been made, the vote of 61 to 6 gave the go ahead to organize a co-op packing company and to raise money to purchase the Duff business.

During the summer of 1951, while the drive to raise capital was just getting under way, lack of funds forced the Duff firm to cease operations. The extreme difficulties forced the provisional board, now known as Hamilton Co-op Packers, to negotiate a new agreement which provided a lower price and included a block and one half of vacant city property. An announcement of the new deal was made as follows:

Co-Op Packing Plant For Ontario Farmers

The Provisional Committee of the Hamilton Co-operative Packers Ltd. announce that negotiations have been completed for the purchase of the Hamilton Plant of John Duff and Sons Ltd.

This plant, covering two and a half city blocks, equipped to a weekly processing capacity of 2,000 hogs, 200 cattle, numerous calves, sheep and lambs, together with a cheese curing plant, dairy products division and a first class egg grading station, will be operated on a true co-operative basis to serve the farmers of Southern Ontario.

The need for a centrally located packing plant in this area is great. The need for a packing industry in which farmers have some control is even greater. How soon this farmer owned and operated plant will begin operations now depends on the farmers themselves. Their long cherished hope of having some measure of control of their industry is within reach.

The Provisional Committee of this Co-operative, Chairman W. Bishop of Norwich; Secretary-Treasurer J. Ewart Brown, Hamilton; R. Bartlett, Jordan Station and J. Carter, Hagersville, together with the Provisional Directors H. R. Metler, Welland; D. Reihl, Lincoln; I. Norseworthy, Wentworth; Alex Hedley, Haldimand; Ford Jamieson, Norfolk; Earl Hopkins, Brant; W. Benton, Oxford; J. Oldham, Elgin; and D. McKinnon, Wellington have organized a campaign to raise this capital among the farmers of these districts.

Every farmer will benefit by the stabilizing effect of this Co-operative Packing Plant. Livestock producers will have their own market, grain producers a ready outlet for their product for grain is necessary before meat can be produced. Fruits and vegetable growers will have better customers for their produce among their fellow farmers and so on down the line will its effects be felt with increased confidence in the agricultural future of this area resulting.

Even though this Co-op will only handle a small portion of the total volume of livestock at the start, it has great facilities for expansion. It will operate closely with a similar Co-op Packing Plant at Barrie which has been outstandingly successful. With local support of all farmers, their combined volume could be sufficient in effect, to control this industry in the producers' best interest, for he who holds the balance of power in any situation, has strength even in excess of those of far greater stature.

This is within reach of the farmers of this district through their purchase of shares to be issued at $100.00 each to raise the required capital. These shares will receive interest up to 4 per cent according to the earnings of the Co-operative, after which participating patronage dividends will be issued. This is an opportunity for the farmer to invest in his own future, to show confidence in his profession and stabilize his industry.

The Committee states that this plant is being maintained in readiness for production as soon as the required capital is raised by the farmers in the area it will serve. Of this capital $300,000 represents the purchase price of land, buildings and equipment with enough more needed to adequately finance its continued operation.

Under the new agreement better progress was made. However, the process of raising capital created the basis of a legal argument. The farmer board felt that the second agreement was not completely in accord with the verbal agreement which proceeded it. Duff then entered into a new sales agreement with Essex Packers who had lost their Hamilton plant by fire.

A registered letter, received in March of 1952 and directed to Wilfred Bishop, Harvey Charlton, Alex Hedley and Alex Anderson sent a shock through the Hog Producers' executive. It stated:

Confirming our conversation with Mr. Bishop on Friday, March 7th, an agreement for the sale of substantially all the assets and undertaking of John Duff & Sons Limited to Essex Packers Limited was signed Thursday evening March 6th.

In as much as the agreement and Option dated November 3rd, 1951 between John Duff & Sons Limited and the said Trustees has not been maintained or completed and has not been re-established within the thirty day period provided it is considered to have lapsed by default.

We hereby notify you of cancellation of the said agreement. Regretting the necessity of this action.

At this point the Ontario Hog Producers' Association made available the legal services of their solicitors, Aylesworth, Garder, Thompson and Stanbury of 67 Yonge Street, Toronto. The legal advice of Mr. Chas. Thompson of this firm was that the agreement with John Duff & Sons Limited could not be enforced. From this point the responsibility of the officers and directors of Hamilton Co-op Packers was to arrange for the maximum payments back to the shareholders. Funds that were in the hands of canvassers were returned intact in most cases. Any loss that was left was for those shareholders whose contributions had already been deposited. Mr. J. E. Brown, a former staff member of the Duff firm who had been Secretary-Treasurer, threw up his hands and quit, abandoning all the financial records, and leaving them in a desk in the plant. The Producers' Chairman, Wilfred Bishop, went to Hamilton, seized these records and turned them over to a neutral party, Mr. David Croft, Office Manager of the Norwich Co-op, requesting that they be put in this co-operative's vault for safe keeping.

The Provisional Board of Directors then established contact with the Ontario Securities Commission. In spite of the deluge of demands for immediate return of investment contributions with the legal advice of Aylesworth, Garder, Thompson and Stanbury, they proceeded with the settlement. One of the solicitors for the Commission calling on the producers' chairman, found him busy with spring seeding, driving a W30 International Tractor, wearing an old coat and sporting a four days' growth of beard. The lawyer invited him to get in the car to discuss the procedures being followed. He listened and looking sideways with amazement observed,

"Why! you are an educated man."

What strange fellows these farmers are.

Mr. Croft was engaged to calculate all outstanding obligations and the amount returnable to each shareholder. Mr. Brown agreed to be a co-signer with the chairman of all the cheques to be sent out.

The minutes of the meeting of the Provisional Board in the autumn of 1952, concerning this matter, follows:

Meeting Of Directors Of The Hamilton Co-Operative Packers

A meeting of the directors of the Hamilton Co-operative Packers was held in the Agriculture Office, Hamilton, October 7th, 1952. The Chairman was Wilfred Bishop. Alex Anderson was appointed to act as Secretary for the meeting. Directors present were A. Hedley; H. Metler; F. Jamieson; D. McKinnon; Mr. Moore; and Mr. Norseworthy:

Wilfred Bishop reported on recent meetings with officials of the Essex Packers, the Duff Brothers and a Government lawyer, and stated that the wind up of the business of the Hamilton Co-operative Packers would be supervised by the Ontario Securities Commission.

Mr. Croft presented a statement of expenses and receipts of the Hamilton Co-operative Packers.

It was moved by A. Hedley and seconded by J. Moore "that there be no payments to directors for per diem or travelling expenses." Carried. Moved by D. McKinnon and seconded by Mr. Norseworthy "that the Hamilton Co-operative Packers pay back to the shareholders the amount or percentage of the share as advised by the lawyer of the Securities Commission". Carried. Moved by H. Metler and seconded by J. Moore "that Wilfred Bishop and J. E. Brown be signing officials for cheques issued from the Hamilton Co-operative Packers bank account in the Royal Bank, Hamilton." Carried.

The meeting instructed W. Bishop to construct a letter which would be suitable to the Securities Commission lawyer to be sent back to the shareholders along with the cheque for their share. The meeting then adjourned.

The letter mentioned above appeared as follows:

Dear Subscriber:

Last spring no one contemplated that it would be more than a few weeks at the most to close up the affairs of Hamilton Co-op Packers and it is a source of great regret to all members of the committee that it was not possible to realize this time schedule.

By last February the basic organization was completed and the campaign was showing enough success to justify a bid for complete success by March 31. The original option agreement with the Duffs had been supplemented by several amendments over the signature of Frank Duff which were accepted in good faith by your committee and the campaign pushed forward with additional vigour. To a largely attended and enthusiastic meeting of the Producers Committee at the end of February the Duffs suggested they would like to break the deal with the farmers in favour of one with other parties at that time unknown. The farmers' reply was that the press would immediately have the story of the farmers' position so that a meeting of all the subscribers might be held to consider possible future action. Mr. Duff begged that no announcement be made and gave an absolute pledge to the committee that no announcement of any kind would be made without the knowledge and consent of the Co-op committee. The next information your committee had was a story in the press announcing the sale of the Duff plant to Essex Packers in direct repudiation of the pledge. Both of the parties have blamed the other. However, this completely unjustified announcement by the President of Essex Packers had the effect of causing Co-op Canvassers to return the funds in their possession to subscribers. Consequently, about a third of the subscriptions, the amounts already paid into the central fund, are being forced to bear the full brunt of the expenses which should have been dispersed to everyone. Cases are few and far between when any other parties have acted in such repudiation of their pledges and so against fair and decent farmer interests. With scarcely a week going by without action your committee since then has gone through detailed negotiations with the parties, government officials and the solicitor of the Provincial Assoc. with the constant objective of acquiring sufficient funds to cover advertising expenses, Mr. Brown's salary, and option payment: so that one hundred cents on the dollar might be paid to all subscribers.

Your committee regards the present payment as only the first payment and will relentlessly battle until complete payments are possible. In different counties the exact method of payment will differ. Haldimand county subscribers will call at the office of the Haldimand Co-op for their cheques and Wellington county members will receive theirs through the county Hog Producers Assoc.

The enclosed financial statement shows the picture as revealed by the audit and also the contributions made by the members of the Committee through the medium of personal spending, time and services towards making a final 100% payment to all subscribers.

Yours truly,
Wilfred L. Bishop
Chairman.

Statement

Receipts		Expenses	
Payments for Stock	25,760.00	Exchange	64.79
Donation	5.00	Salary (J. E. Brown)	1,485.00
Debentures	1,110.00	Commissions	367.00
Memberships	1,050.00	Travelling	605.07
		Telephone	38.20
		Postage	59.99
		Printing & Station.	588.02
		Advertising	203.80
	27,925.00	Duff Option	1,781.50
		Supplies	9.98
		Legal Expenses	178.00
			22,543.15
	Balance		27,925.00

With added bank interest and memberships donated the committee has authorized the payment of $84.00 per $100.00.

Committee Members Expenses which have been Donated

C. E. Lindsay	33.56
Harry Lockwood	10.00
Alex Hedley	1,065.73

A. MacQuarrie	20.96
H. Mettler	132.00
E. Hewitt	25.00
Norfolk Hog Prod.	20.13
Ford Jamieson	138.80
Ray Bartlett	260.90
Wellington Co.	289.77
D. G. MacKinnon	167.40
Alex Anderson	31.80
W. L. Bishop	845.85

On Feb. 12th, 1953, the Ontario Hog Producers Assoc. paid a bill of $231.95 to cover the legal expenses of Hamilton Co-op Packers. So ended one farmer's venture into the field of co-operative processing.

CHAPTER V

BUILDING THE FOUNDATIONS OF CENTRAL SELLING

Central selling, as defined by the Hog Producers' Marketing Board, meant acquiring physical possession of the hogs so that one seller could bring more pressure to bear on the market. The year 1950 saw new legislative questions arise in connection with this new marketing scheme. The annual meeting minutes of March 1st and 2nd reveal these difficulties:

Mr. Tummon reported further that, while it had been expected that our Regulations could be enforced under the Grades and Sales Act, this had been questioned by the Legal Officers of the Crown, who, after intensive study, recommended that a Provincial Live Stock and Live Stock Products Act be introduced. This Act is now before the Legislature. He mentioned further that it is expected the amendments to the Farm Products Marketing Act now before the Legislature will enable commodity groups with Ontario Marketing Schemes to take advantage of Dominion Marketing Legislation. During the present Session of Parliament the Dominion Marketing Legislation will also be amended.

Inadequate funds to handle innumerable tasks facing the industry and to properly finance county associations was creating producer dissatisfaction. But still the Government refused to agree to any increase in the levy per hog over the two cents.

Discussions to determine how central selling might be applied continued. In June, 1950, a meeting with the United Co-operatives occurred and the proposal was advanced that the Livestock Commission Department might be given the responsibility of selling all Ontario's hogs. The Co-op people declined to consider accepting the responsibility. They felt it involved too much responsibility and might increase their problems of selling cattle in competition with the other commission firms in Ontario.

The Producers' Board felt it might fight on in every way possible to obtain better prices. The Department of Agriculture had just released the report of a study showing the cost of producing a hog (2 cwt alive) to be $48.15. At the price of $30.50 dressed weight the farmer received $45.75 for the carcass of a hog weighing two hundred pounds alive. On the way to the Lincoln Annual Meeting in January, 1951, Alva Rintoul, the director from the eastern part of the province and the local director for the zone, stopped for supper at a restaurant between Hamilton and Lincoln, looked at a menu, featuring pork chops, concluded the prices were not in keeping with a minimum expense account, and left to seek a cheaper eating place. Later at the meeting Mr. Rintoul advocated that all Canadians, not just farmers, should pay for sending bacon to Britain at less than cost.

Early in January, 1951, W. E. Tummon and N. McLeod met with the commission firms operating on the Toronto Stock Yards to discuss central selling. Four firms promised to work with the Hog Producers. They were McDonald and Rogers, United Co-op, Black Bros. and McCurdy. Plans were laid for a further meeting.

The first week of February, following a board meeting, all members met with the commission firms in the evening. A smaller sub-committee was appointed to work out further details. A week later, a further report was made to the board and in the evening a session was held with Ralph Bennett of the Federal Government Livestock Services. Mr. Bennett expressed the opinion that the central selling theory was sound and could be made to work. Later the proposal was made to Mr. Bennett that he should accept the management of a central sales organizaiton set up by the marketing board.

On March 7th and 8th the 1951 annual meeting took place. During the reorganization following the annual meeting, the culmination of the differences of opinion on the board resulted in George W. Johnson becoming Secretary-Treasurer in the place of W. E. Tummon, though the latter remained on the board. George Johnson had already been a board member since 1945. He was a breeder of pure bred Yorkshire hogs from Derby township in Grey County where he had served as reeve of that township. No one could have been more thoroughly dedicated to the struggle for a better deal for farm people.

There were changes made in the negotiating committee. But it was to prove a futile gesture to break the continuing deadlock over the issue of minimum price. The new subcommittee charged with responsibility for central selling now became Newton, Johnson, and McInnis. Mr. McInnis, as President of the Association, sat in on all Board meetings.

As the season advanced, efforts continued to obtain a minimum price. By May, 1951, consideration was first given to arbitration to settle the differences with the packers. When the board met in June, Charles Newton reported that the commission firms were prepared to support central selling. In the negotiating committee it seemed possible to settle any questions except that of minimum price. In July the question of central selling was discussed with Ken Morrison, manager of the First Co-operative Packers of Barrie. When the negotiating committee met on August 1st, matters came to a very significant head. The processors declined to participate in further meetings if the minimum price was to be discussed. From the producer standpoint, there was little use participating in further meetings. This was the last time the negotiating committee was to meet. Following are excerpts from the minutes of this very significant meeting:

"Minimum Price: The Producers' Section introduced the subject of 'Minimum Price' by stating that many of their costs were affected by 'Minimum Price' in other industries and that minimum prices were working effectively in the marketing of other farm products.

"Mr. Hugh Murray, speaking on behalf of the chairman of the Processors' Section, re-affirmed a telephone conversation with the Secretary of the Ontario Hog Producers' Marketing Board that "the processors no longer wished to discuss the subject 'Minimum Price' and that they were discussing this matter for their last time at the present meeting". Mr. Murray also stated that he personally agreed with their decision."

The producers section of the negotiating committee immediately asked for arbitration on the question of minimum prices. The processors declined to make any appointment to represent them. The Farm Products Marketing Board was requested to act upon the legal authority vested in it by statutes and provide the machinery for arbitration. The Government did not refuse in so many words. It simply took no action.

The producer marketing board backed its representatives on the negotiating committee. The producers felt that there was undue foot dragging on the part of the authorities. Months earlier, it had seemed that everything was clear, as evidenced by this lengthy exchange of letters between the government on one hand and Mr. Tummon and the board, on the other hand.

Queen's Park,
Toronto 2, Ont.,
April 3rd, 1951.

Mr. W. E. Tummon,
Foxboro,
Ontario.

Dear Mr. Tummon,

I have yours of March 29th re suggestions of Negotiating Committee and negotiating board procedure under the Ontario Hog Producers' Marketing Scheme.

A definite procedure in law has been established under the Act and set out in the regulations under the Scheme. If agreement cannot be reached on any matter properly within the jurisdiction of the Negotiating Committee the matters in dispute go to the negotiating board. The local board has nothing to do with this procedure except to appoint the producer members of the Negotiating Committee. The producer members of the negotiating board in the event of any arbitration, and similarly, the processor members of the Negotiating Committee appoint their representative to the negotiating board in the event of arbitration. The local board has nothing to do with these appointments.

From the point of view of sound administration any body created by a process of law should function and carry out its responsibilities under the law.

Yours very truly,
(Signed)   G. F. Perkin
Chairman.

This letter prejudges the subject to be arbitrated. A letter to the board in September reproduced below would seem to reason rather differently:

Mr. W. G. Johnson,
Secretary-Treasurer,
Ontario Hog Producers' Marketing Board,
77 York Street,
Toronto.

Dear Sir:

The Board has considered at length the issue which has arisen within the Negotiating Committee appointed under the provisions of the Ontario Hog Producers' Marketing Scheme and the request of the Ontario Hog Producers' Marketing Board to have the matters in dispute arbitrated.

The next step, in accordance with the regulations, is for the Processors' Section and the Producers' Section and the Producers' Section of the Negotiating Committee to each nominate one representative to a Negotiating Board and for these two representatives to agree on the third member of the Negotiating Board. Failing to do so, this Board will appoint the third member.

In view of the more or less adamant point of view of each side on the issue involved, the Board suggests your local board consider seriously whether the time is appropriate for you to force matters to this point.

In the first place it is seriously doubted if a minimum price can be enforced in Ontario for all practical purposes until the Ontario Hog Producers' Marketing Scheme is certified under the Dominion Agricultural Products Marketing Act (Bill 82). At least this has been the experience of the Ontario Cheese Producers' Marketing Scheme, the Ontario Bean Growers' Marketing Scheme and the Ontario Winter Celery Growers' Marketing Scheme, all of which have now had their Provincial powers extended under Bill 82. Obviously, a minimum price on hogs in Ontario cannot be maintained with 25% of the production going out of the Province not subject to regulation.

In the second place the whole structure of marketing legislation in Canada is now subject to constitutional examination as a result of the challenge to the Prince Edward Island Potato Marketing Scheme, the Prince Edward Island Farm Products Marketing Act and to Bill 82 under which the Potato Marketing Scheme has been approved, and to the request of the P.E.I. Government to the Supreme Court of Canada to pass upon both the legality of the Prince Edward Island Marketing Act and the validity of the Dominion Agricultural Products Marketing Act.

The reference to the Supreme Court of Canada contains four questions;

"The first is with respect to the power of the Canadian Parliament to enact Bill 82,

"The second is as to the power of the Canadian Government to transfer, by order-in-council, powers under Bill 82 to the P.E.I. Provincial potato marketing board.

"The third is as to the powers of the P.E.I. Government to establish the potato marketing scheme.

"The fourth question is as to the powers of the potato marketing board under their scheme to make the regulations and orders they have made."

It is expected the case will be before the Supreme Court this month. Mr. R. H. Milliken, K.C., Regina, is acting for the Prince Edward Island Potato Marketing Board on this first major test of marketing legislation since 1935 when the then Dominion Natural Products Marketing Act was ruled ultra vires and the British Columbia Natural Products Marketing Act was ruled intra vires by the Privy Council.

Our Board suggests seriously in the interest of your own organization and of all the marketing groups in Ontario that your local board suspend its request in the matter of arbitrating a minimum price on hogs until the decision of the Supreme Court of Canada is announced on the above case.

Yours very truly,

(Signed)   G.F. PERKIN, Chairman.

FURTHER correspondence on the question further confused or clarified the divergent viewpoints.

Mr. Geo. Johnson,
Secretary,
Ontario Hog Producers' Marketing Board,
Room 61, 77 York St.,
Toronto, Ontario.

Re — Minimum Price For Hogs

Dear Mr. Johnson,

I have been going through the exchange of correspondence on the above matter including the recent letter from Mr. George Schell alternate for Mr. Hugh Murray, on the Processors' Section of the Negotiating Committee, wherein it is stated the minutes of the August 10th meeting of this Committee were not in accord with Mr. Hugh Murray's understanding of what took place at that time, and that Mr. Murray had written you as to what he believed more accurately recorded the discussion.

In Mr. Murray's opinion, it appears the processors requested the producers to write to the Industrial and Development Council of Canadian Meat Packers and to the Domestic Meat Packers Association stating exactly what matters the producers wished to arbitrate.

In this way, the question of a minimum price could come before the packers as a whole for final decision inasmuch as the Processors' Section of the Negotiating Committee advise it has not been authorized by its principals to negotiate a minimum price.

As a result, Mr. Schell states the processors feel the negotiations have not been terminated in that they have asked the producers for information which has not yet been received.

An executive meeting of the Industrial and Development Council of Canadian Meat Packers has been called for September 12th, and I understand it is expected the requested letter from the Producer Section of the Negotiating Committee will be available at that time for a full discussion of the question of a minimum price, since this affects all packers in all Canada as well as those located in Ontario.

Before proceeding further in the matter, this is to ask if the information above referred to has been forwarded by the Producer Section of the Negotiating Committee to the Industrial and Development Council to the Canad-

69

ian Meat Packers for tomorrow's meeting.

Yours very truly,

(signed)   G. F. Perkin, Chairman.

September 13, 1951.

Mr. G. F. Perkin, Chairman,
Ontario Farm Products Marketing Board,
Toronto, Ontario.

Re: Minimum Price on Hogs

Dear Sir:

Received your letter of Sept. 11/51, in which you advise that Mr. Schell complains we had not sent our request for "MINIMUM PRICE" to the Industrial and Development Council of Canadian Meat Packers.

I am surprised that Mr. Schell would make such a statement. When I called him to arrange for a Negotiating Meeting, he asked what was going to be on the Agenda. I informed him that "Minimum Price" and "Condemnation Insurance" would be two subjects for discussion. His reply was; he did not want "Minimum Price" to appear on the Agenda again, but, that they would discuss it as long as we wished at this one particular meeting but that their answer was "NO".

At the request of the Chairman of the Producers' Section a meeting of the Negotiating Committee was called for August 1st, 1951, at which Mr. Hugh Murray told the meeting he was substituting for Mr. Schell and wanted to re-affirm Mr. Schell's statement — "THEY WOULD NOT TALK MINIMUM PRICE AFTER TODAY AS IT WOULD NOT WORK."

The discussion on Condemnation Insurance took considerable time and the producers agreed to send, in writing, to the Domestic Packers as well as the Industrial Packers and producers' request in regard to Condemnation Insurance.

At the close of the meeting the Chairman of the Producers' Section brought up the subject — "MINIMUM PRICE" again, but the answer was still "No it will not work."

The Chairman stated the only alternative for the producers to take was to proceed with arbitration.

After receiving a letter from Mr. Hugh Murray stating his version of the meeting, the matter was brought to the attention of our section of the Negotiating Committee, who agreed that the Minutes, as sent out, met with their approval and are willing to take their affidavit to this effect.

Trusting this explanation will be satisfactory.

Yours very truly,
W.G. JOHNSON, Secretary-Treasurer.

It was finally realized that there was no other means of ensuring producer protection in the market place except by establishing machinery for central selling. Fortunately, considerable ground work through discussion with the commission firms had been done already. Thus, progress was more rapid. The United Co-operatives supported the idea of a new company of which they would be a part.

Determination to implement Central Selling caused arrangements to be made for an interview with the Hon. Col. Kennedy, the Ontario Minister of Agriculture. The marketing board and Charles McInnis, President of the Association, met with Kennedy in his office and frankly discussed the difficulty of establishing a minimum price. They pressed the determination of the producer group that authority contained in the original scheme of 1946 be used to establish an agency to sell hogs. To the amazement of the farmers, Col. Kennedy took a more favourable attitude than expected, based on previous experience with having dealt with him. The minister advised the producers to go ahead. The farmers left the minister's office incredulous. Had Col. Kennedy really said what he had seemed to say?

To have record of what had been said, Norm McLeod, "Charlie" McInnis and George Johnson put down in black and white Col. Kennedy's verbal commitments:

1. Arbitration would be delayed only until after P.E.I. Potato Scheme was decided in Courts.
2. He has always been in favor of a "Central Marketing Agency."
3. Ontario Hog Producers' Marketing Board can proceed with setting up a Central Marketing Agency.
4. No "vote" would be required.
5. The Minister would, however, prefer that "Central Marketing" be started in a small way.
6. The Minister to contact:

> Canada Packers
> Swift Canadian
> Schneider's
> Burns Ltd.
> to discuss proposed plan for
> such an agency.

7. The Minister will advise Ontario Hog Producers' Marketing Board as to the attitude of packers.

Later there was a further meeting with the minister. The record of this meeting has been preserved over the signatures of McInnis and Johnson:

Meeting with Hon. T. L. Kennedy, Minister of Agriculture

The Minister stated that he had talked with a delegation representing the Packing Industry. Mr. J. S. McLean (at Canada Packers) was not present. The packers stated that they would not pay a higher price for hogs that were not sold by the Central Marketing Agency than those that were sold by the Agency. The Minister wanted the Ontario Hog Producers' to set up the Central Marketing Agency on a voluntary basis. Before it could be set up on a compulsory basis, a vote would have to be taken.

Throughout the remainder of 1951 and the early months of 1952 efforts by the Ontario Hog Producers continued at an advanced pace to be ready for Central Selling. A new company was formed, called United Livestock Sales. Ownership was vested in the Commission firms selling livestock on the Toronto Stock Yards who hoped to see an increase in the number of hogs passing through their hands. Officers of the United Livestock Sales were President R. M. (Bob) Morrison; Vice-President, D. A. McDonald; Sec-Treasurer, J. Ross Chapman; Manager, C. D. (Pinky) Black; and Assistant Manager, D. R. McDonald.

In the process of developing the new program, the marketing board proposed a draft agreement pertaining to the responsibilities of the board:

a. To act as a liaison between the producers and the Company for the purpose of assisting the company in marketing hogs;

b. where it deems it advisable, to call meetings of producers from time to time and have its representatives attend such meetings to explain the marketing operations to the producers;

c. to provide facilities for conveying grievances of the producers to the Company;

d. to publicize to the producers the functions of the company in acting as the exclusive marketing agency for hogs in Ontario;

e. to assist the company in carrying on a public relations programme aimed at both the producers and processors;

f. to keep the company informed of any changes in the cost of production of hogs, market trends or any other matters which, in the opinion of the local board, might affect the selling price of hogs;

g. to make available to the company the results of any surveys undertaken by the local board to determine the cost of production of hogs, consumer demand or forecasts of the probable number of hogs to be marketed from time to time; and

h. generally to do all such acts and things as deemed advisable to stimulate and improve the orderly marketing of hogs produced in Ontario.

The rate of commission to be paid U.L.S. was a bone of contention in May and early June of 1952. Finally on the 26th of June an agreement was reached supported by Aiken, Bishop, McLeod, Newton and Rintoul. Tummon and Frey expressed dissatisfaction. A month later on July 24 the Marketing Board finally approved the agreement. Mr. Tummon was absent from this board meeting. The board appointed United Livestock Sales as the sale agency to sell Ontario hogs.

By August 8th, when the board met again, the Sales Agency and the Hog Producers had signed on the dotted line. As soon as the United Livestock Sales could be structured it was ready to take over. In September, C. D. Black reported on his efforts to arrange the cashing of all cheques at par. Later "Charlie" McInnis, Norman McLeod and George Johnson were appointed as producer representatives on a co-ordinating board to be made up of representatives of both parties to deal with matters of common importance to both the Sales Agency and the producers.

U.L.S. gradually accumulated experienced personnel, established office facilities and prepared for business. As much as possible the same selling technique as had been used by the commission firms on the stock yards were employed. Contacts were made with the truckers and packers, explaining how business would be handled.

Board members polled themselves to determine when operations should commence. Bishop, Rintoul and Newton proposed, "at once"; Tummon, "when volume is low"; "if and when the other provinces do likewise"; Aiken, "whenever it will do the most good". Nevertheless, January 23rd, 1953, was set as the day to begin. This, however, happened to be the week of the Canadian Federation of Agriculture annual meeting and with it the annual National Swine meeting. Board members attended the national meetings but Secretary George Johnson, who had remained one of the staunchest supporters of the idea, declared his intention of remaining in Toronto lest some emergency requiring attention might arise. Fortunately, everything went smoothly and "Central Selling" had begun.

CHAPTER VI

PROGRESS ON MANY FRONTS

Services in other directions had not ceased while efforts on behalf of central selling were under way. A few events in particular warrant attention.

During the time that W. E. Tummon was Secretary, he had also remained a voting member of the Board representing zone No. 2. When George Johnson became Secretary he followed the same practice until the early autumn when he resigned as the representative of the counties of Bruce, Grey and Huron. A special zone meeting held October 1st, 1951, elected as his successor Mr. Eldred Aiken of Allenford in Bruce County. Mr. Aiken was destined to play an active role in the association and the board for many years. Like most of his early colleagues, Mr. Aiken was not exclusively a hog man, but was also a well known breeder of Polled Hereford cattle. Rather than being an outspoken proponent of militant action, Mr. Aiken was a levelheaded and consistent supporter of the mounting drive for farmer control of the marketing of his own product. He followed Norman McLeod as Chairman of the Board and held office during the difficult days of the late 1950's and early 1960's.

Frequently, throughout the central selling campaign, farmers experienced difficulties in receiving payment for their hogs. One case had occurred in Middlesex County and through negotiation had been cleared up. Meanwhile, just before the beginning of central selling and guaranteed payment, a case arose in Norfolk where a drover had used for his own purposes funds given him in payment for a farmer's hogs. This particular drover was convicted in court of theft. This criminal action was pursued so that a basis might be established for civil action by the farmers to whom funds were owing.

When Essex Packers moved into the former Duff plant in 1952 they required a greater volume of hogs. With a system whereby livestock truckers tended to be agents of one processor it was difficult to entice the extra shipments required. Consequently, they endeavoured to attract the extra volume by contacting truckers and offering a higher price for A hogs and not stating prices for B hogs and lower grades. This immediately raised a new problem. Differentials in price had been established by official negotiation in the Negotiating Committee and were confirmed by both regulation and established practice. In a sense this move by Essex Packers was a challenge to the degree of order that the marketing board had already been able to bring to this limited marketing field of forms, contracts, differentials, etc. At first, when this failure to pay on the basis of established differentials was challenged, the company paid the extra due the farmers in the area from which came the first complaints. It was soon obvious that many more farmers were involved. The company complained to the board that too much office work was involved in mailing the extra sums to each individual farmer.

The board asked to be told the names of the involved farmers and how much was due to each. They requested a cheque to cover the total amount in order to split the sum into the amounts owed each farmer. They handled the individual mailing. There were hesitations by the packers until an ultimatum was delivered on the phone to the company manager by a board member who represented the greater number of the farmers involved. The member demanded, "Either give us the money within forty-eight hours or get your lawyer busy preparing your defence". The money was forthcoming and was mailed from the board office to each farmer.

One of the burning issues of the day was the question of the two cent per hog levy. Both the board and the annual meetings had repeatedly drawn to the attention of the government that the present levy was completely inadequate to do a satisfactory job for Ontario Hog Producers. At the annual meeting of March, 1951, it was determined to try a new approach. The resolutions committee was authorized to go directly to Col. Kennedy on behalf of the delegates assembled in the annual meeting. On April 10th, 1951, under the chairmanship of Mr. Earl Hopkins of St. George in Brant County, the committee met Col. Kennedy and presented their argument in a brief which is worth quoting in full:

Brief of The
Ontario Hog Producers' Association
Presented to The Minister of Agriculture — Hon. T. L. Kennedy
by The Resolutions Committee, April 10, 1951

Hon. T. L. Kennedy,
Minister of Agriculture;

We, of the Ontario Hog Producers' Association, feel that with the increased costs of operations, that we have reached the crossroads, and have to either adopt a more progressive policy involving more finances or we will automatically find ourselves going in a reverse direction.

After years of honest endeavour to secure more practical, adequate and just controls over many and varied branches of the production, transportation, marketing of hog, processing, distribution and research, the Association now finds that their effort to advance further is limited to such a degree that said advance is impossible.

Finances needed to render the services that are not only necessary but actually expected in the interest of the Bacon Industry. True comparisons are that two (2¢) cents per hog, permitted under the present Hog Producers' Association on a product valued at approximately $50.00 is entirely out of proportion to other commodities, such as milk, cream, beans and etc.

Condemnation insurance permitted since 1912 allows a deduction of one half of one percent (½ of 1%). At present hog prices this allows a deduction of about twenty-five cents per hog. The condemnation insurance was permitted without first consulting hog producers and securing a sixty-six percent favourable vote.

The present two cents is nearly all required to maintain an office, board meetings and send back a small amount to the Counties as shown on Financial statement, attached. [Further support is needed for the following purposes:]

1. Several Fieldmen are required to carry on work in the Counties, namely, to assist in organization and setting up a Central Marketing Agency; To investigate any dissatisfaction between producer and processor or between producers and his organization;
   To inform producers the proper settlement forms that should be returned from the processor;
   To make contacts with small processors who are not collecting the two cent producers' fee;
   To study ways and means of;
      (a) Getting producers' hogs to market with a minimum of cost
      (b) Preventing overlapping of transporters
      (c) Bruising and losses in handling
   Investigation of errors made by shippers, truckers and others and the enforcement of hog producers' Regulations designed to protect producers.

2. It is necessary for the Association to co-operate with Livestock Exchange

at public stockyards, to work out a plan whereby more hogs would be sold on the open competitive market, in place of direct shipment to processing plants. Unfortunately, shipments to stockyards are only about eight per cent of total marketing in Ontario.

3. It is essential that we organize meetings in the Counties to inform producer what the Provincial organization is doing.

4. We hope to work out a policy to develop a programme whereby consumers could buy pork products on a graded basis. And further, that this programme would make it possible for the consumers to determine the country of origin of the product before purchasing.

5. Advertising

As the advertising of Ontario Pork Products as presented by the trade has failed to bring to the attention of the consumer the quality, flavour and nutritional value of the pork produced in Ontario, this is an item, we feel, should be immediately undertaken, as a threat of surplus looks evident in the not too distant future, this alone will involve a large amount of money in comparison with what others spend on advertising.

6. Money to counties;

To send more money back to the Counties to assist in Swine Club work and *particularly* in the purchasing of qualified breeding stock, this has been emphasized in the answers to a "Questionnaire" sent out to the Counties.

To enable County Associations to donate prizes to the best type of hogs produced for domestic or export trade and to hold farm meetings to discuss better methods of Hog management and marketing, these would be with the co-operation of the departments of Agriculture and the Ontario Hog Producers.

To enable the Ontario Hog Producers' Association to give support to an all Canadian Hog Producers' organization whereby the producers may have representation on bacon boards, making contracts, and have representation with the Department of Trade and Commerce.

7. Counties are requesting that money be available to take care of increased expenses of delegates attending meetings.

8. If this work is undertaken extra office help would have to be employed.

MOREOVER, no commercial organization would ever reach any degree of success without selling agency or sales department. FURTHERMORE, no secondary industry need either seek approval for or submit to limitations of such assessment on their product, that prerogative remains in absolute control of the industry concerned.

Be assured, the submitting of this brief, in no manner whatsoever, is done with any malice. It is done with the undivided and carefully considered opinion of this Committee and the Ontario Hog Producers. All that is sought, are those things that will assure the greatest returns to those engaged in Agriculture which has and will continue to maintain Canada's National Economy, if, that farmers' interests are safeguarded and protected.

All of which is respectfully submitted for your most favourable, kind and generous approval.

In discussing the question later at a zone meeting Mr. Hopkins said, "Our committee has been said to have got further than anyone had before. If this should be true the others hadn't got very far".

In October, 1953, the county associations of Perth, Waterloo and Wellington co-operated with the Department of Agriculture in arranging for a number of producers to make a study of management and feeding practices on the farm. In all about 60 farmers took part.

Other important events also occurred. Earlier in 1953 the per diem allowance for board members had been raised to $10.00 with a car allowance of eight cents per mile. A factor which influenced Canadian hog prices for some time in 1953 was the imposition of an embargo upon American pork products as a result of disease prevailing in the U.S.

There long had been arguments that a better job could be done in hog marketing if only it were known in advance what the coming volume of production might be. The 1953 annual meeting passed a resolution instructing the Executive of the Association to proceed with such a study. It was decided to select representative areas in each county based upon one producer for every thousand hogs marketed by that county. Thus, some counties would have only one area and others several. The same producers were called upon every four months and four questions were asked each time. The farmers were asked the number of sows bred in the previous four months, the number of piglets under two months, the number of pigs of 2 to 4 months, and the number of market pigs over four months of age. In spite of care in selecting those in each county who made the calls and the co-operation of the producers, the results failed to bear an accurate relation to subsequent marketings and the programme only lasted a couple of years.

Canadian livestock are particularly well protected from outbreaks of disease in other parts of the world. The Health of Animals branch of the Canadian Department of Agriculture keeps a close watch on any material entering Canada which might carry infection. Livestock imported into Canada are in quarantine at the border before being allowed to enter the country. In spite of all these precautions an isolated case of Foot and Mouth Disease broke out in the Canadian West. The infection had been brought in on the effects of a young German immigrant. When the Americans closed their border to Canadian products, it posed a very severe threat to the Canadian Livestock industry. The Government of Canada saved the situation by announcing a support price of $26.00 dollars a cwt. Stability for the industry was provided by the announcement of Hon. Mr. Gardiner that the support would be maintained after the removal of the American embargo. The producers had requested that this support be continued until at least March 1st, 1953. The tragic saga of Foot and Mouth Disease in Canada would need a book in the telling; suffice it to say it was the greatest crisis ever weathered by the Canadian livestock industry.

It seemed that the Marketing Board was faced constantly with legal problems. The packing trade resented any growth of farmer power that would limit their prerogatives. Government authorities, torn by conflicting pressures and desires to compromise, responded cautiously through their indefinite and conflicting answers and actions. The hog producers sought the best legal advice. The outstanding Canadian legal authority on marketing legislation and possible courses of action under such legislation at that time was Mr. R. H. Milliken of Regina. He had established a reputation as the legal representative of Western Canadian wheat growers on numerous occasions and had also acted for the Dairy Farmers of Canada in opposing the legalization of the manufacture and sale of oleomargarine. Furthermore, he was the legal adviser whom the Hon. Mr. Gardiner had often relied upon in the development of federal marketing legislation.

The Hog Producers' Marketing Board arranged for consultation with Mr. Milliken on those occasions when business brought him to Eastern Canada. For instance, in the autumn of 1951, when possible arbitration with the packers on the question of minimum price was being sought, tentative arrangements were made for Dr. Lattimer to be the producer representative on the arbitration committee (which never developed) and for Mr. Milliken to present the farmer case. In the correspondence passing between the board and Mr. Milliken on this issue Mr. Milliken stated his agreement with the board's position. On legal questions aside from marketing problems (such as contract arrangements with United Livestock Sales), the firm of Aylesworth, Garden, Thompson and Stanbury continued to provide legal counsel. Mr. Milliken continued as legal adviser relative to the marketing scheme until the mid-1950's when the growing amount of legal work in this field called for a specialist in Ontario. H. E. Harris of St. Catharines, who had acted as solicitor for some of the fruit marketing plans, became the specialist for almost all of the Ontario marketing boards.

With the rather limited opportunities available, the Association endeavoured to give leadership in relaying information of additional research in the field of nutrition and publicity to producers. One ambitious plan was to bring all branches of the industry producers, packers, feed manufacturers, feed retailers and Government Departments together to give unified leadership in the technical field. In October, 1953, these groups combined in a joint conference. A tentative agreement was reached towards such an objective. However, in spite of continuous efforts, the joint committee of producers, packers and dealers made slow progress even though the Association appointed Bishop, Frey, McInnis and Aiken as members of this all-industry council.

The rapid suburban growth around almost all metropolitan centres following the war years brought a serious problem to many producers in the Toronto and Hamilton areas. The new population spreading out into what had previously been farming townships represented in some cases the majority of the people with ultimate control of the township councils. A few township councils utilized a clause of the Municipal Act giving authority to prohibit the keeping of livestock other than horses and canaries within the municipal boundaries and therefore prohibited the keeping of swine. This happened even when the area where hogs were kept was thoroughly conventional farm land. The law provided no compensation whatever for the farmers affected. Strenuous action by the Hog Producers' Association finally brought legal and legislative redress for the producers involved.

Unfortunately, during 1953 and the early months of 1954, a rift was gradually developing and widening between the Secretary, George Johnson, and the majority of the members of the Board. No particular issue was involved but rather a combination of personal misunderstandings between Johnson and a number of directors. A climax was reached as the board was being reorganized on March 15th, 1954. Mr. N. G. MacLeod, Chairman of the marketing board, was nominated for secretary and in subsequent balloting was elected over Johnson. Miss Orma Clarke, who had been employed in the office for some years, refused to continue to serve in the office and the next day both she and Johnson sent letters of protest to all the county presidents and secretaries. George Johnson, who died a few weeks later, had fought without fear or favour in the cause of a better deal for Ontario farmers and his ideal had sparked the most significant step forward in the marketing of Ontario hogs, a central selling agency.

As the 1950's advanced and the marketing board gained step by step more power to defend producer rights and control the marketing of his product, opposition from those who felt curtailment increased. "Charlie" McInnis, the ever vigorous champion of farmer rights, grew to a stature beyond that of being President of the Ontario Hog Producers' Association. He became rather a symbol of the determination of the farmer on the back concessions to have his position protected in a world of increased pressure. McInnis, with his homespun expressions, never failed to rouse the response of farm audiences and he was constantly in demand as a speaker at meetings of other farm groups. Leaving the farm operations to his son, Charlie was soon giving all his time to the farmer's cause, either in the Hog Producers' office or travelling across Ontario. Books dealing with farm problems were stacked both in the office and in his room in Toronto's Walker House Hotel where he continued to be in consultation with his colleagues or other farm leaders evening after evening. Here, many plans, subsequently put into action, were discussed informally. At several annual meetings different directors offered opposition in the election of the Association president, but "Charlie" always emerged re-elected term after term. People have often remarked what an evangelist "Charlie" McInnis would have made. Perhaps so! At any rate, he was always the sincere dedicated champion of farm people, determined if anything in his power could be done to give them equality with other citizens. In the 1920's a prominent American politician, Governor Alfred E. Smith of New York, was dubbed the "happy warrior." The same term might well have been applied to "Charlie" McInnis, with his bailiwick being the back concessions of Ontario rather than the sidewalks of New York. Perhaps he felt a prophetic inspiration to serve rural Ontario. Without "Charlie's" appeal to rural audiences it might well have been impossible to build the grass roots support which the Hog Producers used so effectively in spearheading the right for farmers of all commodities to control their own product.

At the 1953 annual, Ontario Hog Producers, in a resolution congratulated the Hon. F. S. Thomas on his elevation to the position of Ontario's Minister of Agriculture. Declining health had earlier brought the retirement of the Hon. Col. Kennedy. During his many years in the Ontario Legislature Col. Kennedy won for himself a special niche in the hearts and minds of Ontario farm people. Col. Kennedy was first elected to the legislature in 1919, and served as Minister of Agriculture under Geo. S. Henry prior to 1934. Defeated in 1934 he returned to the legislature in 1937 and became Minister of Agriculture again in 1943. He served briefly as Premier between Geo. Drew and Leslie Frost. Col. Kennedy understood farm people and their problems and constantly expressed a sympathetic and understanding attitude. Sometimes, however, farm leaders were acutely disappointed in the results of their talks with the Colonel. W. E. Tummon no doubt understood very much the problem when he said, "Ministers of Agriculture invariably work in the interest of agriculture and farm people, but too often they are outvoted by the lawyers, doctors and other professional men who have little knowledge or understanding of farm problems". Speaking of Col. Kennedy, Clayton Frey, long a member of the Marketing Board, said, "Col. Kennedy was constantly trying to combine sympathy for the farmer with the determination of Government to stand pat". It was unfortunate for agriculture in Ontario that the Hon. F. S. Thomas was not permitted by his health to serve Ontario farmers for long. Mr. Thomas had been Agricultural Representative in the county of Elgin for many years and had followed Mitchell Hepburn to the legislature from that county. Perhaps it is significant that during Mr. Thomas' tenure of office Hog Producers experienced less difficulty and obstacles in dealing with government agencies.

CHAPTER VII

GROWTH OF CENTRAL SELLING

The selling activities of United Livestock Sales began without any of the facilities that were to be available a decade later. Caution, care and step by step procedures were the only guidelines to employ in beginning to revamp the methods of selling Ontario hogs. The first move was to sell the hogs in the open on the Toronto Stock Yards and to endeavour to have more hogs come on a voluntary basis to the yards. This was aided by the initial arrangement whereby the total fee levied included the availability of the yards with no further charge being made.

The Bank of Nova Scotia early approached United Livestock Sales and the Producers' Board with the proposition that, if they were given the banking business, they would arrange payment of producer cheques at par at all banks in Southern Ontario. The President of the bank appeared before the annual meeting of the Association and Board in March, 1953, and made a public announcement to this effect. However, in proceeding to work out the plan with the other chartered banks, snags developed and the Bank of Nova Scotia was compelled to withdraw its offer.

In January, 1953, when central selling began, all processors were advised that complete details must be provided in all settlement forms, including the two cent deduction for availability of stock yards, and the twenty cents commission charge. These sums were to be forwarded direct to the United Livestock Sales.

Almost from the beginning the biggest question was how to obtain possession of a sufficient quantity of hogs to effectively bargain for their sale price. For instance, if a consignment of hogs were in the yards of a processing firm and the processor was unwilling to pay either the price asked by the agency or a price equal to what some other processor happened to be willing to pay, how should the agency and the Marketing Board react? This question was weighed at considerable length by the agency and the Board. The authority seemed to be there to remove the hogs. This was done once or twice, in bluff, when several freight cars of hogs were shipped out of packers' sidings in Toronto. The final legal opinion seemed to be that authority was there to remove the hogs, but in order to do this, representatives of the board must not trepass on the property of the processor. In practice, there was some doubt whether a helicopter and a lasso would constitute a practical means of removing hogs from a packer's yards! A further complication was a precedent that authority to remove hogs was dependent on whether the processor was prepared to pay a "reasonable price". What constituted a reasonable price?

A further difficulty was the policy of what was referred to as "under table payments", that is special bonuses, paid to truckers to go to this or that processing plant. Whenever a processor wished a greater volume of hogs, he might telephone a particular drover and offer a greater price for hogs, but unless he offered the drover more for his special bonus or agreed to increase the bonus upon a permanent basis he probably would not get any more hogs. The drover might just go to his regular outlet and demand a greater "under the table payment". If hogs happened to be in general short supply the chances would be that he would collect the extra dollars just to keep on delivering the hogs where he previously had been taking them. The problem was how to establish a truly competitive open market under these circumstances.

Truckers who at one time had delivered their hogs to the Toronto Stock Yards were invited to do so again. There was some response and this helped. Still only a small part of the hogs were available to serve as a basis for the establishment of price. Those truckers or drovers, enjoying a commission or bonus arrangement with the packer, naturally attempted to discourage producers from suggesting delivery to the stockyards. They pointed out the greater charges while the drover himself made no charge or, at most, a nominal charge. Nevertheless, all but the most naive knew a cost 'came out of the hog somewhere'.

Unfortunately, some of the old rivalries that marked the relations between some of the commission firms as they did business on the stockyards carried over into relations between individuals serving on the staff of U.L.S. Office facilities had been established at 2824 Dundas Street in Toronto. The Manager, C. D. Black, and the Assistant Manager, D. R. MacDonald, occupied offices side by side with partitions going only part way to the ceiling. In spite of this physical proximity, they were not always on speaking terms with one another. Nevertheless, C. D. Black gave sound constructive leadership in central selling during this period. The co-ordinating board made up of representatives of the Marketing Board and Agency worked reasonably well. Ultimately, however, it was determined that it might better be replaced by joint meetings of the two boards.

The questions of how and whether to direct truckers to bring more hogs to the open market continued to be burning questions. In September, C. D. Black reported to the co-ordinating board that the letter to truckers directing them to deliver hogs to the yards rather than Packer plants was not working as well as it might. At the same meeting the question arose whether more yards should be established for delivery. This suggestion was premature and no action was taken.

During 1953, processors became less sceptical of the new selling programme and, in theory at least, began to admit that it was a feasible approach to selling hogs. In the establishment of price itself, results were significant. Toronto had always provided a higher price than locations such as Kitchener and Stratford, in spite of the fact that meat products were sold over widely overlapping market areas. During the year the disparity between these local markets gradually declined. In the three years prior to 1953, the Toronto price had averaged $1.45 above the Winnipeg price. In the year 1953 the average price advantage Toronto had over Winnipeg amounted to $3.00 per cwt. dressed and this enhanced price advantage was destined to continue in subsequent years.

Central Selling was working almost beyond the fondest hopes, but the idea still had to be marketed. Just a few producers close to events understood the progress that had been made. Periodic news letters were sent out by the Agency and plans were made to develop a program of publicity through the pages of the Rural Co-operator.

As the calendar year 1953 drew to a close 1954 presented new challenges.

United Livestock Sales had experienced a good year financially, but the Marketing Board was faced with its continuing problem of more things to do than the available finances would permit. U.L.S. played it safe, feeling that new services required would be costly.

All autumn of 1954, the Producers' Board had felt that there might be some difficulty in working out a new contract with U.L.S. Consequently, they had asked their solicitors Aylesworth, Garden, Thompson and Stanbury to make a study of the nature of a company they might set up to handle the selling job or the means of doing it directly as a function of the Board itself. Everyone on the Board was now agreed that central selling was a sound idea. But whether or not to continue with just the same type of organization was another matter. The functions of the selling, pricing and mailing settlements were the responsibility of United Livestock Sales, working under the authority granted by the Marketing Board. The Board itself handled all matters in the field of regulations. The Association was responsible for all types of educational work and for organizational effort in the counties.

Continued discussions failed to bring about complete agreement. A point of particular significance was the check by the auditors into the net earnings of U.L.S. In December, it became evident that this sum would be in excess of $40,000. By the end of December, an agreement on a new contract had not been finalized. The last day of the month the two boards met in joint session at the Stockyards. All producer members felt that U.L.S. wanted too much money. V. S. Milburn, Secretary of the Ontario Federation of Agriculture, took an active role in urging that the two parties get together and not risk differences of opinion which might destroy the marketing job that was being done. The Board Members of U.L.S. later withdrew from the meeting and left the Marketing Board members, Mr. McInnis, President of the Association and Mr. Milburn of the Federation of Agriculture, to continue discussions from the farmer's standpoint.

The session that followed constituted the hottest ever held by the Marketing Board, In the first place, everyone was agreed that a good job had been done improving the selling of Ontario hogs. But the threat of a direction programme with more teeth in it was already arousing the opposition of the truckers. If a profit of $40,000 was in the hands of the producer board or was earmarked for programmes to serve the farmer, it could be defended across the province in the face of the criticism opponents of the marketing plan might be able to muster. But how could $40,000 profit in the hands of a private company, as a result of a business monopoly created by a farmer board, be defended? The whole organization was dedicated to maintaining a worthwhile programme. For the individual farmer it would be much better for the producers to take over the programme directly than to risk the development of a new vulnerable position for the farmer.

The seven man Marketing Board was split down the centre. Aiken, Newton and Rintoul were strongly of the opinion that it would be wiser to risk the public relations disadvantage of the U.L.S. $40,000 profit than to take the risk of operating under a new type of organization or directly by the board. The longer the debate, the hotter grew the argument. Tummon, Frey and Bishop refused to budge from their position that a repeat of the private company profit would destroy all that had been gained. In the best of debate Frey challenged the right of McInnis to be present in as much as he was not a member of the Marketing Board. McInnis and Milburn left the meeting. Through the whole argument Board Chairman McLeod remained uncommitted. There had been some indication however, he leaned towards the Tummon, Frey and Bishop position. Finally McLeod felt it might be less disruptive to renew the U.L.S. contracts inspite of the problems it posed. Tummon, Frey and Bishop thereupon called for a recorded vote.

Feeling had run so strongly on this question that preceeding the March annual meeting efforts were made to defeat Frey and Bishop for re-election to the Marketing Board. In their respective zones calls were made upon county officers and they were urged to offer opposition or to find opposing candidate. The county presidents in Oxford and Lincoln were both canvassed. At the Lincoln annual meeting a hot debate developed between McInnis and J. R. Kohler, a senior U.L.S. staff member, on one hand, and Bishop, on the other, over this question. The new contract between the U.L.S. and the Marketing Board was signed January 2nd, 1954. This agreement provided for a commission of twenty cents per hog, pro rating charge of twenty cents per hog and for 20 per cent of the company's gross profits to be paid in quarterly installments to the Marketing Board. A further provision changed the co-ordinating board to a joint board made up of the Marketing Board plus the President of the Association and the directors of the company, plus the Secretary of the Ontario Federation of Agriculture. More authority was given to this joint board.

A renewed effort to reach an understanding with the transporters of hogs was launched through the medium of a joint committee made up of representatives of the truckers, the Marketing Board and U.L.S. In February, 1954, this committee agreed upon a number of questions as to how hogs should be priced, e.g. F.O.B. the farm or at the plant, but no permanent results were obtained.

The theory was developing that there should be some points for assemblying hogs and dispatching to buyers. C. D. Black, U.L.S. General Manager, proposed six or seven such points from which hogs might be sold. He suggested it would not be necessary to unload the hogs but that the truckers would merely report to receive direction orders. During the summer of 1954, negotiations were conducted with the owners of the Kitchener Sales Barn to arrive at terms for the leasing of these facilities for use to assemble hogs. The question was, how would a yard, in addition to the Toronto Stock yards, work? Would it be of help in selling Ontario hogs? A little earlier, a sales branch was established in Montreal to help cope with the problem of Eastern Ontario drovers who went to the Montreal market and defied every aspect of the Ontario marketing plan.

Meanwhile, negotiations were continually being carried on with the banks in efforts to arrange payment of producers' cheques at par. All in all the year 1954 was rather a quiet but significant one. Central selling had become established. Clashes with the transporters were just threatening on the horizon but had not broken out.

The personality of the new Secretary-Treasurer Norman McLeod contributed much to the greater calm on the hog producer front. Mr. McLeod was elected to the executive of the Association in 1945 and consequently was a member of the first marketing board. He brought to the board experience in other farm organizations and municipal experience from his home township of North Dumfries in Waterloo. Unlike his two predecessors he got on well with all his colleagues. He was the epitome of the unperturbed, unexcitable man in going steadily ahead. His associates were often puzzled at his ability to avoid stress and concern. On one particular occasion, a delegation of McInnis, Johnson, McLeod and Bishop was in Ottawa consulting with federal officials. The discussions were over in good time and the plan was to take the mid-afternoon train back to Toronto. Norm McLeod said he had time to make a personal call upon a gentleman in the civil service whom he knew. The other men waited in the station. There was no sign of Norm McLeod, so Johnson and Bishop boarded the train. Finally McInnis joined them, concluding that McLeod would have to take a later train. The last split second before the train was to pull out McLeod appeared, not the least concerned nor in any hurry. Just as the train started to move he made the lower step.

McLeod had suffered from a heart condition for some years. In the late autumn of 1955, after only weeks more than a year and one half as Secretary-Treasurer, McLeod suffered a fatal attack. Norman McLeod must be listed as one who helped to lay the foundation of the Marketing Board.

In the autumn of 1954 the Ontario Department of Agriculture's legal advisers made the claim that a mistake had been made in the hog producer regulations, giving the Board authority to appoint a selling agency. They maintained that, according to the Farm Products Marketing Act, the appointment of an agency must be made by the Farm Products Marketing Board. The Producers' Marketing Board and Association at once replied that this was an error on the part of Government personnel. It was acknowledged, however, that the principle of collective selling was working and, through the efforts of V. S. Milburn, Secretary-Manager of the Federation of Agriculture, the Government agreed. The Government took an attitude similar to that earlier agreed by some Board members. A private company should not be allowed to build up profits as the result of a government delegated monopoly. The terms upon which the Government agreed to accept the principle of collective selling and appoint, through the Farm Products Marketing Board, a selling agency were as follows:

1) That a co-operative be set up to take over the business of U.L.S. so that profits from this business should not fall into the hands of a pri-

vate company but should belong to the producers themselves.

2) The Government would consider amending the Farm Products Marketing Act and would bring in new regulations.

3) A new vote which had been threatened would not be held until the new regulations were in operation.

Friction had continued within U.L.S. and, early in 1955, the agency board dismissed both general manager C. D. Black and assistant manager D. R. McDonald and appointed as acting manager J. R. Kohler.

Following the expression of the Government position as to the United Livestock Sales, negotiations began between the Agency Board of directors and the Marketing Board as to the terms under which a new co-operative might take over the staff and facilities of the Agency.

During April 1955 there was a complete reorganization of the producer's machinery. The Ontario Hog Producers' Co-operative came into being. At the same time, the structure of both the Marketing Board and the Association was altered. The Marketing Board became a board of eleven instead of seven members. The zones remained the same as before but additional provision was made for four members at large. The board of the Co-operative was parallel in nature. The board of the Association provided for three members at large, in addition to the president and vice president who were elected from the floor of the annual meeting. Following this pattern the same personnel were elected to all three boards. The men who had been elected to the zone positions in both the Association and Marketing Board were confirmed in their positions. Three new men appeared on the scene, one of whom was Wesley Magwood, veteran fighter for farmer rights from Grey County. Mr. Magwood had long been a tower of strength through his outspoken support in his own county and at provincial annual and semi-annual meetings. Another, Lance Dickiesen, would play a significant role in the further progress of the Marketing Board. He had been an active director of Wellington County association since 1949. The third new member was Clarence Milligan of Napanee, a former President of the Ontario Federation of Agriculture. A fourth was "Charlie" McInnis himself who had never actually been a member of the Marketing Board, but had been sitting with the Board for years in his capacity as President of the Hog Producers' Association. Now for the first time "Charlie" McInnis had a Marketing Board vote.

The new and enlarged board immediately proceeded to finalize arrangements for the take over of the business and facilities of the United Livestock Sales. Before the end of May, the agreement had been worked out for the Ontario Hog Producers' Co-operative to be in business on June 1st, 1955 and thus began a new era. The agreement itself tells a story in relatively few words and is worth quoting in full:

Agreement Between Ontario Hog Producers' Co-Operative and United Livestock Sales Limited

For the sum of $38,500. payable May 28, 1955, by the Ontario Hog Producers' Co-operative to United Livestock Sales Limited. United Livestock Sales Limited agree to sell and transfer their business, equipment and goodwill to the Ontario Hog Producers' Co-op on the following basis:

United Livestock Sales Limited hereby agree:

1) to lease their offices on Dundas St. as well as parking lot and storage space to the Co-op from May 28, 1955 to December 31, 1957 for the sum of $900 per month for offices, $40 per month for storage space and $60 per month for parking lot (until lease expires)
2) to transfer their equipment free of all incumberances as per Exhibit A [not printed]
3) to transfer all stationery, etc. on hand
4) to terminate present agreement and transfer business as of May 28/55
5) to not interfere or endeavour to engage the present employees of United Livestock Sales Limited without our approval
6) United Livestock Sales Limited agree to pay to present employees the holiday pay in full up to May 28, 1955.

Ontario Hog Producers' Co-operative hereby agree:

1) to assume all responsibility for payment of rent of offices, parking lot and storage space as of May 28, 1955
2) to assume responsibility for adjustment of Insurance Policies as of May 28, 1955
3) To assume responsibility for rental of business machines already on contract, on or after May 28 as per Exhibit B. [not printed]

Mr. and Mrs. W. E. Tummon, of Foxboro, Ontario. Mr. Tummon, one-time Member of Parliament, was a director of the Association 1944-1957, its secretary 1945-1950, and secretary of the Marketing Board 1946-1950.

Three directors of the OHPA at a conference circa 1962: A. H. Warner, Bayfield; George Mannerow, Chesley; and Kenneth Thompson, Kemptville.

The late Mel Becker, a director of the Association, the Board and the Marketing Agency, 1955-1960.

Blake Snobelen, of Thamesville, a director 1961-1972 of the OPPMB.

The "Grey County Rebels" played an important part in efforts to place the selling of hogs in Grey County under the Marketing Board. Taken in September 1951, this photo includes: Wesley Magwood, James Matches, Edgar Lemon, and George Johnson. (Photo: Canada Pictures, Toronto).

Jim Boynton, Secretary, 1957-1975 of the Ontario Pork Producers Marketing Board. (Photo by Canada Pictures).

The late Ted Marritt, Secretary in 1956 of the Ontario Hog Producers Association. (Photo by Nott).

Jim Rollings, Sales Manager, 1976, of the Ontario Pork Producers Marketing Board. (Photo by Hardy).

J. R. (Jake) Kohler, retired Sales Manager of the Ontario Pork Producers Marketing Board. (Photo by Hardy).

Directors of the Ontario Pork Producers Marketing Board, 1955: **Front:** Alva Rintoul, Eldred Aiken, Wesley Magwood, Norman McLeod, Clayton Frey. **Back:** W. E. Tummon, Clarence Milligan, Lance Dickieson, Charles Newton, Wilfred Bishop, Charles McInnis.

The Marketing Board in session, 1961: Howard Huctwith, Emerson Crocker, Gordon Schweitzer, Ken Thompson, Clare Curtin, Jim Boynton, Secretary; Eldred Aiken, Chairman; Ben Steers, Vice-Chairman; Lance Dickieson, Ross McTavish, Vern Kauffman, and Fred Crowe. (Photo by Milne).

SALES OFFICE MARKETING STAFF 1963

Back Row: Bob Carpenter, Marvin Milne, Dave Muir, Zylnowy Knysh, Irving Stinson, Ted Wickens, Bob Sinclair, Ralph Bremner, George Kemeny, Carl Hassell, Bill Fullerton, Bill Thomson.

Fourth Row: Heather Weeden, Helen Pell, Alice Aisbitt, Marion Dick, Cora Velinga, Marion Cushing, Edna Fox, Betty Woolmer, Dorothy Denman, Eunice Arsenault, Joe Beck.

Third Row: Pauline Seymour, Doris Chappel, Helen Henderson, Pat Corrick, Shirley Huber, Marg Taylor, Helen Marks, Annie Smith, Willa Fisher, Gertrude Hachkowsky, Monica Lurs, ... , Mary Graham, Jean Devine, Barbara Keating, Pat Stacey, Sterling Cochrane, Fay McKerrel.

Second Row: Charlotte Moffatt, Marjorie Delorme, Lorraine Chapman, Helen Miller, Corinne Arsenault, J. R. Kohler, Ruth Dalton, Bob Gray, Mildred McCarthy, Tom Joslyn, Mary Conway.

Front Row: Rolly Richardson, Jim Rollings, Steve Kozak, Harold Wheeler, Dayre Peer, Bob Kohler, Barney Old-field, Paul Muir.

A group of producers and association directors at the opening of the Cayuga marketing yards, December 14, 1959.

New directors of the Ontario Hog Producers Association, elected in 1961: Mac Young, Thamesford; Ken Thompson, Kemptville; Tom Pringle, Shallow Lake; John Barnett, St. Marys; Howard Huctwith, Forest. (Photo by Milne).

Eldred Aiken, Chairman of the OPPMB, presenting the respects of the Hog Producers of Ontario to Mr. and Mrs. Charles McInnis, at the annual meeting of the Association in March 1961, when "Charlie" retired as President of the OHPA. The inscription reads, "In gratitude for his complete dedication to our cause; In admiration for his unfailing courage and leadership." (Photo by Milne).

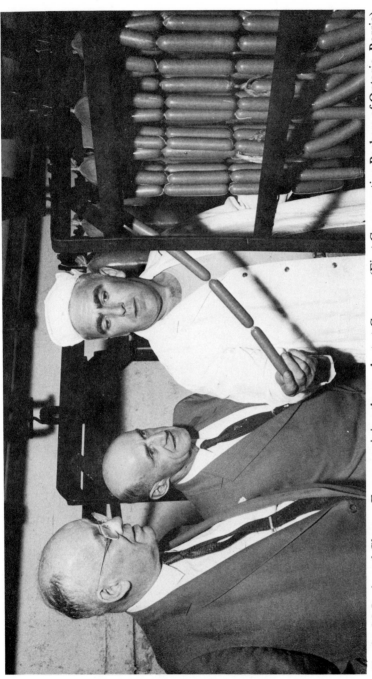

Charles McInnis and Clayton Frey examining the product at Co-paco (First Co-operative Packers of Ontario, Barrie), while seeking out advice for FAME. (Photo by Milne).

Senior Sales Staff, at the central office, Toronto, about 1961: Herb Arbuckle, Gord Oswin, Jake Kohler, Bob Gray, and Mrs. Betty Green, secretary.

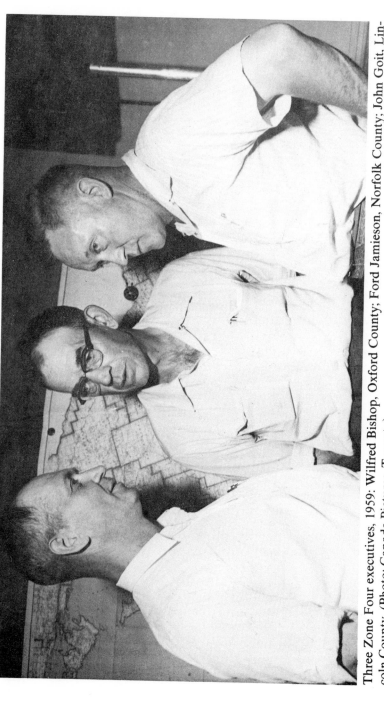

Three Zone Four executives, 1959: Wilfred Bishop, Oxford County; Ford Jamieson, Norfolk County; John Goit, Lincoln County. (Photo: Canada Pictures, Toronto).

Lynn Russell, Chairman, North Simcoe County H.P.A., John Hebgin, Chairman, South Simcoe County H.P.A., and Charles Newton of Barrie, a former OHPMB member. Mr. Newton presents the Newton Cup to Simcoe County for having the highest percentage increase in production, at the OHPA annual meeting, Toronto, March 21, 1962. (Photo by Milne, Toronto).

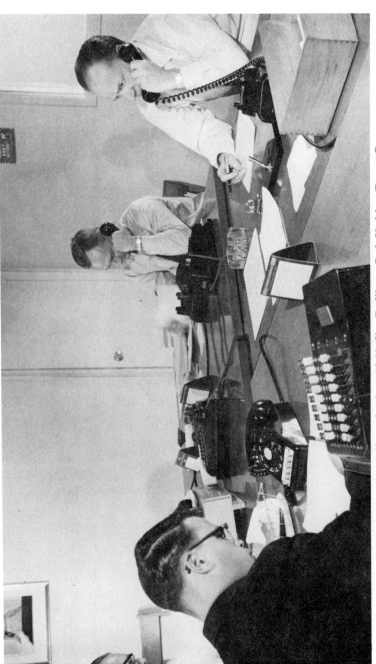

Sales staff at the daily task, circa 1961: Jim Rollings, Bob Kohler, Dayre Peers.

Bob Kohler and a staff member at the Marketing Board's telex machine, the installation of which helped to revolutionize Central Selling. (Photo by Mitchell, Toronto).

Keith Kirkpatrick, president of Dufferin County Hog Producers Association, receives $200 cheque from OHPA director Wilfred Bishop. Dufferin County chalked up second highest increase of Grade A hogs in Ontario during 1964.

This little pig goes to market in the approved manner — and its proud owner becomes a member of the Ontario Hog Producers' Association.

Some Southwestern Ontario county executives: Orville Hogg, Kent; John S. Cameron, Elgin; J. McPharlin, Essex; . . . . , Essex; E. M. Carroll, Elgin; Clayton Frey, Lambton; John Chinnick, Kent.

CHAPTER VIII

A YEAR OF STRIFE, 1955-56

New controversies were becoming ever more acute. Truckers saw "direction" of hogs to the open market as a threat to their extra income. They began to stir up opposition and complained about "compulsion". Packers, accustomed to a system of bonusing truckers to deliver regularly to their particular plants, were skeptical and fearful of change. This opposition was increasingly vocal and legal action was threatened. Lawyers without knowledge of marketing legislation were prone to encourage clients and prospective clients to take action against anything they might imagine to be an infringement upon their rights.

In October, 1955, the Hon. Leslie Frost, Premier of Ontario, announced that the Government proposed to request the Supreme Court of Ontario to pass judgement on the validity of Ontario's Marketing Legislation. The Ontario Hog Producers' Marketing Board went on record as expressing a complete willingness for the Ontario Hog Plan to be used specifically in this legal review.

In the meantime other threats of organizational opposition which were to lead to challenges in the courts were emerging. The suggestion that hogs must be sold through a particular agency or delivered to the open market angered certain farmers. A basic resentment of orders made an increasing number of producers inclined to listen to those truckers who could see their bonuses slipping away and to those processors who had a fear of change.

A local politician from Ellice Township in Perth County, Theodore Parker, had encouraged much of the farmer opposition as far back as 1954. Mr. Parker, the Reeve of his Township, was concerned with the incomplete facts which he insisted on emphasizing. A completely new concept of marketing was bound to contain flaws. Board members were continually endeavouring to iron out weaknesses and increase the soundness of the idea. Add these weaknesses to only partial knowledge and the selfish interests of some in the trade, and the ingredients in the pot were ready to boil.

Under the leadership of Mr. Parker several very well publicized meetings were held in Stratford to attack the marketing plan and to obtain signatures calling for a vote. Supporters as well as opponents of the programme attended these meetings. Some directors attended to answer questions and to reply to charges so the press found ample opportunity for plenty of good copy.

Mr. Parker declined to give a clear answer to the press as to whether he was opposed to collective action by farmers in selling their products or whether he was just opposed to central agency selling. Mr. Parker showed confusion in his knowledge of the functions of the negotiating committee and the sales agency. Perhaps this confusion made it easier to imagine mysterious sums of money which in fact had never existed. Director Bishop readily admitted to one of these meetings that the plan could be improved, that he had not voted to remove George Johnson from office and that he had in the past year been paid $750 dollars for seventy five days work on behalf of the Marketing Board and Association.

Meanwhile President McInnis insisted farmers should control their own marketing machinery and should hire qualified persons to work on their behalf. He claimed that Ontario producers were spending one dollar to get back ten dollars in advantages.

Difference of opinion between persons on the two sides did not always lead to personal bitterness. Following the Stratford meeting with its informal debate, Wilfred Bishop walked into a restaurant on the main street of the city for a cup of coffee. The first man he saw was Fred Slater of Lakeside, also from Oxford County, who was also there for refreshments. Mr. Slater was a trucker who was opposing the marketing program.

Mr. Slater moved over in his seat saying "Come on and join us". A young Dutch farmer who had come with Mr. Slater to the Parker meeting looked on with amazement and confusion in his eyes as Slater and Bishop drank their coffee and chatted as old friends.

The press across the province felt they had a colourful story and continued to report rumours and charges. The Town and Country column of the *Kitchener Record*, sensing that there was considerable opposition among its readers to the marketing plan, took particular care in repeating the ideas and opinions of opponents of the marketing programme. This column queried whether Norman McLeod, who had become Secretary, would also continue as a member of the Marketing Board. What were the circumstances of

Charles McInnis being defeated for the presidency of the Ontario Concentrated Milk Producers Association? The question had nothing to do with the Hog Producers Marketing Board.

The Ontario Farmers Union, a fledgling general farm organization with a strongly militant bent, also presented opposition. In a brief to the producers' Marketing board, a demand was made for the removal of U.L.S. and for a special series of farmers' meetings across the province. In some counties, more particularly those where there was not a distinct clash between the Federation of Agriculture and the Union, the opposition of truckers was the most noticeable. Union members and supporters of the Federation tended to join hands backing the principle of agency selling.

Other prominent hog men took up the torch on behalf of their own organization. Mr. Lloyd Hagey of Preston, writing to the *Kitchener Record*, said he was making "an attempt to correct distorted facts, reveal the truth as I see it, and to refute wrong impressions left by the February 25 *Town and Country* column". Mr. Hagey continued: "The Ontario Hog Producers' Association and its county units were founded on the need for a solution to problems, not suspicion and hate as quoted by the Column".

At a Perth County Federation of Agriculture meeting Mr. Parker asked for ten minutes to express his opinions. When he continued past his ten minute request, he clashed with farmers in the audience, one of whom exclaimed: "This is the first time we've been getting a fair price and have money in our pockets. You would take it away from us".

In February, 1955, Parker launched his challenge to the authority of the Marketing Board in the Supreme Court of Ontario. During this action Mr. H. E. Harris of St. Catharines acted for the producers on advice passed on from Mr. Milliken. Finally the Parker action was dismissed.

The Counties of Bruce and Grey were consistently firm in their constant support of the Marketing Board. The radio station at Wingham, serving the agricultural interests of Huron, Perth, Bruce and Grey Counties, constantly gave expression to the farmer case and reported the news as it happened. In the heat of the argument, Theodore Parker called Mr. Bob Carbert, then in charge of Wingham radio farm programmes and announced; "My lawyer says to forbid you to mention my name again". Mr. Carbert replied, "My lawyer says to tell you to go to Hell". At a meeting in Bruce County two farmers became embroiled in an argument over the merits, or otherwise, of the hog marketing program. The first farmer yelled: "You just called me a pig". The second farmer replied, "I did not, but you sure do act like one".

Mr. Wm. Oswald, Secretary of the Bruce County Federation of Agriculture, was to recall years later coming home from meetings as late as 4:45 a.m. when he had left home at 8:00 a.m. the previous day, all for one day's pay. He had been engaged that evening in a prolonged clash with one trucker who had been collecting bonuses of one dollar per pig in addition to the normal trucking charges.

In order to strengthen the campaign for a free competitive market, the Federations of Agriculture in Bruce and Grey Counties, staffed by fieldmen Oswald and Boynton respectively, embarked in 1956 on a drive to have more hogs placed on the market for open bidding by packers. Farmers were asked to instruct their truckers to make deliveries to the open market rather than to packers' yards. Some truckers co-operated while others defied farmer instructions and went where the packers would pay them a personal bonus.

The Federations responded by preparing weekly lists of truckers and farmers who had ignored their instructions. The two county hog producer associations then published their names in local newspapers.

At the height of the struggle, James Boynton, Secretary of the Grey Federation of Agriculture and later Secretary of the Ontario Hog Producers, was travelling to Toronto with Mr. and Mrs. Oswald. As they passed livestock trucks on the highway, Mr. Boynton would point to a certain truck and say: "This one is going to the open market". Then Mr. Oswald would point to another and say: "this one is going to a packer's yard". Finally, Mrs. Oswald said: "How you men tell them apart". Mr. Boynton replied: "We can tell them by their aroma".

In some instances, truckers offered more money if hogs were shipped directly by them. They even attempted to duplicate the service offered by a producer-owned assembly yard. A minority of truckers continued to ignore direction orders from the Marketing Board and to refuse to apply for licences. Some truckers, in their antagonism, even ignored their own organization, the Automotive Transport Association. One trucker rejected the advice of the A.T.A. to plead guilty to the charge of refusing to take out a licence. Much of the material circulated by the minority of truckers opposing "Orders and Regulations" was of a misleading and malicious nature. But, as the year progressed, more and more truckers gave in and delivered their hogs to the open market. By December, 80% of them were co-operating.

Through these struggles a number of farm meetings were held. Charles McInnis addressed 500 farmers in Chesley on the border between Bruce and Grey Counties. "Charlie McInnis was always at his best when faced by challenges of this kind. He had a deep feeling of outrage that any truckers or any packers for personal gain would stand in the way of changes he was convinced would help farmers' economic position. A great deal, perhaps the major part of the credit for success in this battle and others, must be credited to McInnis' efforts and the confidence he generated by the many platform appearances in these and other counties.

As concrete evidence of the success of the campaign, in July, 1955, the packers were receiving 1000 hogs per week from Bruce and Grey; by October, 1955, they were obtaining only 250 per week, the remainder going to the open market. But much more significant, during the same period the price had gradually improved, The first week of July it had varied from $28.00 to $28.25 and gradually increased almost every week. In the first week of October the variation had been from $30.50 to $31.00. It is interesting to note that opponents to the scheme attributed the increased prices to other factors than the market place.

During this same period the number of yards for open market delivery had been extended. During the previous year only the Toronto and Kitchener yards had been in operation, with Stratford, London and Windsor being added early in 1956. During the time the Grey-Bruce Campaign was under way, yards had been added at Chatham and Barrie.

Board "Orders" at this time, and through the subsequent development of the "Direction" programme, listed all the yards in operation at any given time and instructed that hogs be delivered to any one of these.

Mr. Parker certainly failed in his legal action and whether or not his petition requesting a vote was of any influence in the final calling of a vote may be open to serious question. The Supreme Court endorsed the basic authority of the Ontario legislation and amendments provided a greater degree of enforceability. However . . . the campaign drives of Mr. Parker and other opponents were having the effect of arousing farmer's suspicions, creating misunderstandings and slowing down the process of developing a sound and competitive market for Ontario's hog producers. On the other hand, the attacks certainly caused a careful review of the basic legislation and generated an increased effort to ensure that the principle of collective farmer action to influence the economy really worked. The only method that could make some aspects of this programme work was undoubtedly that of the delegation of some governmental authority to farmer boards. Certainly, in the exercise of this authority on a broad basis, the Hog Marketing Board was the real pioneer. Hitherto, marketing boards in Ontario had relied on the negotiation approach. The Fresh Peach Board at the same time was also experimenting with agency marketing where the board took physical control of the product.

CHAPTER IX

ASSEMBLY YARDS

Early in the campaign to place more hogs on the "open market" it was realized that there would of necessity need to be more assembly yards so that service might be available to all truckers and all producers wherever they might be located. At this stage there were many unanswered questions. What constituted a convenient yard? What facilities were required for a practical assembly yard? Should yards be located reasonably adjacent to packing plants or should the primary consideration be to locate yards centrally in relation to volume of production? Should yards be owned by producers or should they be rented? What would a fair basis for renting be? How many yards would be necessary to provide satisfactory service? Would a dozen be enough or would Ontario require something like fifty? If it would seem wise for producers to own the yards, how could purchase or building be financed?

These questions and others confronted the Directors of the Ontario Hog Producers' Co-operative. At the time it became evident that the competition of an open market at Toronto and Kitchener was enhancing prices received by Ontario producers. The list of yards as shown by Board release of March 15, 1971, included at the end of this chapter, shows what was finally to evolve, but even as this release itself shows there was to be a constant pattern of change and improvement.

Certainly during 1955 and early 1956, when the idea of increasing the yards was developing, no member of the Board or of the staff had any idea of the pattern that was to emerge or of the answers to the questions listed above. The yard at McGregor, or Windsor, as it appears in some of the earlier lists, was established in 1955 to meet the need of having hogs available for sale to smaller plants in that area without a wasteful back haul.

With each successful move to establish a market location, the confidence of the Board grew. In June, 1956, the Secretary of the Board, E. F. Marritt, made a survey of market yard possibilities. The results were seen in an "Order" of the Ontario Hog Producers' Co-operative, listing yards at Toronto Stock Yards, and in Kitchener, Barrie, Stratford, London, Chatham and Windsor. It will be seen at a glance that this offered a fair service coverage to certain parts of the province, but other areas had no yards service available. With the exception of Chatham, there was still a tendency to place yards close to potential packer buyers. Thinking was still in terms of a number of local markets rather than one overall provincial market.

In the meantime other zones of the Marketing Board, the Association and the Co-operative (at this stage the areas were identical) began to study potential sites in their areas. They considered placing a yard or yards where service might be given to producers and also provide a favourable location to packer buyers.

In Zone No. 4, including the counties of Oxford, Brant, Norfolk, Haldimand, Wentworth, Lincoln and Welland, there had been a growing consensus of opinion among the directors of all the counties that a direction programme should be accelerated and at least one assembly yard established in this area. At the annual meeting of March 6th and 7th, 1957, a resolution, sponsored by two of the leading county directors from this zone, Clarence Lee of Brant County and E. Enos of Wentworth County, read as follows: "That we would respectfully urge the Ontario Hog Producers' Co-op to give consideration to using some of the powers entrusted to it under the "Scheme" by directing more of the truckers to deliver hogs to the assembly points." The resolution was given approval. This part of the province went through a long drawn out process of considering various sites that might offer possibilities. Early in the year Essex Packers, who were now operating the former Duff packing plant in the industrial area of downtown Hamilton, approached the Board proposing a deal whereby an assembly yard would be erected on part of the two vacant city blocks they owned near the packing plant. When the Board met early in April, Lance Dickieson questioned the validity of an agreement for such a building as suggested by Essex Packers. At the same meeting Wilfred Bishop, a representative of Zone 4 on the Board, reported that he and the county directors of the area had misgivings as to the wisdom of considering a yard in a large city where farm trucks delivering would find it necessary to travel through a great deal of downtown city traffic. He furthermore proposed that a yard might perhaps be located adjacent to No. 2 Highway between Hamilton and Brantford and proposed a possible location at Cainsville, east of Brantford. This proposed location had formerly been used by a local drover and scales were already there.

Directors from the local counties looked over the proposed Cainsville site and agreed that it would be satisfactory. But the provincial directors, Mel Becker and Lance Dickieson, were not equally satisfied and reported to the Board that an estimated two thousand dollars would have to be spent for renovation before the premises would be suitable for use. As a result, the Board declined to proceed any further with this site. At the same time, Alva Rintoul, Board member for Zone 1 in Eastern Ontario, reported on an investigation as to suitable sites in the Ottawa Valley. At a later date in April, 1957, a joint meeting of the Association and Co-operative studied the operation of the assembly yards already in use and declared by motion that the goal was for full direction 60 days after the remaining legal obstacles could be removed.

With the Cainsville premises definitely eliminated, the Zone Director and the local directors resumed the search for an alternate site in the Brantford district. Barns not in use both west and south of the city were checked as to suitability and availability. No location met the Board's specifications.

In the meantime the collective thinking of the Co-operative was shifting towards the idea of having a larger number of yards. The larger of the two sales barns at Ancaster was rented during the summer and brought into operation in September.

During the spring and early summer of 1957, the search concentrated on the area surrounding Brantford. John Fraser, past President of the Brant Hog Producers and a resident of the Burford Area, half jokingly had remarked that "if nothing around Brantford is satisfactory for a yard, we can provide one at Burford, perhaps on the Burford Fair Grounds." This suggestion had surprising results.

On an August morning, when the dew was too heavy for anything short of mid-day combining, a telephone conversation brought John Fraser and Wilfred Bishop together at the Burford Fair Grounds to look at buildings that might conceivably be modified to serve for the assembling of hogs. A few days later, Mel Becker, on behalf of the Provincial Committee, looked over the grounds and instantly gave his approval. Discussions began with the South Brant Agricultural Society which operated the Burford Fair. Through the wise counsel of Bruce Innes, past President of the South Burford Agricultural Society and a director of the Brant Hog Producers' Association, a mutually satisfactory agreement was reached.

The following account published at the time of the official opening in March, 1958, gives some details of arrangements and facilities provided:

The Burford Marketing Point

The Burford Hog Marketing Point of the Ontario Hog Producers' Co-operative – which was opened December, 1957 – is the product of a remarkable spirit of co-operation between three farm groups. The building, which was designed to serve as a marketing point, is one of the most efficient of the co-operative's 14 marketing points across Ontario. Especially important and noteworthy is that these facilities were erected and are operated at a very modest cost.

How Financed

The Ontario Hog Producers' Co-operative, the South Brant Agricultural Society, and the Brant County Hog Producers' Association are the three farm groups responsible for producing these fine marketing facilities. Here is how it was done.

The Agricultural Society agreed to erect a building (on their fair-grounds) which was suitable as a marketing point for the Hog Producers' Co-operative, and which also could be used during fair-time for Agricultural Society members.

The Ontario Hog Producers' Co-operative advanced the Agricultural Society two year's rent for the use of the buildings, or a sum of $1,440. The Society erected the building at an approximate cost of $4,500 for which the Society becomes eligible for a 25% grant from the Department of Agriculture because the building is on fair-grounds premises and will be used during fair-time. Thus, approximately half of the cost of the building will be borne by advance rent and the eligible grant. Furthermore, as a result of volunteer labour, it is estimated that the Society saved $1,000 on labour costs.

The Ontario Hog Producers' Co-operative agreed to erect and finance the ramps and install the scales.

Because of the volunteer labour, the Agricultural Society was able to erect the building at a cost of $4,500, while they have a building whose worth is conservatively estimated at $6,000. Volunteer labour also made it possible for the hog producers to install the ramps and scales at a total cost, including the price of the scales, of $2,562.

Value of the total facilities – the building, ramps and scales – is placed conservatively at $10,000. Total cost for these facilities was $7,062 which clearly indicates the dollar savings which accrues directly to farmers when they co-operate in ventures of this nature.

The Facilities

The receiving ramps and shipping ramps are separate, which speeds up the movement of hogs through the marketing point. The receiving ramps' platforms are of three heights – 18 inches, 2½ feet, and 3½ feet – to facilitate trucks of various heights. Both the receiving and shipping ramps have shallow, wide cement steps leading down to ground level. Hogs moving up and down these ramps proceed quite readily, and do not show their usual hesitancy and fear of ramps.

As the hogs move along from the receiving ramps to the holding pens, they move across the scales where they are weighed and tattooed. Spacious and clean pens, with sturdy partitions and convenient gates, make for easy movement of hogs in and out of pens. Hogs can be quickly moved from the holding pens down the main passage-way of the barn and out onto the shipping ramp.

There is cement flooring throughout the building, and the ramps are of cement. The surface of the cement has been left rough in order to minimize slipping. Cement flooring facilitates maintaining sanitary premises.

Staff manning the marketing points of the Ontario Hog Producers' Co-operative use SLAPPERS instead of the traditional canes and sticks. The latter frequently leave welts and bruises on the animals. Orders have been issued from the Toronto office of the Hog Co-operative to all marketing points' staff that only slappers are to be used; hogs must be properly bedded and in all instances the animals are to be handled carefully.

The Burford Marketing Point has a direct teletype link with Toronto. This permits instantaneous communication with Toronto, and facilitates the quick movement of hogs to buyers. It is estimated that this marketing point can handle upwards of 1,000 hogs per day – receiving, weighing, documenting, and shipping.

Who Benefits

Through this fine co-operative spirit of the three organizations, the South Brant Agricultural Society, the Ontario Hog Producers' Co-operative, and the Brant Hog Producers' Association, all three organizations and their members benefit. The Agricultural Society has additional barn-facilities for fair-time; the Ontario Hog Producers' Co-operative has excellent marketing facilities at a very reasonable rental; and the Brant Hog Producers' Association derives benefit from the location of the marketing point, and from the increased bargaining power which this marketing point has given the salesmen of Ontario hog producers.

Credit is due to all three organizations and their members for their co-operation, and for the voluntary labour which was donated. Special credit is due Wilfred Bishop, zone-director; Clarence Lee, president of the Brant County Hog Producers' Association; and to Bruce Innes, past-president of the South Brant Agricultural Society, whose leadership inspired the erection of the Burford Marketing Point.

The previous September, when basic plans were being laid, a delegation made up of Mr. Campbell, representing the Agricultural Society, Mr. Enos, President of the Wentworth Hog Producers, Mr. Mel Ball, President of the Oxford Hog Producers, Mr. Clarence Lee, President of the Brant Hog Producers, and Mr. Ford Jamieson, President of the Norfolk Hog Producers, called on Mr. Floyd Lashley, Director of the Fairs and Exhibitions Branch of the Ontario Department of Agriculture. They discussed the acceptance of Fair Board properties, being used for the erection of assembly yards, and whether government grants would still apply, provided the buildings were also used for fair purposes. The favourable answer by Mr. Lashley not only provided the green light to go ahead at Burford, but established an important precedent to be applied later at a number of other centres.

The hero of the Burford project was Mr. Clarence Lee, a veteran of the First World War, a graduate of the Ontario Agricultural College and a one time employee of the Ontario Department of Agriculture. He was involved in every aspect of the project.

The Board of the Co-operative, with little capital for expansion, declared that it could not afford new scales. The local people were just as determined that there must be scales at Burford. The old scales at the Cainsville site were available at a nominal price. The Board agreed to pay for them and for their re-installation. There was still the task of taking them apart and driving them some fifteen miles to Burford. Clarence Lee, a good mechanic and an excellent carpenter, was ready, assisted by Harry Lockwood, a former President of the Oxford Hog Producers, and Wilfred Bishop. He took the scales apart and drove the parts to Burford. When it came to erecting the building, Clarence Lee was again the man of the hour. As the members of the Fair Board worked organizing bees, Mr. Lee worked with them to produce a practical building in line with the proposals made by J. R. Kohler, the Manager of the Co-operative. Funds were also scarce to carry out construction of the ramps. Under the leadership of Mr. Lee, directors from the counties of Norfolk, Brant and Oxford organized local work bees to get that job done.

The yards were opened for use in December, 1957, and were formally opened the following March. As time went on, improvements were to be made by the Co-operative and later by the Marketing Board, but the scales remained in use and were still giving satisfactory service in 1972. Through the years the Burford Yards have remained one of the most efficient assembly points, consistently handling hogs at a lower fee unit cost than any other yard, except Kitchener.

In the meantime the progress in the rest of the province was steady. In June, 1957, a committee was set up to study assembly yard locations for the counties of Bruce and Grey. At the same time another committee was set up to develop a direction programme.

Later in the same month, an assembly site was selected at Harriston. At the end of August, plans were made to bring compulsory direction into force on September 16 in the counties of Grey, Bruce, Huron, Dufferin, Halton and Wellington. A few weeks later, the counties of Essex, Kent, Elgin, Middlesex and Lambton were added to those under direction. Board "Orders" to bring these yards into operation were the first experience of delegated power, requiring hogs to be delivered to these yards and requiring packers to buy only from them. In March, 1958, authority was given to J. R. Kohler to borrow up to $50,000 for the further construction of yards. At the same time, W. E. Tummon, Clarence Milligan and Clare Curtin were asked to study yard possibilities in the Belleville area. Two months after the official opening of the Burford Yards, a delegation of Wentworth Producers met the Board to suggest that a new Ancaster yard be built on the Ancaster Fair Grounds, following much the same approach which had been used at Burford.

Early in 1958, yards were added at Lindsay and Clinton. Almost at the same time, a delegation from Elgin County met the Board to request yards at Dutton and Aylmer. At the annual meeting in March, 1958, a resolution was passed requesting that more yards be established and that they be accessible to all producers. Direction was to be made mandatory in all parts of the province. Elgin's request was at least partially answered by the establishment of a new yard at Talbotville. Early in 1959, consideration was being given to yards at additional points in Bruce, Grey, Dufferin, Lambton and Middlesex Counties. In May the amount provided for additional building was set at $120,000. For the new yard being developed on the Fair Grounds at Dundalk, it was agreed to advance three years rent in order to assist the Fair Board with construction costs. Shortly afterwards came an agreement for a new yard on the Ancaster Fair Grounds.

With the number of yards being increased across Western Ontario, it was readily agreed that Burford and Ancaster were not adequate to serve producers across the seven counties of Zone 4, stretching eastward from Oxford county to Niagara. The question that first arose was whether it would be feasible to have one yard that would serve Haldimand County as well at Lincoln and Welland counties. As in the case of the earlier efforts to locate a suitable site in the Brantford area, numerous trips were made by local directors to sites centrally located and reasonably priced or to barns that might lend themselves to modifications to create suitable premises. Altogether, ten or a dozen sites were inspected, mostly between Binbrook and Number 3 Highway, or in the area of Canfield. None seemed to be suitable.

In the meantime, based upon experience across the province, the idea was gaining ground that it was sound and practical to have more yards then had originally been planned and to have them located with more emphasis upon availability to producers who might want to deliver their own hogs. Hence, the idea developed that a central location in Haldimand would be practical. What was there at Cayuga or nearby that would serve the purpose? The old railway shipping yards at Cayuga had not been used for years and were in a questionable state of repair, but were located centrally to serve Haldimand County. A committee, set up by the Haldimand Hog Producers' Association, recommended to the Ontario Hog Producers' Co-operative that these yards might be rented and improved. A request was directed to the Canadian National Railways inquiring under what terms the yards in question might be rented. What followed was a tangle with railway bureaucracy. Requests were repeated and still no reply came as months slipped by. Finally, in desperation, an appeal was made to Mr. John Charlton, M.P. for Brant-Haldimand, to see if an approach could be made through the Department of Transport of the Federal Government in order to at least speed up the answer.

A favourable reply came through quickly. The C.N.R. was prepared to lease yards for the sum of fifty dollars per annum, but the Hog Producers' Co-operative would be responsible for all repairs and modifications to make the yards suitable. These terms were satisfactory and work began using local men to put the yards in proper shape. Later, from time to time, further modifications and improvements were made.

From the start, the Cayuga yards were unique in that almost all the hogs were brought in by farmers, using farm trucks and trailers. So to a greater degree than in the case of most yards an economic assembling service was given to hog producers. After a few years of operating the Cayuga yard, Mr. Gordon Skinner, who was then Agricultural Representative in Haldimand, said that he had yet to hear any dissatisfaction with the service being given by the yard.

With the needs of Haldimand taken care of, Zone 4 was still not adequately served by yards. The counties of Welland and Lincoln were still without convenient services. The search for suitable yard facilities, that had been conducted in co-operation with Haldimand, had eliminated a number of possible sites. In the midst of further search it was found that a suitable barn was available at Jordan and that the owner was available on a part time basis as operator.

During this same period, a similar expansion of yard facilities was taking place all over the province. One of the more significant stories occurred in Northumberland County, east of Toronto. Before a new move there must always be someone with an idea. Fred Skinkle, like most of his colleagues in the County, had been dissatisfied with the location of the yard in Northumberland, since it was in a far corner of the County. When Mr. Skinkle became county President in 1961, he did something about the problem.

With the support of the county directors, he asked J. R. Kohler as manager of the Co-operative to draw up plans for a building that would be suitable. A site was procured south of Campbellford. The local banker lent the funds required on the personal notes of all the sixteen county directors. The Beaver Lumber Company was given the contract to construct the required building. Bees were conducted to clean up the grounds around the building and to do some of the auxiliary work. In the words of one of the directors at the time, Carman Bray, who became the manager, the project worked because of "Free time, free labour, interested people". The first hogs were received in the summer of 1962 even before the scales were installed or the ramps built. Bank loans had been repaid by the revenue the central organization had paid in the form of rent. Thus, Fred Skinkle's idea had developed into a good yard owned by the Northumberland Association and contributing income, enabling better service to be given to county producers. In a similar manner all across Ontario county directors and local producers took an interest in their local yards and contributed to improvements.

At Madoc in Hastings County, producers were dissatisfied with the water and mud which prevented good service at the only facilities that could be rented. So the local producers went to work to develop a plan with the local Fair Board similar to what had been done at Burford, Dundalk and Ancaster to provide a new building on the Fair Grounds that would be adequate and suitable. In 1965 the new building was officially opened with wide community support.

Today, as hog production shifts, some yards are closed or moved, some new ones are brought into operation. With continuing producer participation the network of yards has become more efficient.

Ontario Hog Producers Marketing Yards 1971

Yard Location	Date Opened	Days of Operation (and remarks)
Addison	April 18, 1960	Wednesday
Ancaster	Sept. 10, 1957	Monday, Tuesday, Wednesday
Antrim	April 19, 1960	Tuesday
Arthur	Dec. 16, 1959	Tuesday and Wednesday
Barrie	Oct. 18, 1956	4 day operation (Grey Bruce - July 23, 1956) (Rented Yards - Aug. 12, 1956) (First sold hogs - Oct. 18, 1956)
Blenheim	July 21, 1964	Wednesday after July 21, 1969
Burford	Dec. 9, 1957	4 day operation
Campbellford	Aug. 8, 1962	Wednesday

Cayuga	Dec. 14, 1959	Monday
Chatham	Aug. 7, 1956	Monday and Tuesday
ˑ'		(Prior to Sept. 18/67 was a
		4 day operation)
Chatsworth	Aug. 4, 1959	Tuesday (closed Oct. 2/68)
		(Prior to Nov. 20/67 was also
		open on Mondays)
Clinton	Jan. 21, 1958	Tuesday
Cobden	June 9, 1959	Tuesday
Corbett	June 10, 1959	Wednesday
Dundalk	Aug. 4, 1959	Tuesday and Wednesday
Elmwood	June 24, 1959	Wednesday and
		(Thursday Mar. 18/71)
Finch	Feb. 6, 1961	Monday
Franktown*	Jan. 10, 1966	Monday
		*(opened Dec. 17, 1959 and known
		as Smiths Falls; on April 18,
		1960, name changed to Perth)
Harriston	July 15, 1957	4 day operation
Jordan	April 18, 1960	Monday
Kemptville	Nov. 2, 1964	Tuesday
Kincardine	June 10, 1959	Wednesday
Kitchener	Sept. 6, 1954	5 day operation
Lindsay	Jan. 16, 1958	Wednesday
London	Feb. 6, 1956	4 day operation
Lucknow	June 10, 1959	Monday (Prior to Apr. 17/61,
		operated on Tuesday)
Madoc	Feb. 23, 1959	Monday (Had been local since
		Dec. 15/58)
Maidstone	April 5, 1971	Monday and Tuesday
Milverton	Mar. 25, 1964	Wednesday and Thursday (Thurs.
		added May 12/66)
Newburgh	Feb. 24, 1959	Tuesday (local since Mar. 19/57)
Newbury	June 9, 1959	Monday and Tuesday
		(originally opened on Tuesday and
		Saturday)
		(Effective Mar. 29/67 operated
		on Monday and Tuesday)
Orangeville	Dec. 17, 1959	Wednesday
Peterboro	Feb. 26, 1959	Thursday (Originally operated
		on Tuesday also, but discon-
		tinued June 15/64)

Petrolia	June 10, 1959	Thursday (Prior to July 21/69 open on Wednesday)
Picton	Feb. 23, 1959	Monday
Ripley	June 10, 1959	Wednesday
Stouffville	April 15, 1958	Tuesday
Stratford	Feb. 6, 1956	4 day operation
Talbotville	June 17, 1958	Tuesday
Teeswater	June 10, 1959	Monday and Thursday (Thursday added Sept. 18/67)
Thamesville	July 20, 1964	Thursday (Prior to Sept. 18/67 open Monday)
Toronto	Jan. 26, 1953	5 day operation
Tupperville	July 20, 1964	Wednesday (Prior to Sept. 18/67 open Monday)
Vankleek Hill	June 9, 1959	Wednesday (Prior to Mar. 29/67 open Tuesday)

Marketing Yards No Longer In Operation

Yard Location	*Date Opened*	*Date Closed (and remarks)*
Hoard's Station	Feb. 25, 1959	Closed Aug. 8, 1962 (Replaced by Campbellford)
Lancaster	June 10, 1959	Closed May 17, 1961
Alexandria	June 29, 1959	Closed May 16, 1960
Seeley's Bay	Dec. 16, 1959	Closed June 30, 1965
Smith Falls	Dec. 17, 1959	Closed April 18, 1960 (Replaced by Perth)
Tweed	July 21, 1964	Closed June 29, 1965
Perth	April 18, 1960	Closed Jan. 10/66 (Replaced by Franktown)
Belleville	Dec. 15, 1959	Closed Oct. 1, 1969
*Hurdemans Bridge	Mar. 31, 1959	Closed Sept. 1, 1970 *(Opened May 21, 1957 and known as Leitrim, and operated on Monday and Tuesday - Hurdemans Bridge also operated on Tuesday, but stopped January 26, 1965)
Montreal (West End)	May 15, 1961	Closed Nov. 1, 1970

Chesley	June 25, 1959	Closed Mar. 11, 1971 (Replaced by Elmwood open 2 days)
Comber	May 25, 1959	Closed Mar. 30, 1971 (Replaced by Maidstone)
McGregor	Nov. 14, 1955	Closed Mar. 31, 1971 (Replaced by Maidstone)

CHAPTER X

POWER STRUGGLES

In the mid-1950s, fears of change, especially of different methods of pricing, aroused tempests and controversy on all sides.

Secretary Norman McLeod passed away suddenly from a heart attack in the late autumn of 1955. Until the end of the calendar year, Herb Arbuckle, who had been working with the sales staff, became acting Secretary. He was followed by Ted Marritt, a graduate of the Ontario Agriculture College, who, with his farm experience, had also been a member of the Canadian Department of Agriculture hog grading staff. Mr. Marritt, a nephew of W. G. Marritt, many years Agricultural Representative in Wentworth, in no time at all acquired a grasp of the struggle by the producers' organization to maintain a precarious hold on its fair share of control in the industry. However, by the end of the year, Mr. Marritt had received an offer from a large seed firm too tempting to refuse. From this position he went on to several positions of increasing importance in the agricultural field until his premature death a dozen years later.

Fortunately, upon the resignation of Mr. Marritt, the Hog Producers' were able to secure the services of a person who already had been emphatically identified with the efforts to place hogs on the open market. Mr. James Boynton had served in the Canadian Army during the war years and had returned to farm in Grey County when he immediately became involved in farm organizations and soon became Secretary of the County Federation of Agriculture. Mr. Boynton took over his new duties as Secretary Treasurer of the Hog Producers' Association, Co-Operative and Marketing Board on January 1st, 1957.

Hectic battles were to mark the next few years. Board personnel had been changing during the same period. Norman McLeod had retained his seat on the Board during the time he was Secretary. On his death he was succeeded by Melvin Becker, also of Waterloo County. Charles Newton of Simcoe County retired and was succeeded on the Board by Ben Steers also of Simcoe County. Mr. Newton, a graduate of the Ontario Agricultural College in the late 1930s, afterwards managed the Barrie Assembly Yard for the cooperative. At the time of the 1958 Annual Meeting, W. E. Tummon, who had made a tremendous contribution to the development of the organization through the years and had served as Secretary, retired from the Board. Mr. Tummon had been suffering from poor health for some time. At a Board meeting on May 14th, following his retirement from office, W. E. Tummon was presented with a travelling bag and a scroll in appreciation of his services. In his reply, Mr. Tummon said he had never served with a body as conscientious as the Marketing Board in carrying out the wishes of those whom the members represented. An even more specific opinion had come from Mr. Tummon in a letter to the Secretary the previous March: "The Board, as now constituted, is composed of individuals of which any organization should be proud. During my lifetime I have been a member of many Boards, but none more sincere and wholly dedicated to the task and purpose of their election."

Clarence Milligan, who had been a member at large, became representative for Zone No. 2 and his place as member at large was taken by Clare Curtin of Victoria County. Team work between Board members was always strong. Mr. Curtin, a prominent and active leader of the Knights of Columbus, remarked with a twinkle of Irish wit when he joined the Board: "I don't mind in the least sharing a room with a Protestant – as long as he is not an Orangeman." The very first time members of the Board found it necessary to stay overnight, Mr. Curtin found himself sharing a room with Eldred Aiken of Bruce County, an ardent Orangeman who had followed Norman McLeod as Chairman of the Board. In the late sixties, when Mr. Aiken was being honoured upon his retirement, it was Clare Curtin who, at the annual banquet of the Board and Association, paid the most emphatic tribute to Mr. Aiken, affectionately calling him "Uncle Eldred".

The next year, Mr. Milligan, who had entered the House of Commons in 1957, retired and his place on the Board was taken by Roy Sills of Hastings whose sound judgement and bland humour made him a valuable addition to board membership.

Through the whole of this period the large packers, now represented by the Meat Packers Council of Canada, were complaining to the press and to the Government about the methods of sale. They claimed that they did not have a chance to bid on all hogs being offered. At the same time the smaller packers, or as they have usually been called, "Domestic Packers", not under Federal Inspection and able to sell only on the domestic market, were expressing agreement with a full direction programme and the methods of sale. From the commencement of central selling by United Livestock Sales and later by the Hog Producers' Co-op, the method of sale had been that of private treaty, or negotiation, similar to what had always been employed by the Commission salesman on the Toronto Stock Yards and elsewhere. The Packers' Council subsequently listed in chronological order the significant events of this period. Time after time they mention proposals made to the Premier of Ontario, the Minister of Agriculture, the Farm Products Marketing Board and to joint meetings with either the Hog Producers' Co-operative or Marketing Board, relative to methods of sale.

Often on the pages of history, the earliest efforts to carry out innovations meet with violent opposition while a similar program or policy a few years later scarcely creates a public ripple. The very limited controls of placing hogs on the free market caused such a violent furor in Ontario that it seems almost impossible to believe that far more control over milk by the Milk Marketing Board a decade later was accepted with hardly a flicker of public interest. The method of selling hogs by private treaty was spoken of as allocating hogs. Suggestions were constantly made that the sales staff of the Hog Producers' Co-operative could show favouritism. Yet no charges were ever made to indicate that such was the case in any instance. A decade later the Ontario Milk Marketing Board was to frankly allocate milk supplies to various processors without price competition. Yet not a voice was raised in any kind of protest.

Questions were constantly being raised as to the legality of sales methods. For example, was a levy imposed upon a product by any local board acting under provincial legislation a tax? Was this not an instance of indirect taxation which lay within the authority of federal and not provincial legislation? In 1955 the Hog Producers' Marketing Board expressed complete willingness to review its legal position before the Supreme Court of Canada. In the spring of 1956 the case was heard. The argument for the legality of the licence fee or service charge was presented by C. R. Magone, Q.C., who appeared on behalf of the Attorney-General of Ontario. H. E. Harris, Q.C., of St. Catharines represented the Ontario Federation of Agriculture, and R. H. Milliken of Regina appeared for the Ontario Hog Producers' Marketing Board. A letter sent to each county association at this time contained the following report: The lawyer who represented the Board argued that "the licence fee or service charge was not passed on to the consumer through the retail price and therefore could not be declared an indirect tax levied by the province. They maintained that it was merely a fee paid by the producer for the purpose of financing the administration of the Scheme and for the services rendered the producer of a regulated product, and for these reasons came under the jurisdiction of the province. Further, Mr. Harris and Mr. Milliken outlined in detail to the court the operation of our Hog Marketing Agency and the Fresh Peach Marketing Agency."

The noted trial lawyer, J. J. Robinette, was appointed by the Court to submit argument against the legality of the licence fee or service charge and maintained that the service charge or licence fee was an indirect tax by the province. The Supreme Court verdict, announced in January, 1957, was highly favourable to the Marketing Board, but did suggest some further legislative changes to strengthen provincial marketing boards. In 1957 the federal law was amended to meet these suggestions.

Some years later, Mr. Alex Turner, afterwards Deputy Minister of Agriculture in B. C., who had been the main representative of the Federal Department of Agriculture in negotiating with the Ontario Hog Producers' Marketing Board, wrote as follows: "There were many times I went over with representatives of the hog producers the limits of the extension of power in interprovincial and export trade under the Agricultural Products Marketing Act of 1949. These were particularly difficult interpretations in Eastern Ontario where shipments to Hull and Montreal packing plants were involved. As I recall the Ontario Hog Producers' were one of the early groups to obtain this extension of powers. It was not until 1957 that the Agricultural Products Marketing Act was amended to allow Boards, with the approval of the Governor-in-Council, to collect levies which might be construed as indirect taxation and therefore beyond provincial authority. However, the extension of control powers in inter-provincial and export trade had been approved for many Boards including, if my memory serves me correctly, the Ontario Hog Producers' Board during the early fifties."

In June, 1956, the packers agreed to discontinue so called "under table payments". These were the extra payments to truckers by packers for making delivery of hogs to a particular plant. "Charlie" McInnis had repeatedly declared in speeches that more than 2 million dollars of producers money was paid out annually to drovers and truckers. The ensuing headlines in scores of newspapers across the province telling of these under table payments never once was challenged by packers, truckers or drovers. Most truckers had been receiving at least some under table payments, and some truckers much more than others. The Marketing Board and its supporters had long argued that truckers were entitled to a fair price for the transportation service that they were providing, but not to special commissions by the plants. The smaller or domestic packers often reported efforts to obtain extra hogs by contacting a trucker and offering a little extra per cwt. The trucker, however, would go back to the larger packer and negotiate an increased commission for himself, leaving the small packer to cool his heels.

After the announcement forbidding packer's "under table payments", truckers were more inclined to vent their rage against the Hog Producers' Marketing Board. Some truckers were, of course, far more concerned than others. Those with the least involvement with the larger packers or who divided their "under table" receipts with their farmer clients most resented the criticism that the Hog Producers' directed against truckers. Scorching letters appeared in the mail received by the Board. Individual directors and county officers were also on the receiving list. Mr. Ball, President of the Oxford Association, was sent an anonymous letter, telling him not to associate with the local director, Wilfred Bishop, or with the past president or both would have their barns burnt down. Bishop had two stone posts at his gate destroyed. A red livestock truck was seen backing up at one post and battering at it until it was broken down.

In the midst of this angry atmosphere the Oxford Association was determined to play a role in the current provincial programme by conducting special information meetings. A hall was procured in a local area. Mr. Ball chaired the meeting and local director, Wilfred Bishop, undertook for twenty minutes to explain the programmes and policies of the Provincial Board. The meeting divided itself into about fifteen supporters of the Board on one side of the hall and about fifty opponents on the other side. The room was quiet until the meeting was thrown open for discussion. Then bedlam broke loose. Questions were hurled at the director from every corner of the room. Some questions were realistically and genuinely in search of information. Others definitely were not. The *Woodstock Sentinel Review* of the next day (in May, 1956) reported calls from the floor such as "We don't want you" and "Let's throw him out". There were accusations of attempts to run farmers' business against the farmer's will. Attacks were even levelled at the late G. R. Green, the first Oxford Agricultural Representative, who was accused of working too closely with farm organizations. Truckers and drovers who were opposed to the programmes and policies of the Marketing board saw their structure of income and methods of doing business crumbling. It was a head on clash between these men and those who were leading a reform in marketing on behalf of the individual farmer. Farmers who were opposed were influenced by their trucker friends and also by many businessmen dealing with farmers who saw in the Hog Producers' the rise of an independent farm force which to them posed a threat to their influence in the farm sphere.

Ontario farmers have inherited from their United Empire Loyalist ancestors and from their oppressed European ancestors an intense love of freedom from legal restraints. The Ontario farmer enjoys the tradition of rural independence. Their fear of delivering hogs through a system of yards and collective selling opened visions of more and more regulations. The fact that the Hog Producers' Marketing Board, by unanimous consent, has never developed controls comparable to many other marketing boards perhaps shows hog men in Ontario to be more independent minded than other farmers. Clayton Frey, member of the Provincial Board representing the South Western part of the province in addressing a meeting of Middlesex county producers, condemned the undertable payment practice in these scathing words: "Ontario Hog Producers' best interests are being bartered, bought, scuttled and sold with their own money."

The battles of the later 1950s brought Charles McInnis, the dynamic and indefatigable president of the Hog Producers' Association and Co-operative, to his highest level of prominence on the agricultural stage. The colourful battles made good newspaper copy; the Ontario struggles to establish farmer rights stirred interest all across Canada. "Charlie" constantly had invitations to speak in other provinces; where his appearance was advertised in Ontario, there was sure to be a full house of farmers. The number of hours he worked per day, whether in his office or in his own Room 202 in the old Walker House Hotel, remain unrecorded. Often consultations on policy and strategy lasted all evening. At the same time he covered the province to meet speaking obligations.

Mr. J. R. Kohler, manager of the Co-operative, who had responsibility for selling the hogs and for business operations in general, also lived a hectic life. From farm groups came a demand to hear at first hand what was happening in the selling of the hogs. Later Mr. Kohler was to recall travelling with "Charlie" McInnis to a meeting in the Ottawa Valley, back to another at Hamilton, and the next day to another meeting for Bruce and Grey Counties. "Charlie" McInnis was able to catch some sleep while Jake Kohler drove.

Wherever "Charlie" McInnis went, he was at his best inspiring producers to firmly stand together to resist pressures from packers, truckers and government agencies. One such challenge came from the *Chesley Enterprise* in an editorial in January, 1957. It called the Hog Marketing Scheme a major farm problem and went on to say that "Producers' are seeking an open market to establish free competition". Dr. H. H. Hannan, President of the Canadian Federation of Agriculture, addressing the 1957 annual meeting said: "In view of the tremendous bargaining power which these large corporations (Massey-Harris Ferguson, etc.) have it seems to me a bit strange for serious criticism to be leveled at a rather unimportant regulation of a Producers' Marketing Board whose objective is simply to direct and control the initial sale of one product."

On one of the hottest summer days on record (June, 1957), Presidents and

Secretaries of the County Associations met with county Federations of Agriculture Secretaries for a frank discussion and exchange of information on all the current Producers' activities.

In October the Hon. W. A. Goodfellow, provincial Minister of Agriculture, announced that a plebiscite on the Hog Plan would be held in March or April. This did not come as a surprise to the Marketing Board. For several years there had been constant suggestions that a vote might be called. The first priority was to negotiate with the government of Ontario as to the terms and conditions of the vote. With the help of the Federation of Agriculture efforts also began immediately to organize support for the Marketing Plan.

When a special meeting was convened on November 4th in the Lord Simcoe Hotel, Toronto, nearly three hundred people attended. They represented county Hog Producers' Associations and local branches of the Federation of Agriculture. All were determined to make the plebescite a victory for the hog producer marketing programme. On the suggestion of the Reverend Bert Daynard of Perth County, the hat was passed to provide funds independent of the income from the sale of hogs for the support of the campaign. Over eight hundred dollars was raised. Another concrete action of this meeting was the election of a special campaign committee to assist the directors with the coming vote campaign. Those named to this vote committee were C. M. Lee, Duncan Wallace, Bert Daynard, J. Vanden Bosch, Emerson Crocker, William McCarthy and John Alton. A second meeting was held on December 10th to provide further foundation for the campaign.

At a board meeting held on December 30th, 1957, a committee composed of McInnis, Frey and Aiken reported a discussion with the Minister of Agriculture on how the vote should be conducted. The Board itself proposed that the following points act as the basis of the vote:

1) Hog Producers were not opposed to the holding of a vote.
2) The vote be taken so that uncertainties that exist may be cleared up.
3) The previous annual meeting had requested a full year of operation for the direction programme before a vote was taken.
4) The Board did not favour a vote being taken between May 1st and the following January.
5) That a fair basis for recognition of a favourable vote would be sixty per cent of those voting.

An early Government proposal that a favourable vote should be at least 51% of all those eligible to vote brought strong disfavour from both the Ontario Federation of Agriculture and the Hog Producers'. It was pointed out that this meant all those unable to vote would be counted opposed. During the ensuing month regulations were pounded out to provide for a thoroughly authoritative vote. Provisions were made to provide as much care for the preparation and revision of a voters' list as would be the case in a provincial election. Using the services of township clerks in most cases, provisions were made for balloting in each township. But all this took time and it was soon evident that a vote could not be taken as soon as the Hon. Mr. Goodfellow had at first announced. The date was finally set for Friday, July 25th, 1958. (In the meantime the administration office of the Hog Producers' Marketing Board was moved in Toronto from the old location at 77 York St. to the ground floor of the Prince Edward Building at 4198 Dundas St. Simultaneously, the sales offices moved there from 2824 Dundas Street and, for the first time, the entire organization operated under one roof.) With the date for the vote set and four pages of regulations provided by the Farm Products Marketing Board to establish the basis of the vote, the campaign went into high gear. Fronts for those parts of the packing trade who disliked the producer programme possible ran ads in newspapers. Under the signatures of producers they condemned the present methods of sale.

With the support and co-operation of the Ontario Federation of Agriculture, the Producers' Marketing Board launched an aggressive educational campaign. Even the urban press began to take an interest in this miniature provincial election campaign. Mr. Devon Smith, Financial editor of *The Toronto Telegram,* visited the sales offices and wrote a story, comparing the methods used in selling hogs to those used on the Toronto Stock Exchange:

Each Little Pig Goes to Market

Looked under a bushel yesterday – and found a light.

Realizing that just about everybody in Ontario who owns any bacon-on-the-hoof will be voting July 25 on whether or not he wants to sell through the Ontario Hog Producers' Association, we went to have a look at what this marketing method was.

It is easy these days to take it for granted that farm marketing plans are socialistic, calculated to turn farmers into pressure groups. After all, a lot of strange characters have used the farmers' problems as personal stepping stones to fame and fortune.

So it's encouraging to see how the Hog Producers work. Led by big, good-natured and shrewd Charles W. McInnis, association president, they have hammered out an application of the most effective form of auction market.

Maybe you'll cheer and maybe you'll snarl at this: they have provided for hogs just the sort of setup that makes buyers and sellers of stocks happy to have their shares listed on the big stock exchanges.

If the OHPA scheme is approved on July 25th, then every little porker born in Ontario will be listed for trading by a sort of birthright.

The best way to describe an auction market of this sort is to say that it offers sellers the whole available market and offers buyers the whole available supply; all traders, large and small, meet as equals.

This is how it's done.

Producers, the hog raisers, take their hogs to gathering points scattered across the province.

Teletypes flash the information on incoming hogs to the trading room at Dundas and Prince Edward dr. in West Toronto. There, the four highly skilled traders go to work.

They already have a wealth of information on processors needs (these traders are every bit as capable as you'll find in securities and commodities markets).

Like any bond dealer, they calculate from this flow of information just what they figure hogs should be worth today, and they set the offering price.

It's up to the processors' representative to figure what they think the squealers are worth, and to set their own bidding price.

One or the other or both must give a little before a deal is made. When a deal is made both sides know that particular deal reflects the buying or selling attitudes of all producers and processors.

That is the essential point of an open auction market. Whether he does it or not, everyone has the power to bid or offer as long as his bid or offer is backed by the ability to pay or deliver.

The consequence is an orderly rise and fall in prices, in supplies and in demand.

It is difficult to see how the existence of this sort of market can do anything but inject new health and prosperity into both sides of the pork business – producing and processing.

And, most important of all, the rapid and accurate reflexes of the open auction market are good for consumers' interests.

County Associations played an active role by advertising in local papers and in organizing campaigns to get out the vote on election day. Board supporters were dismayed at the great effort the Farm Products' Marketing Board made to emphasize the compulsive aspect of the question. Huge display posters containing all board regulations were supplied to polling booths.

Marketing Board supporters had some severe shocks as the first ballots were counted. A number of the heavier producing counties of Western Ontario voted "No". However, the total count was more favourable.

2	counties gave over	90%	"yes"
13	counties gave from	80 to 90%	"yes"
11	counties gave from	70 to 80%	"yes"
8	counties gave from	60 to 70%	"yes"
1	county gave from	50 to 60%	"yes"
7	counties gave below	50%	"yes"

The total score showed 68.2% in favour. This was more than the 66 2/3% favourable vote required by the final draft of the Government Board regulations.

The ballots were scarcely counted when complaints of voting irregularities were made. There was no doubt that there were persons who voted who were not eligible and who were not producers of hogs at the time of the plebiscite as the regulations demanded. In a general election it is relatively simple to determine whether or not a person is of age and lives at a certain point. But to determine whether a farmer was an owner of hogs at the designated time is more difficult. No doubt there were a number of farm people who were opposed to farmers having more authority in the market place. Similar problems had arisen when wheat producers voted some months earlier.

An organization known as the "Free Enterprisers" appeared on the scene as the organized and official opposition to the Marketing Board. Their position was that the individual would be much better off if the marketing fee were not a necessary cost and that producers should have the individual right to choose whether they wished to deliver their hogs to a plant rather than a Board yard. The president of this group was Peter McDonald of Bright who was to serve later as a Board Member for several terms.

The Marketing Board's investigation of irregularities indicated that the majority who voted improperly had been expressing strong opinion against the marketing plan. In the ensuing Court challenge to the legality of the vote, the Free Enterprise group was the plaintiff and the Farm Products Marketing Board the defendant. The ultimate decisions of the Supreme Court of Ontario, a ruling by Chief Justice McRuer, released in March, 1959, declared the vote invalid. The reason given was that the proper procedure had not been followed in the calling of the plebiscite. This, however, did not set the marketing plan aside as a negative vote would have done. It merely meant a falling back on the earlier authority established after the 1945 vote. Selling of hogs continued as usual.

From now on there was a continuance of pressure from Government agencies and from the trade for changes in both the organizational structure of the Marketing Board and in the methods employed in making sales. The producers' organization felt that a favourable vote of over 68% was clearly a demonstration of farmer support. A sharp difference of opinion in the interpretation of the basic legislation was definitely coming. The farmer board took the attitude that producers were entitled by legislation to the same principles of internal self-government as that exercised by the Bar Association or the Medical Association. The Government position was that all actions of the producer board must be carefully scrutinized by the over all Farm Products Marketing Board. Irresistible forces were meeting immovable objects.

A press headline of November 15, 1958, declared that the Government demanded a new plan.

During 1958, both before and after the plebiscite, the Marketing Board was continuing efforts to ensure that "Direction Orders" were being carried out. A practical difficulty was the obtaining of evidence that would stand up in court as to the specific business practices of a particular trucker. To provide clarification of what the particular facts might be, the Board and the Co-operative had procured jointly in February, 1958, the services of Mr. H. J. Fitzallen, a retired R.C.M.P. investigator. Mr. Fitzallen served during most of the year organizing evidence that was finally to place the "Direction" programme on an accepted legal foundation.

The net effect of the July vote seemed to intensify pressure for changes in the marketing format. Addressing the semi-annual meeting of the Board and Association and the annual of the Co-op on September 18, the Hon. W. A. Goodfellow, the Minister of Agriculture, declared that only two parties need to be concerned with the method of sale, the producers and the packers. Already a month before this, both groups of packers, the Council Members and the Domestic had met in the Minister's office to press for the resumption of negotiations concerning the methods of sale.

In October, the Premier, the Hon. Leslie Frost, convened a joint meeting of producers and processors. Thus began a series of meetings in camera, under government auspices, to consider the method of sale. Different proposals were made by each party. A subsequent review of some of the proposals made during this series of discussions suggests that a struggle for power was of greater importance to the participants than the question of sale methods. The Packers Council afterwards maintained that progress was being made until a special meeting of producer representatives in December refused to compromise.

Mounting pressure on the farmer group led to a search for technical assistance. The spotlight of publicity continued to be turned on Charles McInnis, the President of the Co-op and the Association, through this period of confrontation. This in turn brought him contacts with many in other fields of activity who were interested in the farmer effort to maintain marketing control. He happened to meet on one occasion Dr. David D. Monieson, a native of Montreal and a graduate of McGill University, who was currently a professor of marketing at the Wharton School of Commerce and Finance at the University of Pennsylvania. As a result of talks with Dr. Monieson and consideration by the Marketing Board, arrangements were made for the three producer organizations to procure Dr. Monieson's services on a part time basis as a marketing consultant. Much of the argument material issued during the next two years was to bear the mark of the thinking of Dr. Monieson.

Early in the new year the producers' group again met with Premier Frost and presented to him a number of points explaining the producer position. The following proposals outlined the position being taken by the producers at this time:

1. The producers were prepared to accept auction selling as proposed by the packers, provided 35 buyers out of the total of 51 would always be present.
2. The producers also were willing to receive bids by auction on condition they could contact other buyers if less than the 35 were present.
3. All processors might bid by teletype so that all bids would be on record, thus retaining for producers the advantages of good salesmanship.

Early in 1959 the Government appointed Mr. George Gathercole, an economist on the staff of the Premier, to preside over joint meetings of processors and packers in an effort to find a solution to the impasse. Throughout the early part of the year there seemed little progress. Some of the meetings were held in one of the regular Legislative Committee Rooms with the press admitted. By mid-summer little was achieved. At the March elections, Board members were re-elected with the exception of Clarence Milligan, who, as mentioned earlier, was succeeded by Roy Sills.

President Charles McInnis remained in the public eye. Without his platform popularity and ability to muster farm support the producers might very easily have been forced into a position of retreat. Mr. McInnis repeatedly stated from public platforms that the method of sale issue being pushed by the government was due to packer pressure. Government spokesmen denied this.

In 1959, the Hon. Mr. Goodfellow announced a very far reaching re-organization of the Farm Products Marketing Board. New appointments were made. Mr. Frank Perkin, an able civil servant with a long career behind him, who had been chairman of the Government Board, became Commissioner of Marketing. The new Chairman was Mr. George McCague, a very able leader in farm organizations who, over the years, had combined success in farming with equal success in business. Mr. Hugh Bailey, General Manager of U.C.O., also combined experience in business. He had at one time served as President of CO-Paco, the farmer owned packing plant at Barrie. Mr. Bailey, in fact, had been instrumental in re-organizing that business and putting it back on its feet. The third new appointee was Mr. Wm. Nickerson, a fruit growers' from the Niagara Peninsula, who had a lengthy period of service as a member of local fruit growers' boards, operating under the Farm Products Marketing Act.

Mr. Goodfellow also announced that the Government was thinking of combining those organizations that were associated with any commodity marketing board. Some weeks later the Minister spoke further: "Marketing Boards had the freedom to bargain but commodity groups must safeguard the rights given them by the Government Board . . . No local board should seek to influence its commodity group to take any action that might be beyond the authority delegated to it by the Farm Products Marketing Board . . . Necessary amendments to the legislation would be made after deliberation." He went on to say: "I am of the belief that a local board having a monopoly on a product must assure themselves that their selling methods are not open to question . . . Speaking as Minister of Agriculture I must say that in my opinion the present selling method in the case of hogs is not in the long term interest of orderly marketing."

Opponents of the producers' board went so far as to seek space in church publications and an opportunity at formal church meetings to take "pot shots" at the producer board, basing their attacks on imagination rather than facts.

In the autumn of 1959 presentations were made by the producers group, the Farm Products Marketing Board, the free enterprisers and the Meat Packers Council, to the Committee of Enquiry which had been set up by the Government of Ontario to investigate the whole state of agriculture.

Even with the change of personnel on the Farm Products Marketing Board, negotiations seemed little improved as continued efforts were made to solve the deadlock.

Roy Sills, always with a flair for the unusual approach, arrived at one of the joint meetings bearing two long-stemmed clay Indian pipes, Presenting one to George McCague, Chairman of the Farm Products Marketing Board, and the other to Eldred Aiken, Chairman of the Hog Producers Marketing Board, he suggested the use of the pipes of peace might be conducive to an early settlement.

Again there were rumours of a new plebiscite and of changes in the marketing legislation of the province which would place the authority in the hands of the government's board.

Supported by the technical advice of Dr. Monieson and by continued endorsement across the province, Charles McInnis unrelentingly declared that the producers stood firmly by their basic rights in claiming the same authority over their business as was granted to professional groups.

In September 1959 the farmers procured the services of Lucien Parizeau in public relations. Mr. Parizeau had just returned to Canada from service abroad with the Food and Agricultural Organization (FAO) of the United Nations. For the next few years Mr. Parizeau wielded a most skillful and devastating pen on behalf of the hog producers groups.

In an atmosphere of mounting tension, delegates from the counties to the

Ontario Hog Producers Association met in special session on January 20, 1960 at the Seaway Hotel, Toronto. A highlight of the meeting was the showing for the delegates of a new film production entitled, "The Better Way." Prepared by Crawley Films, the presentation displayed for the public across the province just how the Marketing Board and their selling office actually functioned.

James Boynton, Secretary of the Board, read the government's press release announcing yet another plebiscite in the spring. Charles McInnis told the meeting that with continued pressure from the trade to change the method of sale and the government's announcement of the pending vote it had been considered wise to call the current meeting. At this meeting suggestions were made from the floor that a vote might not be called if some changes were made in the sale methods.

Certainly, in the year 1960, the great agricultural question in Ontario was "What was going to happen to the Hog Producer Selling Program?" In February, Board members were amazed to hear that Everett Biggs, the Assistant Deputy Minister of Agriculture, was scheduled to deliver a special address to the annual meeting of the Canadian Holstein Friesian Association on question of hog marketing. What was going on here? What connection was there between Hog Marketing in Ontario and the problems of the largest dairy breed association in Canada? Years later, Everett Biggs, as Deputy Minister of Agriculture in Ontario, stated that it was definitely planned that a major speech be made at the Holstein meeting so that the position of the Government might be properly clarified. His philosophy was misunderstood at the time. Since then he has more often been criticized for being too pro farmer in the field of marketing. There was a feeling on the part of the Department of Agriculture that there was a danger in the philosophy of leadership when Charles McInnis spoke as though he had magic authority, challenging the delegation of powers provided by legislation. It was necessary for a referee to be provided. In his position as Assistant Deputy Minister of Agriculture in charge of marketing, Mr. Biggs felt that he was entitled to be trusted. He had talked with McInnis at the convention of the Ontario Concentrated Milk Producers' Association and then later at the Hog Producers' offices and received the impression that, if the Hog Producers' were not bothered, everything would be fine. There appeared in the opinion of Government to be serious dangers in the situation. The question was being asked: "What was the Government's position?" "What did the Government really want?" If Government officials really knew, they did not tell anyone, least of all the Hog Producer officers. Consequently, a state of confusion was bound to continue.

At local meetings Hog Producers were being denied both sides of the story. The information was given out that Biggs and McCague would be happy to attend county meetings. Mr. Biggs received an invitation to speak at one of the county meetings north east of Toronto. A provincial director from a neighbouring county was called upon for a few remarks and continued to tell stories until four o'clock. Mr. Biggs broke in and said that he had been invited to speak, but if he was not wanted he would head back to Toronto.

Following the speech at the Holstein meeting, which had been cleared with the Minister of Agriculture, McInnis went on the CBC Television program, "Country Calendar", calling the action of the Department of Agriculture a use of the "Big Stick", illustrating his point as he brandished a length of "two by four." Later, speaking at the annual meeting of the Flue Cured Tobacco Growers Marketing Board, Mr. Biggs said there was a possibility that the marketing legislation might be withdrawn should friction continue at the prevailing level.

Following the Holstein meeting speech, the Communications Department of the Ontario Hog Producer's Organizations, under the direction of Mr. Parizeau, issued a seven page reply to Mr. Biggs. Approval was expressed of Mr. Biggs' remark that we need "a warmer climate in the market place" and his reference to the "efficiency of the administrative machinery". On the other hand, he was severely criticized for quoting material out of context from *The Market Place,* the official organ of the Association, and from the pen of Dr. Monieson.

The bone of contention continued to be the method of selling. The producers' communications department remained critical of any so called "Auction" system. They emphasized the inability to store, the difficulty of protecting the anonymity of the bidder, the relatively small number of buyers, and the continual packer pressure on the Government.

All through the winter of 1959-60 tension remained high. *The Market Place* was vigorous in its editorial comments. The Government was accused of being pushed around by the big packers. In the meantime "Direction" had been extended to Eastern Ontario so that the whole province was now covered. The position of the producer board was being strongly supported by both the editorial page of *The Market Place* and by a flood of letters from producers. Again no one was more constantly in demand as a speaker than the President of the Producers' Association, Charles McInnis.

Early in the new session of the Ontario Legislature, amendments to the Ontario Farm Products Marketing Act were presented in the form of Bill 86. In farm circles, and more particulary in hog producer circles, Bill 86 immediately became a "dirty word". The most noticeable of the amendments was one to increase the authority of the Farm Products Marketing Board to step in and to exercise more control over local boards, even to the point of taking over their operations.

The annual meeting of 1960 registered strong protests over the question of Bill 86. Already an idea was beginning to germinate that there might be methods of producer action to circumvent Government authority. Was there a place for a co-op slaughtering project in Ontario? At this annual meeting a report was given of a visit made to the U.S. the previous autumn to study not only a slaughtering operations, but also the merchandising of carcasses. In his presidential address Mr. McInnis thanked the Minister of Agriculture and the members of the Farm Products Marketing Board for at long last promising that, if a new system of selling were tried and found not to work, it would be possible to revert to the former method. This question had been a source of major concern to the producers since Frank Perkins, chairman of the Farm Products Marketing Board, had expressed doubt to "Charlie" McInnis as to whether this would be possible. Present at the annual meeting wer Mr. C. D. Graham, the Deputy Minister of Agriculture, as well as Mr. Biggs.

Amid this continuing atmosphere of debate and disagreement the Government suddenly announced that a firm of business consultants, Price, Waterhouse & Co., had been engaged to make a study of the operations of the Ontario Hog Producers' Co-operative Association and Board. Following the release of the Price Waterhouse Report, a reply was made through the Marketing Services Department of the Association. With the assistance of Dr. Monieson, criticism was expressed that the terms of reference given Price, Waterhouse and Co. had not been made public and that the consultants had not gone into many of the details. Thirteen specific recommendations were listed and a reply was made to each of these in turn. They were as follows:

Recommendation (1): There should be one organization rather than three. The reply was that three organizations gave greater freedom of operation and that apparently the Government did not wish an independent Association.

Recommendation (2): Policy should be determined by Board Members but should be implemented by staff. The Marketing Services Department replied that there was considerable difference between an ordinary business corporation and a farmer company and that the contacts of directors were a particular asset in the countryside.

Recommendation (3): All Board members should be elected in zones rather than some in zones and some at large. The reply was that, with variations in production, a more equitable representation was being achieved.

Recommendation (4): A member of the Farm Products Marketing Board be appointed a non-voting member of the Hog Producers' Marketing Board. In reply it was suggested that Bill 86 already provided absolute veto power.

Recommendation (5): The service charge should be reduced to 30 cents and then reviewed every three months. The Association's reply was that a stable fee was more satisfactory than one that had to be raised and lowered as volume of marketing should vary.

Recommendation (6): Assembly yards and other fixed assets should be leased. The Association replied that this would raise costs.

Recommendation (7): At the beginning of the fiscal year an expense and capital budget should be submitted to Farm Products Marketing Board. The Association's response was that control over the Producer Board would just be that much more complete.

Recommendation (8): At least once a year a comparable financial statement be made available to all hog producers. No objection was raised in response.

Recommendation (9): A punch card system should be prepared for the records. In reply it was stated that this had already been studied and had been found to be less efficient and more costly than the method in use.

Recommendation (10): Service charges collected should be transferred early to the general funds instead of being mingled with trust funds. The Association replied that this would merely reduce the interest on behalf of hog producers. Ward, Welch, Hall and McNair, the auditors, added that methods in use were proper, and daily instead of monthly transfers would result in loss of interest and additional expense.

Recommendation (11): Approval should be obtained by the Hog Producers' Marketing Board for payment made to the Ontario Hog Producers' Association on April 13th, 1960. The Association's reply was that this action was legal because the authority of Bill 86 brought into effect to prevent such payments without the authority of the Government Board was not law at that date.

Recommendation (12): The Ontario Hog Producers' Association should further be required to return the additional sum of $80,000 to be deposited with the Ontario Credit Society. In reply it was pointed out that part of this sum had already been used to finance the day-to-day operations of the Association and that the money had been set aside to ensure the continued operations of the Association.

Recommendation (13): An independent study should be made of the operations of the assembly yards to ensure the most economic returns. The Association agreed that this was a sound suggestion and plans had already been made to do this very thing.

On June 30, 1960, the Directors of the Ontario Hog Producers' Marketing Board engaged another consultant firm, Stevenson & Kellogg, to make another study of the operations of the three producer organizations. The Report submitted in September, 1960, contained two main points. We quote:

124

In the course of our investigations we have come to two basic conclusions which underlie the subsequent report.

(1) The surrounding legislation is basically fair, establishing as it does, a balance of responsibility and control on one hand with the privilege of monopoly on the other.

(2) The Ontario hog marketing monopoly is the strength of the O.H.P.M.B. the O.H.P.C. and even to some extent the O.H.P.A. and all else must be second to retaining this position.

With this interpretation and opinion, on our part we were forced to the conclusion that living within present legislation in order to retain compulsion was mandatory since it was in the best interests of producers.

There have no doubt been courses in recent years and months, for frustration and loss of faith, but we consider them secondary in importance to the monopoly privilege. In our opinion, to accept it is to survive, to reject it is to succumb.

The main part of the report accepted, in general, the structure as it existed at that time. While the continued existence of the selling co-operative from the board itself was not really essential, it offered the opportunity for additional activities not within the scope of the authority delegated by the Marketing Board. The remaining part of the report was largely given to an analysis of details of structure and a review of the duties and responsibilities associated with different offices. Thus, a contribution was made towards the achievement of greater efficiency.

At the same time as all this study and investigation was going on, the Marketing Board spent two days in New Brunswick and Nova Scotia to confer with the Maritime Marketing Board and also to see the Nova Scotia Co-operative Abattoir which was then nearing completion.

In the summer of 1960, the decision was made that an effort would be conducted to establish a major co-operative meat processing plant. As an independent company, it would owe no responsibility to any Government Board. At the same time, there was a continuing effort to resolve the differences dividing the Farm Products' Marketing Board and the Hog Producers' Marketing Board. In July, 1960, Dr. Monieson, writing in *The Market Place,* accused the Farm Products' Marketing Board of trying to destroy the Hog Producer leadership. On August 18th, a joint statement was released by the Farm Products' Marketing Board and the Hog Producers' Marketing Board, expressing agreement on a number of points. In addition, a study was to be made of selling methods by a joint committee. Dickieson and Frey were to represent the producers with Bailey and McCague speaking for the Government Board. It was agreed that the Co-op and the Marketing Board should have the same fiscal year, and it was agreed to accept the Government proposals for eleven new zones to replace the seven formerly used by both

Co-op., Association and Board. This was to apply only in the case of the Marketing Board and elections were to be held prior to the annual meeting. Furthermore, there was agreement that the Co-operative was to remain as the selling agency.

In the meantime, the plebiscite, which had been earlier announced, was postponed indefinitely. After several meetings, the committee on method of sale found itself unable to make any progress.

The July meeting, approving the construction of a Co-operative Abattoir, was followed by a larger meeting in the Seaway Hotel in Toronto on October 19th, 1960. Here the new Co-operative was formally born and officially named the "Farmers Allied Meat Enterprises." The die was now cast for the new co-operative enterprise which automatically would mean an ultimate action on the part of producers without Government legislation. The board of the new co-operative was made up of the same directors as the Marketing Board, the Co-op Agency and the Association, plus a number of additional members. This, however, was only a temporary arrangement. Mr. Pat Dickey, who had served briefly in the new position of Fieldman for the Hog Producers' Association, took the role of an organizer for "FAME", the abbreviated name of the new company. The tightened restrictions on the freedom of the Marketing Board to make grants to the Association to finance its extra services of publicity and research had begun by this time to have effect, thus, the services of Dr. Monieson were curtailed and finally dispensed with.

It was recognized by the Farm Products Marketing Board and by the Marketing Board Directors and Co-op Agency Directors that those who might choose to continue as directors of "FAME" would not be eligible for re-election. In the case of the Association, the situation was somewhat different in as much as the functions of the Association were promotional and educational and did not involve any business dealing with "FAME". In this way possible conflicts of interest were avoided. There was general agreement that the Association must carry on even though the day might come when it would have no funds from the Marketing Board.

The January-February issue of *The Market Place* carried a letter from the Ontario Farm Products Marketing Board, stating that the producer Board must abide by the new regulations or lose the powers of direction. Furthermore, a new method of sale must be in effect by April 1st. As a result of further consultation, a new joint committee was set up to proceed with new studies.

The new joint committee was made up from the Producer Board of Steers, Dickieson and Curtin, and from the Government Board of Bailey and Teasdale. This committee was able to achieve some concrete results and accepted a teletype system of selling. Almost two years earlier a system of this kind had been proposed by the producers and had been rejected by the packer buyers. Later a very similar proposal by the packers had been rejected by the producers.

In its essence, the teletype method now agreed upon proposed a master machine in the head office that would list "lots" being held at assembly points. One lot would be listed at a time and would appear on teletype machines in the office of each packer. A tape listing asking prices with a range of one dollar, going down from the highest level at five cent steps, would be used. A button on each buying machine would allow the buyer for each packer to declare the level of price his firm would be willing to pay. This action would disconnect all machines except his own from the line to the central sales office so any details regarding the particular sale might be discussed. The salesmen might decide that the price on a particular lot of hogs should be close to $35.00 per cwt., dressed weight, on the basic grade. Then the tape being carried on the teletype network would read $35.00, $34.95, $34.90, $34.85, $34.80, etc. The button would be pushed at the particular price level the prospective buyer would be willing to pay. Should the hogs in question not be sold within the range suggested, the sales staff could then present the same lot again at a later time.

On January 3rd, 1961, the delegates of the Ontario Hog Producers' Co-Operative were called for the last of a series of special meetings called from time to time to consider crises. These meetings had marked the growth of the Hog Producer organizations to a position of prominence on the Ontario agricultural stage. The purpose of this meeting was for consultation on the situation as it had been developing. The delegates present endorsed the stand that their Board had been taking in opposing the increasing pressure from the Government Board, but, at the same time, they voted in the morning to invite the Honourable Mr. Goodfellow, the Minister of Agriculture, Mr. Biggs and Mr. McCague to address the afternoon session. All three gentlemen agreed to accept the invitation. Mr. Biggs said he had addressed the Holstein meeting the previous winter on hog marketing questions through the lack of any other available forum. Mr. McCague met several challenges from the floor, but Mr. Goodfellow was not interrupted, probably because he was Minister of Agriculture. Wilfred Bishop, a producer director, in the course of the discussion, criticized the selling proposals for not making adequate provision for the smaller packer who would not be able to provide a buyer to handle a teletype throughout the buying period. He pointed out that it was unfair to ask the smaller packer to buy through the medium of a large buyer. Criticism at this time may have contributed to later modifications to assist the smaller buyer.

During the ensuing weeks, Charlie McInnis, and a substantial part of the producer Board, came to feel that working under Government legislation

127

was largely a lost cause and the only way left to fight for farmer rights was through the medium of "FAME". This reasoning resulted in a lull or state of truce. The other section of the producer Board felt it was still possible, within the scope of the new regulations, to serve farmer interests.

In February came the necessity for the Directors of the Co-op Sales Agency to make the formal decision as to whether the teletype method of sales was to be approved and, if so, what steps should be taken to bring it into operation in the spring. If insufficient directors attended this meeting, there would be no quorum and no action could be taken. Mr. Wesley Magwood was sick and unable to attend the meeting. McInnis, Rintoul, Frey and Becker decided not to attend or have anything to do with the new selling method. On the other hand, Dickieson, Aiken, Steers, Curtin, Sills and Bishop, constituting a bare quorum of the Co-Operative Agency Board, participated in the meeting and formally approved the teletype method of selling and, in so doing, declared for the continued existence of the hog producer organizations.

Interest now came to centre upon the elections under the new system for a new Marketing Board. Provisions were made for this to be carried out by the Department of Agriculture personnel before the time of the March annual meeting. Again a time of decision was at hand for each individual member of the producer Boards. Would he be a candidate for the Marketing Board and Co-Op Agency Board, or would he choose instead to be a candidate in the new election for the "FAME" Board, scheduled for early April? Of course it would be possible to retire from all offices, but the only director making this choice was Wesley Magwood of Hanover in Grey County who retired because he was in ill health. Mr. Magwood had long been a most outspoken and courageous exponent of the farmer cause and had made a very valuable contribution not only to the hog producer organizations, but also to the Federation of Agriculture and other farm organizations. The other directors all decided to go in one direction or another. McInnis, Frey, Rintoul, Becker and Bishop made the choice of declining to be candidates for the new Marketing Board and stating they would be candidates for the "FAME" Board; Aiken, Dickieson, Steers, Curtin and Sills choose to be candidates under the new terms.

It very soon became evident that over most of the province there would be a very heated contest for election of committeemen in most of the eleven new zones. The committeemen in each zone, in turn, would elect members to the Marketing Board. Nominations were conducted by the Agricultural Representatives in late February with provision for voting by secret ballot early in March. In some counties two rival slates of candidates for committeemen were nominated, there being a firmly drawn line in most cases between those pledged to do away with the marketing plan and those

128

pledged to support the position being taken by the candidates from the old Board. These gentlemen took the attitude that it was still possible to serve producers through the medium of the new regulations. In counties where this contest was hottest, each side circulated lists of candidates for committeemen to help partisans to remember who their candidates happened to be. There was not the overall advertising that marked the 1958 plebiscite, but there was more personal canvassing. Many truckers who hated the system of direction and assembly yards saw an opportunity to influence enough votes and change the complexion of the Marketing Board so that either the whole marketing plan might be dissolved or, at least, the Direction could be done away with, permitting them to deal directly with the packers and to probably reinstitute the old under the table payments. In some counties the secrecy of the customary polling booth was broken. Lines of waiting voters created almost an impasse. Consequently, voters were handed ballots and allowed to sit at tables in a large room to mark them. A noticeable feature in one county was that of several persons wandering from table to table giving advice as to how the ballots were to be marked. Significant among these was a man who had been a vocal opponent of the marketing plan who was clearly wearing on his jacket the insignia of a well known firm active in both the feed and meat packing industries.

When the committeemen in each zone had met to elect Board Members, and the smoke of battle had cleared away, it was evident that the supporters of the marketing plan had won a clear victory. Of those elected, four of the five members of the old Board, who had been candidates, were re-elected; of the new members, three definite opponents of the Marketing Plan were elected and the other four were known supporters of the Marketing Board system.

In the meantime, the official announcement was made that the new selling system would be brought into operation in April or as soon afterwards as possible.

Attacks against the Marketing Board System, however, continued to be carried on at many of the county annual meetings. In some counties the majority of the directors who had been on record supporting the marketing programme were defeated and replaced by opponents. In some counties where this happened the local directors were changed, but not the provincial delegates to the Association or to the Co-operative selling agency. In some other counties there were only partial changes. A whole new approach was evident at the 1961 annual meeting which met in March, 1961.

For "Charlie" McInnis the stage was thus set for his valedictory after twenty years of leadership of the hog producers of Ontario. Mr. McInnis told of the inadequate share of the consumers' dollar being given to the farmer. He criticized state control of marketing which he saw taking the place of what had been producer control of marketing. He felt it would be impossible to salvage anything from what he called a stepping stone to dictatorship. Continuing, Mr. McInnis expressed the opinion that the only hope for the future lay in the development of "FAME" to serve producer interests. In conclusion, he made an appeal to hog producers to keep the Association vital and independent, and able to criticize friend and foe alike. That same evening, Mr. McInnis was honoured at the annual banquet. He received a commemorative plaque and a purse from county associations. The purse he immediately designated for the purchase of common shares of "FAME" to be the common property of all share holders. At the same time, Mrs. McInnis was the recipient of a bouquet of roses.

Whatever had been said about "Charlie" McInnis, there can never be any doubt of his absolute personal honesty, integrity and total dedication to what he felt to be in the best interest of farmers. During his twenty years as President of the Ontario Hog Producers' Association, he constantly gave more and more of his time to what to him had become a dedication to a burning cause. Never, at any time, was he the recipient of a salary. He never received more expenses or a per diem allowance which, during his term of office, varied from five dollars to fifteen dollars per day. His general practice, travelling at night, was to sleep in a day coach rather than to increase expenses by using a berth. His name was known not only in almost every farm home across the province, but also to city newspaper reporters who always could see a story in his constant demands of justice for Ontario farm people.

At the banquet, leaders of the hog producers of the province were joined by many others in paying deserved tribute to the retiring leader. Among these were the Hon. William Goodfellow, the Minister of Agriculture, with whom he had so often clashed; the Hon. Farquhar Oliver, speaking for the Liberal Party in the Ontario Legislature; Donald MacDonald, leader of the C.C.F. in the Legislature; and Mr. Wm. Tilden, President of the Ontario Federation of Agriculture. The following tribute appeared in *The Market Place* for April 1961:

A Tribute to
Charles W. McInnis

It is sometimes difficult for those of us who came late to organized agriculture to grasp the significance of the struggles that made to-day's farm movements possible. It is even more difficult to understand as we should the role that human dedication and industry have played in this constant progress.

Yet it is to the men who pioneered in the field of organized agriculture, to

130

the men who had courage and vision when the task seemed impossible – it is to them that we all owe our gratitude.

Such a man is Charles W. McInnis of Iroquois.

Some twenty years ago, the hog producers of Ontario were without economic power. Their labours stopped at the farm-gate, each man struggling for himself, his hopes for better to-morrows still-born in a world of uneven competition. Charles McInnis fought on.

The Ontario Hog Producers' Association was born, first as a tribune for uncertain goals and aspirations, then as a more formal organization, and finally, after many years of trials, as a solid front of producers, determined to improve their lot, determined to obtain a just reward for their labours, determined to secure strength in the market place.

Charles McInnis tirelessly spearheaded a movement which, in its formative years, seemed to carry little chance of success. Chiefly due to his dogged persistence and his foresight, the Association worked hard to lay the groundwork for marketing legislation that would enable the hog producers to sell their commodities collectively through a central agency and to achieve a position of equality in their vertical competition with the processing trade.

The rest is history – the passage of the Farm Products Marketing Act, the creation of the producers' marketing agency and marketing board, and finally, out of these considerable achievements, a new idea in co-operative meat-processing and marketing known throughout the country as "FAME".

The new co-operative is now a reality. It would never have been possible, as a logical extension of collective marketing, without the dedication and courage of Charles W. McInnis and of the men who later joined him from the ranks to guide the destinies of the Hog Producer Organizations in Ontario.

To such a man, who embodied the hopes of two generations of farm producers, we owe an enormous debt of gratitude. But most of all, we owe Charles W. McInnis the self-respect and the respect of others that we have gained through the years as a group of men engaged in a noble, but oft-neglected, profession.

Withdrawing from the Hog Producers' Marketing Board does not mean, could never mean retirement for Charles McInnis. It means a renewed drive, within the "FAME" Co-operative, to earn even greater rewards for Ontario's farm producers.

To a man like Charles McInnis, one does not say, Good Luck! He makes his own. To a man like him, one does not say, Thank you! He finds his thanks in thankless tasks. To a man like him, one does not say, Farewell! He will be around for a long time, making his presence felt and his voice heard as long as there is an injustice or an evil in our midst.

131

To Charles McInnis, we can only say, "We are with you." This assurance we all want you, Charlie, to carry with you to battle. We are truly with you in the years ahead.

THE HOG PRODUCERS OF ONTARIO
MARCH, 1961

The address delivered to this annual meeting by Mr. Eldred Aiken in his capacity of Chairman of the Marketing Board was of particular significance. He clearly spelt out the Board objectives for the year 1961:

a) The right to determine the amount of money producers spend on marketing and matters pertaining to marketing.
b) The right to determine the basis of electing officers, to effect changes in the corporate structure of the board and the marketing agency, and to make their own policy decisions.
c) The right to decide how the product should be marketed.
d) The right to choose a marketing agency.

He went on to say that unless the meeting otherwise gave direction these would remain the goals for 1961. Speaking of the pending change in the method of selling, he said: "I am pleased to report that the change in the method of sale to teletype communications and recording is quite similar to a proposal we made two years ago". Continuing to discuss the question of study and investigation, he said: "The year being reviewed was one of investigations, firstly by Price, Waterhouse and Co., then by Stevenson and Kellogg Ltd., and then by the Farm Products Marketing Board, and finally by our own auditors. Indeed, I feel tempted to paraphrase a war time statement of Winston Churchill's and describe 1960 thus: never in the history of farm organizations have so many investigations been done by so many to so few."

Also at the meeting, a resolution from Bruce County, endorsing the stand taken by the local board to change the method of sale "under duress", was endorsed by the annual meeting.

The attitude among those present was that the Association should not be separated from "FAME" which was to contrast to the agreement which separated the Marketing Board and the Co-op selling agency from "FAME". In fact, all three were being spoken of as the products of the progressive thinking and leadership of the Association.

When it came time for the 1961 election of zone directors to serve the Association, Wilfred Bishop, who had earlier announced he would not be a candidate for re-election to the Marketing Board or Co-op Agency but would contest a seat on the "FAME" Board, was re-elected a director of the Association and thus was able to continue as a connecting link between the Association and "FAME".

Another chapter in the dramatic farm struggle waged by the hog producers in their first twenty years had come to an end. The old leader had

switched his activities to a new field of venture, feeling there was no hope in further operation under Ontario marketing legislation. In so doing, he had been joined by a substantial group from the old board who shared his misgivings of the future.

Another group, however, felt there were still possibilities of using the marketing machinery to serve farmer interests. Only the gradual unrolling of the future would tell which was right. More significantly, there was no quarrel between the two; each wished the other the best of fortune in the continuing struggle to serve farmer interests.

CHAPTER XI

FARMERS ALLIED MEAT ENTERPRISES: THE "FAME" STORY

During the early 1960s, the name "FAME" became almost a household word across rural Ontario. The name "Farmers Allied Meat Enterprises" was selected in fact so that the initials would have a real impact. Hence, "FAME" became the symbol of a new movement.

During the late 1950s, the investigations, the legal battles, and the quarrel with Government personnel and agencies over relative authority gradually convinced many of the leaders of the Hog Producer Organizations that the power of farmers through the medium of delegated governmental authority was breaking down. Some new basis of independent farmer strength had to be found. In June of 1960 the directors of the Hog Producers' Association went to the Maritimes to confer with the Maritime Marketing Board in Moncton, New Brunswick, and proceeded to Nova Scotia to see the co-operative abattoir which had just been built near Halifax. An evening discussion with the President of this co-operative showed the Ontario men how funds were raised and an organizational structure developed.

Another exploratory trip took place in 1959 when the directors went to Sioux City, Iowa, in the American Corn belt. Here was an opportunity to observe a modern slaughtering plant which was shipping carcasses to both the Atlantic and Pacific coasts.

In July 1960, under the auspices of the Ontario Hog Producers' Association, three hundred delegates, representing the forty-two county associations, met in Toronto. This meeting gave the final signal to proceed with plans for producer abattoirs. Speakers at this meeting, foremost among them the ever determined Charles McInnis, expressed emphatically the opinion that with rigid government control hanging over the marketing board the only way to assert producers rights and authority was for farmers to build their own slaughtering plants. Then, if necessary, expansion could develop these into facilities for processing and marketing beef. Support for the idea was given by all directors of the Association and also by other prominent farm leaders such as Leonard Larenture, a member of the Executive Committee of the Ontario Federation of Agriculture.

Now backed by a clear indication of popular support, hog producer leaders began in earnest to develop details of a co-operative structure for the slaughtering and marketing of meats. On October the 19th in the Seaway Hotel in Toronto, a similar and larger meeting than that of July convened to formally launch the new co-operative Farmers Allied Meat Enterprises, "FAME". The four hundred producers assembled gave unanimous support to the new co-operative and elected as the first provincial board the same men who were already the directors of the Marketing Board, the Hog Producers' Association and the Hog Producers' Co-operative. Charles McInnis was the obvious and natural choice for President. On this founding occasion, "Charlie" McInnis declared: "Crisis also means opportunity. This is our opportunity to build for the future." Clayton Frey became Vice-President and said: "With the willingness to work it can be done, it will be done". Eldred Aiken, Chairman of the Marketing Board, declared: "If we work together, nothing, absolutely nothing can hold us back".

The plan, placed before this meeting, differed somewhat from the proposals that were to be evolved over the next several years. Originally, the plan was for a federated co-operative with the responsibilities of handling, selling, advisory research, and perhaps specialized processing. The slaughtering and some cutting and processing would be done in conveniently situated local plants across the province.

Several other leaders and representatives of various organizations were present at the launching of "FAME". Dr. H. H. Hannan, President of the Canadian Federation of Agriculture, said: "If farmers are to have an economy working in their favour, they are the ones that should control it and have the right to control and manage it". Mr. Gordon Greer, President of the Ontario Federation of Agriculture, expressed words of caution in his remarks. Harold Schmidt of the Ontario Co-operative Union welcomed "FAME" as an important new member of the co-operative family. The rather sensational guest speaker of the day was Mr. J. A. Courteau, Chairman of Quebec Farm Loan Board and former Manager of the Meat Packing

Division of Co-op Federée of Quebec. Mr. Courteau told the story of co-operative meat packing in Quebec, its success and its rapid growth. As he concluded, Mr. Courteau handed "Charlie" McInnis a personal cheque for $5,000 as an investment in "FAME" debentures. Immediately following, the county hog producer directors present contributed another $26,000 for debentures.

Thus, "FAME" was off to a colourful and vigorous start. Volunteer canvassers prepared to go on the road and sell "FAME" debentures. *Market Place* listed them for half the counties in Ontario. The promise was made that the next issue would contain the names of canvassers from the remaining counties.

An encouraging sign was the favourable press comment across the province. The *Globe and Mail*, *The London Free Press* and much of the local Ontario press joined in a chorus of approval for the concrete business action being initiated after years of quarrelling with the packing industry and government agencies.

The first snag encountered by "FAME" was the prohibition of this initial sale of debentures. The reason given was that, in as much as "FAME" was not yet in business as a co-operative, the leeway given co-operatives by statute in selling debentures did not apply. "FAME" returned the sums raised in this first move and immediately revised its plans to raise funds through the medium of the sale of common shares. Unfortunately, however, much of the drive generated by the organizational meeting had been lost. Between this time and November 30th, 1964, 12,518 subscribers purchased common shares to the extent of $1,414,800. Late in 1962 arrangements were made to again sell debentures. By 1965 a total of $1,029,750 had been raised by debenture sale.

No campaign to raise funds for farmers starting a business venture ever raised as much as was done by "FAME".

Unfortunately, too many problems arose as to the proper use of these funds. It had been agreed early that the same men should not continue as directors of the Marketing Board and "FAME" at the same time. Consequently, early in 1961, directors who until now had been serving in a dual capacity were faced with the decision of which organization to serve. As mentioned in the previous chapter, McInnis, Frey, Becker, Rintoul and Bishop made the decision not to be candidates for another term on the Marketing Board and, instead, offered themselves as candidates for re-election to the "FAME" Board of directors. On the other hand, Eldred Aiken, Chairman of the Marketing Board, along with Lance Dickieson, Clare Curtin, Ben Steers and Roy Sills elected to be candidates for the reorganized Board. Wesley Magwood was compelled by ill health to retire.

The basis of representation was enlarged by additional farm leaders coming forward to complete both boards. Only an indirect connection was left. Wilfred Bishop, while leaving the Marketing Board, was re-elected to the Board of the Ontario Hog Producers' Association which, from here on, was to have an interlocking directorate rather than a directorate identical with that of the Marketing Board. Now "FAME" stood clearly on its own feet.

During the summer of 1961, progress continued to be made in the sale of shares. But it was realized that the shareholders and the public were looking for definite, concrete action in the form of a building somewhere. Perhaps this influence was the more specific because of promises made at the beginning.

In his capacity of President of the Ontario Hog Producers' Association, "Charlie" McInnis had some time earlier been guest speaker at the annual meeting of the Consumers Co-op of Kansas City. This large and varied co-op operated, among other enterprises, a substantial meat packing business. Through correspondence the President of this Co-op advised "FAME" to procure the services of a consultant and architect specializing in the meat packing business, namely Mr. John Troy of the firm of Troy and Stalder of Omaha, Nebraska. Later, Consumers' Co-op advised that they had found Mr. Troy unsatisfactory and had dispensed with his services. Furthermore, the Grain Pool people of Manitoba, who were planning a new packing plant at Brandon, Manitoba, used his services temporarily and came to the same conclusion as Consumers' Co-op of Kansas City.

In the meantime, however, Mr. Troy had met with the Executive Committee of "FAME" on October 12th, 1961, where the following motion was passed: "That we engage Mr. Troy of Troy and Stalder to conduct research with respect to meat processing operations and to make recommendations relative to producer processing in the Province of Ontario, including plant locations, type and design and the fee for a complete survey not to exceed $5,000." Troy gained the confidence of many of the directors. Much of Troy's work had merit. He emphasized the importance of modern techniques and plotted the location of plants in relation to markets and sources of livestock. On the other hand, there were charges that his estimates of earnings were unrealistic and overly optimistic.

Troy, not being a recognized architect in Ontario, was compelled to engage an Ontario architect to work with him in preparing plans for the proposed plants. Later this architect was to testify that his accounts for services had never been paid. "FAME" directors who had become suspicious of Troy objected to some of the payments that were being made, maintaining that these were in excess of the amounts due for what work had actually been done. Finally, a motion passed by the "FAME" Board declared that payments were to cease at the end of three months, pending further proof of what might be then owed to him. However, the Royal Commission of

Enquiry appointed later to inquire into "FAME", was to discover that these payments did not cease as directed by the Board. Mr. Justice Grant estimated that Troy was overpaid $50,000 to $60,000. Troy was invited to testify and was guaranteed payment of his expenses by the Commission. The only response was in the form of a letter from Troy's lawyer which charged the enquiry with instigating "a witch hunt . . . by those "FAME" directors dissatisfied with McInnis' leadership". Judge Grant's response from the bench was to declare that should Troy's lawyer ever cross the Canadian border and come within the jurisdiction of the court he would be charged with contempt of court.

From the beginning of the "FAME" drive Charles McInnis and Clayton Frey the Vice-President demonstrated their unselfish devotion to the farmer cause by spending full time in the "FAME" office and on the road speaking at "FAME" promotion meetings. Neither received more than $10 per diem and expenses. Later on it was necessary to do away with any allowance for per diem or expenses.

As with most other farmer financial campaigns, the early decision to use volunteer canvassers was found to be inadequate; professional salesmen were then hired. Some were "high pressure types" who proved to be out of place in selling for a farmer cause. Disappointment in the rate of raising capital did stimulate hiring of some personnel and the use of promotion that was to lead Justice Grant in his report to question the wisdom of an expenditure of nineteen cents cost for every dollar raised.

Overall construction plans called for a major plant to be built adjacent to Highway 401 about two miles east of the junction with highway 97, sometimes referred to as the Ayr plant. Supplementary plants were to be built near Lindsay, Smith Falls, Mitchell, Neustadt, Chatham and Belleville. Land was selected and purchased for the Ayr, Mitchell, Neustadt and Lindsay plants, or more often called the Mariposa plants. Negotiations were never completed for a contemplated site near Smiths Falls. Survey work was done on several of these locations. Major expenditure was made on the Ayr site, including the grading and gravelling of a roadway and the drilling of a well. As a follow up to this work and as an answer to shareholders who were expecting more visible action, a gala sod turning ceremony was conducted in September, 1963. This event served as a stimulant to capital raising. As time went on, however, it was found that costs of construction were advancing and fund raising was tending to slow down.

Early in the summer of 1964, information came to the attention of "FAME" officers that it might be possible to purchase the Fearman packing plant in Burlington. This plant, owned by E. R. Gunner, an English meat packer, had been constructed in 1961 to replace an obsolete plant which had operated in downtown Hamilton for many years. It was a modern plant that appeared to offer real possibilities for the future. The entire "FAME" Board inspected this plant on July 31, 1964, and were impressed with its modern facilities. The minority of directors who had gradually become more critical of many of the policies being followed proposed an option on the plant rather than an outright purchase; but their amendment was defeated on a recorded vote. The main motion to purchase the shares of the Fearman company was approved, provided satisfactory financing could be procured.

Many aspects of the details of checking the finances and even the nature of the contract finally made with Mr. Gunner have remained clouded in doubt, even after the hearings before Mr. Justice Grant in 1965.

A few salient points, however, are definite. One and one half million dollars were paid to Mr. Gunner in cash with an additional million to be paid in ninety days with Mr. Gunner holding a mortgage for one half million. This agreement was signed on the authority of only the Building Committee and the endorsement of the "FAME" Board was sought later. Assurances were given to the Board at this time that only one third of the shares were committed as security for the additional million to be paid during the ninety days. The facts as they were recorded later were that all the shares were committed. This circumstance was the core of what was to lead to the collapse of "FAME".

When the knowledge of the commitment of all the shares came into the open, directors Schmidt and Bishop called a meeting of representatives of various farm organizations to discuss the the threat of the loss of the "FAME" capital. At this meeting Mr. R. S. McKercher, later President of U.C.O., summed up the situation by saying: "If you dissatisfied directors [Schmidt, Pridham, R. Anderson and Bishop; others were soon to share their opinion] controlled "FAME" we could do something for you. But you are only a minority of the Board. What can we do?"

On August 31st, 1964, the "FAME" organization took over the Fearman business. Plans were immediately made to improve the operations. Mr. James Allardyce, a former Canada Packers executive, became General Manager and Mr. Gordon McSweeney, who had extensive experience with Swift Canadian and a meat brokerage business, was placed in charge of quality control and product sales. During the following three months, statements given to the "FAME" Board showed an improving financial position which was somewhat at variance with evidence given later before Mr. Justice Grant.

Charles McInnis had counted upon the purchase of the Fearman plant stimulating sales of shares and debentures. In practice, the opposite seemed to be true. Desperate efforts were made to obtain capital from American sources. A fee of twenty thousand dollars was sent to Willard Securities of New York as payment for raising the required capital. The critical group of directors demanded a recorded vote to show their opposition, but the plan was endorsed anyway.

The mystery man of "FAME's" relationship to the Fearman purchase was Edward Walton, the English accountant, who became employed as Treasurer of "FAME" in 1962. He was the official who had been designated to examine the Fearman books and report on the financial position of this firm prior to the purchase. In his report as Royal Commissioner, Mr. Justice Grant stated, and we quote: "Walton says Ritchie [Treasurer of Fearman] did not show him the financial statements but from other evidence I am convinced that he is wrong about this. If such were the case, one would have expected him to relate such refusal to his own board immediately. This he did not do. His recollection is that Gunner told them at the airport of the one and one half million dollar losses. McInnis attempts to say that, although he asked Walton for his report on the financial structure of the company and that he never gave him any information in respect thereof and did not show him the financial statements of Fearman or tell him of the current liabilities and that he knew nothing of the financial position of the company at that time. It is difficult to understand that the President would send the Treasurer over to examine the books of the company which was under consideration of purchase and not insist on getting a report or some information as to the financial position of the company when he returned."*

At any rate, the statement made to the "FAME" Board at the time of the approval of purchase was definite. The Fearman company had suffered severe losses at the time of a strike in 1962, but had recovered to a break even point.

*Report of the Commissioner under the designation "FAME" Inquiry in respect of the affairs of Farmers' Allied Meat Enterprises Co-operatives Limited, p.72.

In the Royal Commission's Report, Justice Campbell Grant states:

The purchase of the shares of the F. W. Fearman Company Limited was a completely unsound business undertaking, made without proper consideration as to the value thereof, the loss record of such company or the ability of FAME to procure the funds for payment of the balance of the purchase price. It displayed a complete bankruptcy of business ability on the part of the majority of the Board of Directors. The President of the Company, Charles W. McInnis, must be held primarily to blame for the mistakes and irregularities associated with such purchase. He purposely refrained from seeking the advice of FAME'S auditors in connection with such purchase or informing them thereof and deprived the Board of Directors of such professional guidance. He knew that such Company had been for some considerable period of time and still was, operating at a considerable loss but misled the Board of Directors by assuring them that it was then at a point where such losses had ceased. Although he knew that the Fearman Company was heavily indebted to the Bank of Nova Scotia and that such liability was to be a continuing liability, he made no attempt prior to closing the transaction to secure the assurance of such Bank that it would continue such loan or advance sufficient to allow the reorganized company to carry on its usual business. With the exception of a few Directors, the balance of the Board exercised no judgment of their own, but blindly followed the dictates of McInnis. The latter dissociated himself with anyone giving advice contrary to his ambitions but surrounded himself with advisors who yielded to his opinions in any matter.

Mystery about Ed Walton has been enhanced by a number of facts that have never seemed to fit into a conventional pattern. Walton persuaded McInnis to engage a particular law firm to handle the deal with Mr. Gunner. During the later part of his employment, Walton flew to London, England. He claimed to be on "FAME" business, but was not sent and none of the directors knew what he was doing. During the same period transatlantic telephone calls came to the "FAME" office for Walton. During the period when Mel Becker had taken over the presidency of "FAME" in a futile effort to save the situation, he received a telephone call from Mrs. Walton in England. She said her husband was out of the city and she would like the money owed to him. Mr. Becker explained that "FAME" had paid him completely and owed him nothing. Back over the wire came the amazing remark: "What about Ed's contract with Mr. Gunner?" Mr. Becker was thoroughly alert: "Ed had a contract with Mr. Gunner did he?" Perhaps realizing she had said too much, Mrs. Walton refused any further reply.

At the time of the "FAME" annual meeting on November 25th, the serious situation was covered up. Raymond Anderson, the former M.P. for Norfolk, retired and was replaced by James Hill of Delhi. William Anderson of Stratford, a former director, returned to the Board.

Opposition to the business policies of Charles McInnis was growing among Board members. In the reorganization immediately following the annual meeting, he encountered for the first time opposition from the Vice-President, Clayton Frey, for the position of President. Realization was growing that there must be a complete change of policy if "FAME" was to be saved. On December 3, Charles McInnis offered to submit his resignation as President. By a secret ballot, the Board of directors accepted the resignation. Mr. Frey became acting President and one week later was formally elected to the position.

Now began strenuous efforts to save the situation. A clear majority of the directors favoured a different business approach. Unfortunately, the Fearman shares had been surrendered to Mr. Gunner without the consent of the Board of Directors at the end of the ninety days (November 30th) when the additional million was not available. For the next few weeks, Mr. Frey gave of his time and abilities most unselfishly without any remuneration in efforts to preserve "FAME". Discussions were held with the Government and other farm organizations, and a new agreement was negotiated with Mr. Gunner. Unfortunately, Gunner was now in the driver's seat, having both "FAME'S" money and the Fearman shares. Some further financial aid was coming from the shareholders, but was not enough. The Directors were determined to call a shareholders' meeting in January and place everything before the members, including their own resignations.

This well attended meeting endorsed the new policies and voted to request a Royal Commission to investigate the whole situation. Several directors who had supported the old policies did not attend this meeting and did not resign. Mr. Frey declined to accept office again and several Board changes were made. Mr. Melvin Becker, who had been one of the original "FAME" directors and who had left the Ontario Hog Producers' Marketing Board to serve with the new Co-op, now returned to the Board. In the earlier "FAME" organization, he had been Secretary, but gradually had become critical of the lack of business astuteness being displayed. When the controlling group had tried to unfairly restrict his normal role, he had resigned. At the first meeting of the reorganized Board, Mr. Becker was elected President and William Anderson of Stratford, Vice-President. Again there were determined efforts to recover the monies in the hands of Gunner, to raise fresh capital, and to negotiate a new deal to regain possession of the Fearman plant.

In June, the Royal Commission appointed by the Ontario Government and headed by Mr. Justice Grant conducted hearings for a two week period into the whole "FAME" operation. During the summer and early Autumn of 1965, "FAME" directors and shareholders expectantly awaited the report. The long awaited Royal Commission report was at last released on October 21st, 1965. It carefully reviewed and analyzed all the policies and activities of "FAME". But it failed to make recommendations towards courses of action by any authority.

In the meantime, Mr. Becker, after following the self sacrificing example of Mr. Frey and receiving nothing for even his out of pocket expenses, felt that he could carry on no longer. His place was taken by Mr. William Anderson, a shrewd and capable retired farmer from Perth County who continued the same unselfish leadership. The Board had been reduced to nine members and the last of the directors who had supported the earlier mistaken policies had left the Board. In as much as a number of items of knowledge to directors, including a number of points mentioned in the report, led outside of Canada, there was reason to consider further investigations. Some informal advice from a former R.C.M.P. detective suggested that an approach should be made to the Solicitor General of Canada. By arrangement, James Hill and Wilfred Bishop spent a couple of hours with the Hon. Larry Pennell, Solicitor General, placing the facts before him and requesting that the R.C.M.P. look into the remaining mysteries of the case. However, the matter was not followed up.

Among former directors and shareholders there has remained a feeling that the provincial and federal governments, for whatever reason, were reluctant to become further involved.

For some months longer the directors sought to consolidate the assets, to cut expenses, to re-negotiate with Gunner, and to raise new capital. The adverse publicity made the task impossible and by March, 1966, it was useless to carry on further. At this point the directors could see no alternative to going into bankruptcy.

In summary, two bare facts stand out in bold relief. Mr. E. R. Gunner of England was the beneficiary to the extent of more than a million dollars, and many public spirited farm people were the losers in terms of effort and cash to the tune of more than two million dollars.

CHAPTER XII

NEW BEGINNINGS

Following the 1961 annual meeting, of necessity a new approach emerged. There had been a significant change in leadership; the personnel of the three Boards was no longer identical and new restrictions from the Farm Products Marketing Board were in effect. In the eyes of some people, at least, the hog producer organizations had fallen on evil days, losing much of their prestige and authority. A formidable task lay ahead to restore the organizations to their place as one of the main commodity groups in the province.

When the Marketing Board met to reorganize, Mr. Aiken was re-elected Chairman and Ben Steers became Vice-Chairman, replacing Bishop who was no longer a member of the Board. The Association was reorganized with Ben Steers as President and Bishop as Vice-President. Lance Dickieson became Chairman of the Co-op selling agency.

With the distinct difference in personnel between the Boards, it was necessary more than ever before to designate clearly the responsibilities of each. The responsibility of selling was given to the Co-op; the licencing and over-all authority was delegated to the Marketing Board; the responsibilities of the Association became those of promotion and public relations, including that of relations with local county associations.

In the four years prior to 1961, Jim Boynton, the Secretary-Treasurer, never had an opportunity to exercise his full capacities. "Charlie" McInnis had overshadowed each Secretary and had in reality handled many of the duties that would normally be the responsibilities of a Secretary. With neither the Chairman of the Marketing Board, nor the new Presidents of either the Association or the Co-op finding it feasible to spend any substantial amount of time in the office, Mr. Boynton was faced with both new responsibilities and new opportunities. The gradual rebuilding of the whole organization became, in large measure, his responsibility.

We have already mentioned that Mr. Boynton had been Secretary of the Federation of Agriculture in Grey County and played an active role in the campaign to place the hogs of Grey and Bruce Counties on the open market in the early days of "direction". James Boynton was born in the eastern part of Grey County and obtained his secondary schooling at Collingwood. He served in the Canadian army during the war and saw action in North Africa, Italy and Western Europe. From 1961, Mr. Boynton was gradually to come into his own. He had down to earth farmer approach to the discussion of hog problems which, at farmers' meetings, served to establish a bond on contact with hog producers across the province. His careful and reasonable approach to Government agencies helped to heal the breach with the Farm Products Marketing Board. Much of the credit for the increasing prestige and influence of the Association and the Marketing Board within the farm organization spectrum was traceable to the contributions made by Jim Boynton.

The firm stand taken by Eldred Aiken at the 1961 annual meeting in expressing the objectives of the Marketing Board has already been noted. The maintenance and continued follow-up of this position by Mr. Aiken was the proper expression of opinion at the right time. Mr. Aiken had entered the directorates of the Association and Marketing Board ten years before when George Johnson had resigned to become Secretary. A background in community and fraternal groups had provided an experience which was valuable in manoeuvring around the shoals in the troubled waters of 1961.

Ben Steers, the new President of the Association, had joined the Board in 1956. Mr. Steers, born in England, came to Canada with his parents while a small child and was raised in Simcoe County where he had long been known as a purebred Yorkshire breeder. Mr. Lance Dickieson, who now became Chairman of the Co-op Sales Agency, had long been a director of the Wellington County Association, before joining the Board of Directors. At the time the Co-op was first organized, and the Boards of the Association and the Marketing Board were enlarged, he was elected provincially. Mr. Dickieson brought to his increased responsibilities a lifetime of experience in the livestock industry.

The new teletype selling system, being set up by Bell Telephone, was not ready until May, a month later than was originally planned. It was found that it was possible to negotiate changes and make improvements until arrangements were developed whereby the small packers, instead of having a teletype machine in their own offices, could telephone their requirements and the prices that they were willing to pay to one staff member in the central office who would do the actual buying as their agent much the same as any other buyer.

Further changes in the organizational structure were not long in coming. The studies of 1960 had raised doubt of the need to continue the Co-op Selling Agency as a separate entity. Even this was not altogether new. In 1954 some directors of the Marketing Board, before the formation of the Co-op, had proposed a direct take over by the Marketing Board. Also, a provision of the controversial Bill 86 would allow the Board to operate as its own agency, thereby removing any legal barrier. In September, final approval was given to this merger which was to come into effect on December 1st. From that date until the March annual meeting, the Co-op Agency directors were to meet with and become a part of the Marketing Board which then was to be increased by three members, elected at large by the committeemen of all eleven zones voting as one unit. Another change in regulations provided for nominations of committeemen in the future to be conducted at the annual meetings of county associations.

During its first two decades, the Ontario Hog Producers', and those groups that had sprung from it, had been inspired by a crusading spirit in the struggle for economic justice and a better life for farm people. Under the impact of this drive, strong local associations had come into being in each of Ontario's Counties. Every provincial meeting that had ever been called had been well attended and had enthusiastically endorsed whatever forward steps were presented to it. When the organization was first formed, very few producers were hog farmers only. The great majority were producers of milk or cream, with hogs as a side line. Even men who were principally beef producers in a day when feed lots were unknown usually milked some of the beef cows and sold some cream, so as to have at least some skim milk left for the pigs. These circumstances lent themselves well to commanding the interest and support of large numbers of farmers all over the province.

By the early 1960s marked changes were coming over rural Ontario with ever increasing rapidity. Farming as a way of life was coming to a close. Dedication to the farmer cause was becoming less emotional and more inclined to find expression in the use of technical and business knowledge.

The great question mark, more real than expressed, was, would the Ontario Hog Producers' Association and the Ontario Hog Producers' Marketing Board adapt themselves to the new conditions and, in so doing, retain the massive public support expressed through the medium of county locals and well attended provincial meetings?

Other marketing boards were going much farther in the establishment of rigid controls of one kind or another than anyone with responsibility in the

Hog Organizations had ever imagined in his wildest dreams. No longer were questions being raised as to the legality of any of the foundations of the direction or selling programmes.

The major problems were no less important and challenging. The task on the horizon was to maintain the maximum personal and individual freedom for hog producers and also to enable them to meet the competition of the North American continent and to have for themselves a fair share of the production of the economy amid expanding costs.

The success of teletype selling became significantly apparent even after a few months of operation. The opportunity to establish a range of asking prices and to refuse to sell if the lowest point of this range was not satisfactory to the buyers was significant. The competition demanded by critics had been met and the opportunity to use salesmanship on behalf of producers had not been lost as so often had been feared.

Interest in these methods was such that as early as December, 1961, J. R. Kohler, the General Manager, was invited to speak to the Farmers' Union of Alberta to discuss the advantages of teletype selling. In an address to the Automotive Transportation Association of Ontario, Mr. Kohler emphasized that competitive bidding was bringing higher prices at Kitchener and Toronto, yet still preserving salesmanship as an essential factor to the proper functioning of daily trading.

With increased emphasis being placed on the promotion of pork and less services being provided by Mr. Parizeau on a long distance basis, there arose a need for greater professional services in this field. John Badger, an advertising agent and public relations man, was hired by the producers' organizations for promotional work.

The early 1960s was a period of agricultural uncertainty. What was the relative value of marketing boards and co-operatives in solving the economic difficulties of farmers? Towards the solution of this question a number of annual marketing conferences were to be held each January at the University of Guelph. In discussions, the continuing development of the great experiment in the collective selling of hogs was always to the fore as the relative advantages of marketing boards and conventional co-operatives were weighed and considered. In his annual presidential address to the Canadian Federation of Agriculture in January, 1962, at Banff, Alberta, Dr. H. H. Hannan declared that the Ontario Hog Marketing Plan, with its teletype selling, was the greatest step forward by any marketing group in Canada. Mr. Everett Biggs, commending the system, warned the packing industry that the compulsory offering of all hogs for sale through the Board offered protection against vertical integration.

Speaking of vertical integration, which was happening in many branches of agriculture across the continent, it came to be recognized that this compulsory selling was what removed the advantages that would have come to the packers by having hogs produced for their own individual plants under some type of contract. Thus, a bulwark was created to save the individual farm as a business concern. Regarding vertical integration as a major threat to agriculture, the Hon. William Stewart, the new Minister of Agriculture in Ontario, proposed further amendments to marketing legislation to protect the individual farmer.

At the time of the annual meeting in 1962, it was becoming increasingly evident that the reorganized leadership of the Board and Association was firmly established and was ready to give positive forward guidance. Eldred Aiken, as Chairman of the Board, advocated a National Board and issued a firm declaration that not a cent of any funds raised by the Board had gone into any "FAME" shares. Ben Steers, speaking as President of the Association, called for a more aggressive pork promotion programme. The financial reserves of the Board being exhausted, the annual meeting voted to raise the marketing fee by 10 cents per hog.

With the merger of the Co-op with the Marketing Board, Lance Dickieson became Vice-Chairman of the Board. In the elections of 1962, Blake Snobelen, later to make a very significant mark as Chairman of the Board, was elected, replacing Howard Huctwith in District II. Mr. Huctwith now became a member of the Board at large. In the Association, Fred Crowe, later President of the Association, and Alfred Warner replaced Roy Sills and John Barnet as directors. One change approved was for the nomination of committeemen to occur at each county annual meeting.

Also in 1962, sales operations began to attract visitors from beyond Canadian borders. In June, Mr. C. R. Mitchell, editor of the American based *National Hog Farmer*, visited the offices and returned to write in his periodical that the operation he had seen was the most efficient on the continent.

Mr. Parizeau severed his connection with the Association's periodical *The Market Place*. Another event in 1962 was the formation of the "Swine Improvement Council", an effort to bring together the producers, pure bred breeders, meat packers, feed manufacturers, feed dealers, technical men at Guelph, and the Department of Agriculture. Steers, Pringle and Young were appointed representatives of the Association, with Boynton serving as Secretary for the new group. The year also saw increased efforts to promote pork and also to contact producers, with exhibits for the first time being established at both the International Plowing Match and the Royal Winter Fair. Tom Pringle of Grey County passed away; his place was taken in a special election by George Mannerow of Chesley.

No sooner had the year 1963 begun than visitors started to arrive from the Prairie Provinces under the auspices of the Farmers' Union for each of those provinces. Of particular interest to Ontario people was the news that Alberta was considering a marketing plan of its own. In the spring of 1963, Howard Huctwith became Vice President of the Association and Lance Dickieson, Chairman of the Board. The Perth County Association developed very active support for the promotion programme by acquiring its own barbecue facilities and making available its services to any other county or other organization.

In the summer, the Ontario Swine Improvement Council sponsored the first of a series of annual conferences at the University of Guelph. At the time of the semi-annual meeting, the question of a National Board came up again, with Bishop, reporting for a special committee on export trade, advocated a producer controlled National Board to handle export trade. On another question, approval was given to electing members of the Marketing Board on a three year rotating basis.

By continuing booths at the International Plowing Match and the Royal Winter Fair, the educational policy was becoming firmly established.

International visitors continued to arrive, with Malayan guests looking over the whole marketing operation. In January, 1964, at the annual Economics Conference, or Workshop, at the University of Guelph, Mr. Ed. O'Meara of the staff of the Ontario Department of Agriculture declared: "Farmers need the authority Marketing Boards can give them". One of the services it has been possible to give producers has been the guarantee of payment for hogs sold. The early days of 1964 illustrated the effectiveness of this. A small packer in the southern part of the province went into bankruptcy owing $49,542. In the old days there would have been heavy losses for the producers who had recently supplied hogs. In this instance, all the producers were paid by the Board in the usual fashion. Afterwards, the Board recovered $24,000 which was the extent of the guarantee bond. The remainder of more than $25,000 came from the general funds of the Producer Board. The general practice is to have assurance of the ability to pay for hogs purchased, or to insist upon adequate bonding.

In February, the South Western Ontario counties organized the first Regional Conference based upon the joint effort of academic, personnel, government people and producer organizations. Jack Underwood, then on the staff of the Ridgetown Agricultural School, was the principal motivator of the idea. This programme was to establish the pattern for similar conferences at Guelph, Kemptville and for the Peterborough area. Professor Robert Forshaw played an important role in the overall leadership of these conferences. An outstanding guest speaker was brought to the province to deliver addresses at each of the four conferences which followed.

At the time of the annual meeting, more changes in personnel than usual occurred. The death of John Barnet from Perth County removed one of the younger and most promising members of the Marketing Board. Emerson

Crocker of Middlesex County announced, prior to the elections, that he was retiring for health reasons. Vernon Kaufman of Oxford county, who had come to the Marketing Board three years before as a pronounced opponent of the marketing programme, retired from the Board to devote more time to other interests. Association Directors elected for the year 1964-65 were, from the districts, Thompson, Crowe, Steers, Bishop, Dickieson, Aiken and Huctwith and, at large, Warner, Curtin, Mannerow and Young. Board Members elected at the same time were, from the districts, Thompson, Crowe, Curtin, Steers, Aiken, Schweitzer, Lupton, McDonald, Conlin and Snobelen and, at large, Mannerow, Warner and Huctwith. Mr. Mannerow came to the board with a background of active community and municipal participation; he had served as a director of the Ontario Ploughman's Association and as Warden of Grey county. Mr. McDonald, a former Warden of Oxford County, had formerly been a critic of some of the Board's programmes. Mr. Conlin, like his predecessor, Mr. Crocker, hailed from Middlesex County where he and his sons carried on substantial commercial farming in hogs and dairy production.

Addressing the annual meeting, Everett Biggs, the Deputy Minister of Agriculture, said: "Your Hog Board is the best in the world", and in reference to the disputes of three years earlier: "It has been a scramble. In the process you taught me and I learned a lot." In the west, campaigns were proceeding to establish similar selling programmes in Alberta and Saskatchewan. The Association, to help provide a factual picture of the achievements in Ontario, sent Aiken and Boynton to address meetings in Saskatchewan, and Dickieson and Curtin to speak in Alberta. Visitors from Saskatchewan continued to arrive in Ontario to study Ontario sales methods.

Another provincial swine conference was held on the Guelph campus in the month of June. During the mid summer, a project was initiated with the support of the local Associations in Kent and Essex and directed by Professor Bob Forshaw to study the shrinkage of hogs in transit.

In the spring of the year, further progress was made towards the establishment of a national organization at a Canada wide conference held in Montreal.

The Market Place of September, 1964, carried a story about Willard Bilderback, a mechanical engineer from Indiana who had arrived in Ontario four years earlier. He first operated as a cash crop farmer and then became a successful hog producer. Mr. Bilderback soon took an active part in provincial meetings and finally became an active member of the Marketing Board. He went into production with the determination to establish economic equality with those in other vocations.

Addressing the semi-annual meeting in September, 1964, Professor Bob

Forshaw declared that it would be a reasonable sum to spend between three and four million dollars a year in Ontario for research and pork promotion. Also at the meeting, the principle of a special check off to finance the promotion of pork was supported. Blake Snobelen, addressing a delegation proposing some changes in the location of assembly yards, declared that "The location of yards is never a closed issue". This illustrates well the fact that efforts to improve yards to better serve producers has been a continuous process.

In 1964, product promotion at the plowing match included a semi-sponsorship of the sale of baconburgers by one of the local groups, which added another phase to an every growing promotional programme.

The creation of a Swine Improvement Council in Manitoba marked another step towards organization across the nation. Towards the end of the year a special loss account was established in Manitoba with the support of producers, packers and truckers. This was to cover the losses involved between the assembly yards and the packing plants. As a result of a study made by a special committee of the Manitoba Legislature, a Hog Marketing Commission was set up in that province to sell hogs, voluntarily using a teletype system similar to that used in Ontario. Another significant event was that which occurred following a study of breeding trends in the U.S.A. An organization known as "Quality Swine" was organized in South Western Ontario to bring individual swine breeders together in one organization that could provide realistic competition to large breeding corporations marketing special hybrids or special bred lines. Some of these private companies were gaining a Canadian foothold.

Addressing the annual meeting in the spring of 1965, General Manager J. R. Kohler urged producers to market more evenly through the week, predicting that this could lead to an increase in average prices obtained.

At the spring elections, Clayton Giesel of Waterloo County was first elected to the Marketing Board and Brian Ellsworth of Welland was elected to both the Marketing Board and the Association, and Glen Willows became the eastern zone member of the Board.

During the summer a significant change took place in the personnel of the Farm Products Marketing Board. George McCague became Chairman of the new Dairy Commission and his place as Chairman of the Farm Products Marketing Board was taken by Herbert Arbuckle, the former Secretary of the Ontario Federation of Agriculture and briefly the acting Secretary of the Ontario Hog Producers Association and Marketing Board during the latter part of the year 1955, following the death of Norman McLeod.

The growing support for a vigorous programme of pork promotion was shown by the approval at the 1965 semi-annual meeting of a resolution proposing the sum of $26,000 to be so used. At the same meeting Boynton outlined proposals for a National Board. Word was also received from Manitoba to the effect that teletype selling there was meeting with success. A readjustment in the basis of elected committeemen from the various counties called for representation to be based sixty per cent on production and forty per cent on the number of producer members. Again plans were being formulated for another National Conference in the early part of 1966.

Also during 1965, Rodger Schwass, who originally came from Bruce County, became editor of the *Market Place*. Mr. Schwass was a graduate in economics, a former secretary of the National Farm Forum, and a free lance economics researcher. Mr. Schwass assumed this responsibility on a part time basis.

As the tide of time rolled along during the mid 1960's, there were continuing changes here and there and indications of further changes across the country. The Swine Improvement Council continued its activities and the information kept coming that the Americans were producing a leaner hog that offered the prospects of more competition. Aggressive leadership was appearing in the ranks of participants in general meetings and in county personnel. Malcolm Davidson, a young man from the U.K., who had established a hog operation in Huron County, was demanding a step up in youthful and aggressive programmes for the industry and that more effort be devoted to pork promotion. From Alberta were coming stories of a revived demand for a system of teletype selling, perhaps like that of Manitoba.

At the 1966 annual meeting, J. R. Kohler issued a warning of the dangers of over production adversely effecting prices. First proposals were made for the name "Pork" to be substituted for that of "Hog" in the names of both the Association and Marketing Board.

A dispute raging between the White Bean Marketing Board and the Farm Products Marketing Board over the rights of a local board in the field of product merchandising led to all the Boards collectively requesting public hearings in cases of disputes between producer Boards and the Government Board. The significance of this action left no doubt that the Boards could be critical of the Government regardless of the restrictions resulting from the amendments of 1960.

Strength was being maintained in the national field as producers in Nova Scotia registered strong support for their Board.

In Zone No. 4 (Oxford County to Niagara) the county association began an effort to either duplicate or to extend eastward the breeding programmes of Quality Swine. Producers in the eastern region felt that commercial breeding programs were on the horizon and the involvement of producers themselves was much superior to the task being handled by large commercial corporations. In 1966 the Marketing Board was organized with Lance

Dickieson as Chairman, Clare Curtin, Vice-Chairman, and executive members Howard Huctwith, Ben Steers and Blake Snobelen. The new member of the Board was Milton Elliott. More emphasis was being placed upon the need for swine research. Towards this end a total of five thousand dollars was granted to the furtherance of clinical studies at the Animal Science Department of the O.A.C.

In the ever active county association of Lincoln, at the time of the annual spring banquet, John Goit, for many years county president and a very active participant in provincial meetings, was honoured for his services and he was praised for "his most valuable contribution to a most successful marketing system."

In July, 1966, at the Central Experimental Farm in Ottawa, the most significant and successful national meeting to date was held under the auspices of the Canadian Federation of Agriculture. National meetings had been going on in something of a hit and miss fashion since 1943 when the first was held in the Chateau Laurier in Ottawa at the instigation of the Ontario Hog Producers' Association and with the help of the Canadian Federation of Agriculture. Between then and the Montreal Conference of 1964 a national meeting was held most years at the time of the annual meeting of the Canadian Federation of Agriculture. Ontario was usually represented by a substantial group from the Ontario Board and so were the Maritimes; representation from the other provinces was less direct. No formal organization was maintained from year to year. The discussions were the means of establishing a consensus from which the Canadian Federation of Agriculture might develop swine policies. The 1964 and 1966 conferences finally brought to a definite form a realistic national organization, the Canadian Swine Council, later to become the Canadian Pork Council. Stan Price of Alberta became the first President and Ben Steers of Ontario the first Vice-President. A budget of $700,000 was planned with research to be conducted in the scientific field and in marketing. In July the Ontario Association directors approved an initial payment of one thousand dollars and later the semi-annual gave approval to annual payment from Ontario of $3,700. Unfortunately, the lack of properly financed groups in the other provinces was to delay similar contributions. A very significant feature of the 1966 conference was the thorough review and producer approval of the new index grading system for hogs.

Ben Steers continued as President for 1966 with Howard Huctwith as Vice-President. In June, Roy Sills, a former member of both Boards, passed away.

County associations were becoming active in pork promotion, more particularly in that of organizing barbecues. The International Ploughing Match was held in Huron County that year. The county association had excelled itself in erecting a special building to provide for pork product and hog quality demonstrations; then to everyone's sorrow it rained and rained, making the grounds a sea of mud, almost destroying the planned effect of all the efforts of the Huron producers.

Interest in and a sense of responsibility for further pork promotion was shown when the semi annual meeting voted a 30 per cent increase in funds to be so used for this purpose in the coming year. In reporting to the semi-annual, the chairman of the Stabilization and Markets Committee of the Association advocated Federal legislation, similar to that establishing the Wheat Board, and went on to say that this would offer the means of expanding markets and stabilizing prices.

In 1966, farmer discontent reached a high pitch. Responding to the farmers' discontent with price levels of farm products the Ontario Government called a conference of representatives of all farm organizations which convened in October in Vineland. Both the Association and Marketing Board sent delegations to participate. The main result of this conference was the establishment of a special Income Committee to investigate all aspects of low farm income. Before the end of the year the Marketing Board and Association jointly presented a brief to this committee. Among the proposals made were a national commission to handle sales of hogs and pork products beyond Canada, income transfers, additional capital grants, and the granting of increased bargaining power to farmers with subsidies only as a last resort. Early in the year Board Member Brian Ellsworth, as one of two Canadians winning Nuffield scholarships to study in the U.K. for six months left for overseas. The Association planned for him also to go to Denmark and study the pork industry there.

It had become apparent that the large summer conference sponsored by the Swine Improvement Council in June, although well attended, was not involving hog producers to the extent desired. The result was a decision to hold a series of conferences duplicating the successful one already operating at Ridgetown. In the first week of February, winter conferences were held at Guelph and Kemptville, using much of the same material as Ridgetown. After 1967, the summer conference was dropped and a fourth winter conference was added for the Brighton-Peterborough area. The series of winter conferences became a regular part of the annual educational activities of the industry.

At the 1967 annual, Howard Huctwith retired and was succeeded by Sid Fraleigh. Clayton Geisel was elected to the Association Directorate. He hailed from Waterloo County where he was a spokesman for the livestock men. Tom Broughton was elected to the Marketing Board. He was a large and successful commercial hog producer from the Oakville area. Glen Willows, elected previously, was also a prominent commercial breeder from

154

Eastern Ontario. Clair Curtin became Chairman of the Marketing Board and Blake Snobelen, Vice Chairman. Ben Steers remained President of the Association with Fred Crowe becoming Vice-President. At the time of the annual meeting every county was represented and twenty-six had perfect attendance of all their delegates. Again a National Pork Commission was suggested by the committee studying market expansion.

A significant event of the Canadian Centennial Year was the holding under the auspices of the Ontario Swine Improvement Council of the first Ontario barrow show. To meet the challenge of some of the more heavily muscled popular breeding strains below the border, an American judge was invited to place the classes and do it on the same basis as he would in the U.S. Barrows of the conventional bacon type, long accepted in Ontario, fared rather badly in competition with heavier muscled barrows, most of which were cross bred. At one point, the announcer at the ringside listed the winners of a particular class, paused and then added: "At least according to the judge these are the winners". Surprisingly to many Ontario people the muscled hog showed up well on the rail and maintained the positions won on the hoof. This show really established hybrids and some of the newer American full ham and muscled loin lines in Ontario.

Canada's centennial year also gave county barbecues another big boost. Lincoln County began a barbecue programme that was due to grow and expand. Perth County, already active with its own equipment, became more involved and these counties were joined by others, including Elgin, Brant, Durham, and Wentworth.

By mid-summer, the Farm Income Study Committee, set up at Vineland, had a preliminary report to offer representatives of farm groups gathered at the Kemptville Agricultural School in Eastern Ontario. Soon after its formation, the Income Committee had hired the consulting firm of Hedlin and Menzies to conduct studies of a number of farm problems. A reduction in the number of packing firms using teletype buying occurred when Swift's closed their plant and purchased the plant of Presswood Bros. A decline of one in the number of buyers was not serious in itself, but it did raise the question of what might happen if the decline should continue and the total number be reduced by three or four or even more plants.

The Manitoba Hog Commission, in its annual report, said that the sixty per cent of the hogs that had gone through its selling machinery was not quite as it would wish and was in fact down by two per cent from the previous year. Alberta was still only talking of setting up a commission.

In 1967 the Federal Government appointed a group of prominent agricultural economists who were to be known as the Task Force to make a study and to make recommendations as to future policies.

American interest in Ontario's marketing programme continued with Bob

Kohler, a staff member in charge of marketing yards, being asked to speak in Wisconsin on the subject.

The Marketing Committee of the Association, which had been making a series of reports to provincial meetings, met with senior officials of the Federal Department of Agriculture to discuss its proposals for Federal marketing legislation to provide means for collective promotion of pork at home and abroad. Suggestions were made for the control of imports from countries other than the U.S. in much the same manner as the Canadian Dairy Commission was functioning. Secretary James Boynton told the Government officials that importations from Northern Ireland had broken the price in Ontario. Other members of the delegation were Dickieson, Crowe, Bishop, Crone of the Ontario Federation of Agriculture, and William Hamilton of the Canadian Federation of Agriculture.

At the semi-annual meeting, J. R. Kohler suggested the renovation of a number of the assembly yards and the establishment of some controls over what volume could be marketed.

In 1968, the Ontario Association gave an extra punch to progress by providing an additional five hundred dollars for awards to be given at the 1968 Provincial Barrow Show.

The annual meeting in 1968 rejected a proposal first made a year earlier that directors be limited to a nine year term. Keith Weeden and Eugene Carroll were elected to the Association Board for the first time and Sid Fraleigh and Alf Warner were elected to the Marketing Board, the latter after an absence. Keith Weeden took the place of Eldred Aiken on the Association Board while Mr. Aiken continued on the Marketing Board to complete the term for which he had been elected. Like his predecessor, Mr. Weeden came from Bruce County where he operated a commercial farrow to finish co-operation. Mr. Carroll came from the Ottawa Valley where he had long been active in farm and community organizations, serving his local municipality, the Federation of Agriculture, Farm Forums, the Beef Improvement Association, and the local Hog Producers. With his election to the Marketing Board, Mr. Fraleigh broadened his activities from his earlier participation on the Board of the Associations. Warner's return to the Marketing Board brought the experience of an old veteran of many years of active participation at the county and provincial level. Ben Steers retired as President following the annual meeting of 1968 and was succeeded by Fred Crowe; Brian Ellsworth became Vice-President. Clare Curtin was re-elected Chairman of the Marketing Board as was Vice-Chairman Blake Snobelen. In the spring the Board and Association made a joint presentation to the Federal Task Force. Their brief listed the average weighted prices for the last several years:

1967 — 30.70
1966 — 35.90
1965 — 32.40
1964 — 26.30
1963 — 26.80

They declared that, if the public was to have cheap food, income transfers were necessary to give the farmer economic justice.

President Steers of the Association and Sales Manager J. R. Kohler both complained that, while Ontario farmers had responded to requests to cut back production, increases in the West made the Ontario decrease non-effective.

Alberta was now considering three different proposals: one, a Marketing Board and selling system similar to Ontario's; another, a Hog Merchandizing and Development Authority, naming the sales companies as agents with a compulsory check off and selling over a teletype system on a progressive bid basis; and the third, a voluntary Swine Commission.

In an effort to procure a greater degree of participation, it was decided in the fall of 1968 to have four regional semi-annual meetings instead of one. By mid-summer, the Canadian Swine Council and the meat packers agreed that the new grading was satisfactory and could be brought into operation by January, 1969.

During the summer and early autumn, while the fall fairs were in progress, barrow shows were sponsored for the younger generation of from ten to twenty years.

Early in the period following the 1968 annual meeting, discussions in both the Marketing Board and Association directorates developed the idea that greater leadership and service should be given to producers in both technical and economic fields and that the whole organizational structure should be reviewed. Among the earlier suggestions, it was proposed that an economist who would also have organizational responsibilities be added to the staff. Applications were even entertained. The final decision was to have instead a complete study made by a qualified firm of consultants. After due consideration, the firm of Hedlin and Menzies, which had conducted the research work for the Farm Income Committee mentioned earlier, was engaged to make a study of both the producer organizations and the hog industry in the province.

Late in the summer, an announcement was made of the planned study and of the registration of all hog producers as a basis of determining the varying nature of hog production units so that there might be a better idea of just what position producers were in. All producers were to be registered by February, 1969.

157

In the autumn, among the continuing flow of international visitors, was a group from Czechoslovakia, the first from beyond the "Iron Curtain". They were interested in studying the method of merchandizing being followed in the sales office.

A further endorsement of Ontario methods came with the news that, of the various methods being considered in Alberta, a survey questionnaire showed a strong majority favoured a system similar to that of Ontario. A further tie in with developments in Alberta was a visit of young Albertans to see assembly yards as well as the sales office.

As the postal strike at this time hampered all business operations in Ontario, the network of sales yards offered a means whereby cheques and settlement forms might be delivered by courier to the various marketing yards, there to be picked up by producers. During the autumn months efforts to encourage producers to register met with increasingly favourable response.

On January 1st, 1969, the long awaited new grading system, setting up the index method of expressing hog carcass quality, finally came into effect. Hogs were now to be bought on the basis of an index of one hundred with individual carcass prices scaled up or down depending upon the index established by back fat measurements.

Also in January, the Farm Income Committee, first appointed in October, 1966, and which had given a preliminary report in the summer of 1967, called another conference to present their final report.

This report was revolutionary throughout. An overall supply management programme was proposed. Supplies of some products might, from time to time, be reduced while supplies of other products might well be increased. Towards this end it was proposed that the Marketing Boards in the province be reduced to a total of seven by combining boards handling related products and that they all be brought into co-operation through the medium of a so called "Food Supply Agency" upon which each of the Boards would be represented and which would function in this field of supply management. Closely related was a proposal to establish one general farm organization which would replace both the Federation of Agriculture and the Farmer's Union. It was proposed that this General Farm Organization would:

1. Co-ordinate the activities of farmers.
2. Develop policies on farm income.
3. Advise the government on problems relating to industry and rural affairs.

The reaction of farmers and farm organizations was both mixed. Almost all the proposals, except that of one general farm organization, were soon to be forgotten in the controversy that now arose. Persons associated with the

Ontario Federation of Agriculture almost unanimously gave their support to the proposal. On the other hand, leadership in the Ontario Farmers' Union was divided. Many large scale farmers, particularly those engaged in beef cattle feeding, reacted against such an idea, perhaps fearful that their large volume of turnover would create a heavy fee responsibility to such a general organization. Then there was that always present group of farmers unable to see the advantages coming from any farm organization. Discussions between the Farmers' Union and the Federation had been going on before the release of the final report, endeavouring by negotiation to find a common basis for combining the two organizations to form one general organization, but without tangible results. The support from the Federation of Agriculture and from a section of the Farm Union leadership, however, was substantial; the Ontario Legislature passed the enabling legislation to provide the opportunity for one general farm organization to be set up and financed by levies upon all the different agricultural products. A special committee was organized to give leadership to the movement towards farm organizational unity and a date in June was set as the time for a province wide plebescite on the question.

During the period of the campaign, the Hog Producers' Association and Marketing Board gave support to this unity drive both by participation of their personnel and by financial aid. In the polling booths, the opposition of the groups mentioned above combined to turn down the idea of unity. Now the organization view across Ontario was extremely confused. In as much as the unity idea, supported by the Federation of Agriculture, was discredited, there were people who thought the Federation should itself be dissolved. Even some of the Marketing Boards whose members had given at least nominal support to the unity proposal joined in this chorus. The two hog producer groups representing more producers than any other commodity came to the fore in this hour and took a very strong stand in support of the Federation of Agriculture.

If credit should be given to any one man for turning the tide of defeat toward the emergence of a new day for the Federation of Agriculture that man was Clare Curtin, Chairman of the Ontario Hog Producers' Marketing Board. Mr. Curtin was spokesman for the single largest group of ordinary farmers who had supported the leadership of the Federation of Agriculture. At commodity group meetings and at general meetings, the stand taken by Mr. Curtin gradually turned discouragement into a realization that those who had opposed one general organization were not by any means a unified group, but had given opposition for a variety of reasons and offered no basis for providing service on general issues. Soon it was to be realized that a reorganized and revitalized Federation of Agriculture was the only current answer. The Hog Producers' organizations had not faltered in their stand behind Mr. Curtin and had told those within their group who were critical that there was no other way hog producers could avail themselves of services in the fields of tax reform, land expropriation, general research and many other problems. Farmers were waivering, as the Federation's financial position was critical. Without the clear and courageous voice of Clare Curtin, the Ontario Federation of Agriculture would almost certainly have come to an end and farmers would have been left without a general organization with strength all across the province. The rebuilding of the Federation from this point forward under the leadership of the soon to be president, Gordon Hill, is another story to be told elsewhere.

At the annual meeting of March, 1969, new strength came to both boards when Carl Clayton and Keith Weeden were elected to the Marketing Board, and Eric Alderson, Murray Aberle and Darwin Lannin were elected to the Association directorate. Mr. Weeden was already a member of the Association Board. Mr. Clayton, who was born in South Africa and had experience in the U.K., was the operator of one of the largest swine operations in Ontario. He was qualified and was able to add materially to the Board's leadership. Eric Alderson, a University trained Englishman and the manager of McLeod Farms of Aurora, came with an already long record of positive, unselfish leadership in the field of swine technology. His presence added prestige and strength. Murray Aberle and Darwin Lannin brought to the Association the views and background of the younger generation of commercial hog producers to whom the policies of the future had to be oriented.

CHAPTER XIII

BUSINESS LEADERSHIP

At the time of re-organization, Clare Curtin, as has been indicated previously, was reelected Chairman of the Board, with Blake Snobelen as Vice-Chairman. Fred Crowe remained President of the Association as did Brian Ellsworth, Vice-President. The Association, at the time of re-organization, set up three standing committees.

(1) Breeding, selection and weanling sale.
(2) Product Promotion and Supply Management.
(3) Reconstructing organization at the county level, grants and delegate compensation.

J. R. Kohler, General Manager, reached the age of retirement early in 1969 and left on February 5th of that year. After a lifelong career of selling livestock, Mr. Kohler had joined the staff of United Livestock Sales when that company took over sales for the Marketing Board in 1953. When that company was re-organized in 1954, Mr. Kohler became manager, a position he retained until the Sales Co-Operative was formed in 1955. During the years following he played an active role in developing changes in methods and perfecting the teletype system.

The Marketing Board, instead of appointing another General Manager, decided to set up three departments all directly responsible to the Board. Robert Gray, a veteran livestock salesman, who had served since the start of collective selling in 1953, became Sales Manager; Dayre Peer, in charge of office activities since 1953, became Comptroller and Treasurer in charge of office operations; and Robert Kohler became manager of the assembly yards. Later in the same year, when he reached retirement age, Mr. Gray was succeeded by James Rollings.

The report of Hedlin, Menzies and Associates was presented to the Marketing Board and Association prior to the 1969 annual meeting. We quote briefly from the Summary and Recommendations: Goals of the Ontario Hog Industry. A study such as this must be focussed clearly on certain objectives that are at the same time achievable and acceptable to Ontario Hog Producers. "We believe that the following three goals meet these tests."

(1) To have the largest possible net income for Ontario hog producers as a whole, over the year.

(2) To have the largest possible number of producers achieve a reasonable income from hog production over the years.

(3) To maintain as much decision making power with individual producers as possible, consistent with realizing the previous objectives.

The recommendations made to the Marketing Board and Association were extremely varied and covered a wide range of possibilities. It was recommended that the producers' organizations support the formation of breeding stock development groups with the backing of local county associations. It was also proposed that organized markets be developed for weanling pigs. This could be done by the proposed breeding development groups. Compliments were paid to the system of assembly yards that had been developed, but it was proposed "in transit selling" be added as an alternate to selling at the yards and that competition might be greater if actual selling were not done at all yards but rather at specific yards. Speaking further about yards, it was recommended that the Toronto Yards be moved out of the city to encourage greater price competition. A major recommendation was for greater effort in the promotion of pork sales.

In the field of supply management it was proposed that more efforts be put into forecasting of hog supply and prospective prices. Also, that efforts be made to influence sow breeding in Ontario. Furthermore, that detailed and careful study be made of the allocation of the rights to participate in the hog industry. In the organizational field the report proposed the dropping of the Association and combination of the Marketing Board and the county associations, with the Marketing Board members being elected from the county associations.

During the next year and a half, considerable thought and study was to be given to the various recommendations both by the two boards and by provincial meetings.

The year 1969 was one of significant happenings and events. At the beginning of the year changes were announced in postal rates, some to apply at

162

once and some to come into effect later. As far as the monthly periodical, *The Market Place,* was concerned, the new rates threatened an additional cost which good business practice demanded a careful study. Negotiations resulted in a business contract being signed with the *Farm and Country,* published by the farmer owned Agricultural Publishing Company. The agreement called for an insert to be known as "The Market Place" to be contained in the regular issues of the paper at least fifteen times per year and that a new publication to be known as *The Market Place Quarterly* be mailed to all registered hog producers four times a year.

When he was Secretary-Treasurer of the Association and Marketing Board in the early 1950's, George Johnson had begun sending out newsletters to all hog producers who were listed at the provincial office. This, however, had not continued on a regular basis. When Ted Marritt was Secretary in 1956, he had initiated a publication known as the *Hog Producers' Bulletin* which was continued when James Boynton became Secretary a year later. When Lucien Parizeau became public relations staff member he took over the editorial responsibility, enlarging the paper and making changes in the format. For a time after he left the Association, Mr. Parizeau continued to edit *The Market Place* on a part time basis. Later his place was taken by Rodger Schwass, as has already been mentioned. When it ceased to exist as an independent publication and direct organ of the Hog Producers', *The Market Place* had reached Volume 14, Number 3.

During 1969, much was being said about new breeding programmes and about new breeding companies endeavouring to establish themselves. Giving expression to this emphatic interest, the Canadian Swine Council organized a National Conference on the Breeding needs for the Canadian Swine Industry. This conference was convened in Winnipeg during the first week of November and was attended by all branches of the industry across Canada. Ontario producers were well represented by both pure bred breeders and by the Association and Marketing Boards.

Outside interest continued in the Ontario system of hog marketing. Bob Kohler was invited to speak at an extension service programme, sponsored by the University of Nebraska. In Canada, New Brunswick began selling hogs by a teletype system, modeled on that of Ontario. James Boynton was invited to speak at a series of meetings in Prince Edward Island. Mr. Orval Anderson, manager of the Alberta Board, visited the Ontario offices to check on methods being used. Closer at home, Quality Swine of Western Ontario began selling weanling pigs, using a modified telephone system.

In comparison to 1969, the year 1970 moved at a slower pace. Pork promotion continued at a high level with several copies of a new film "New Facts About Pork" being made available on request.

The Board proposed that the service fee be henceforth on a percentage basis rather than so much per hog. The annual meeting in March gave its consent.

At the 1970 annual meeting, former Chairman of the Marketing Board Lance Dickieson retired from the Board and was succeeded by one of Wellington County's veteran supporters of the hog marketing programme, Fred Noble. Mr. Noble, who engaged in general farming in the northern part of that County, brought to the Board considerable experience in the municipal field as well as in farm organizations. At the time of the re-organization of the Marketing Board, Blake Snobelen was elected Chairman and Sid Fraleigh, Vice-Chairman. Mr. Snobelen, in his own words, was "a graduate of the University of Hard Knocks". He had left the farm as a young man, went into the machinery business, became a successful practical engineer and developed his own manufacturing business. He then established a pure bred hog and corn business in his native county of Kent. At a time when the hog industry was about to go through one of its most severe depressions where the emphasis had to be on the sound business use of technology, the experience and business abilities of Blake Snobelen were of great value to the Marketing Board. From now on it became increasingly important that the affairs of the Board had to be conducted in accordance with sound business practices. The leadership of Mr. Snobelen in this field provided another step up the ladder of progress. Sid Fraleigh, a specialized hog farmer of Lambton County, came from a Lambton family long prominent in agricultural and public affairs. A graduate of the Ontario Agricultural College, he had already brought to the Association and the Marketing Board evidence of his ability to provide constructive and forward thinking.

When the Association was re-organized, Fred Crowe was re-elected President and Keith Weeden became Vice-President.

At the 1970 Barrow Show, cross bred entries swept all classes, showing clearly the continuing trend towards a more heavily muscled type of commercial hog.

In the 1970's a great deal has been heard about pollution. With suburban residents complaining about smells emanating from neighbouring livestock operations, it has become more important to give attention to pollution problems.

Eric Alderson, a member of the directorate of the Association and one of the representatives from Ontario, became President of the Canadian Swine Council. This marked a distinct step forward in the real assumption of national leadership for the industry. Under his leadership, the Canadian Swine Council affiliated with the Canadian Federation of Agriculture, giving a firm basis for the carrying out of policies and programmes. The name was later to be changed to Canadian Pork Council in keeping with the trend developing in Ontario and elsewhere to keep promotion of product to the fore.

In July a new programme was initiated to conduct a marketing seminar for young people interested and involved in the swine industry. All expenses were paid for several days of sessions where programmes dealing with the producer organization, and processing and merchandizing of pork products were discussed. The goal was to train and to develop leadership for the future. The county associations were asked to recruit participants.

Another step forward was the establishment of an "In transit Loss Committee" made up of representatives of producers, truckers and packers to study transportation losses and make plans to reduce them. For the first time, in the summer of 1970, American buyers purchased sows through the Marketing Board. Orders were placed in the same manner as used by small buyers whose purchasing is done over the teletype machine in the central office.

Hog population was building up in the west, pointing towards the low prices that were to prevail in 1971. In the early autumn, hog population increase in Western Canada was estimated at 45%.

The year 1970 was also significant for the increased promotion of products. Early in the year information came through of an American mobile automatic barbecue machine. In order that its value for promotional purposes might be assessed at first hand, the operator of one of these machines was invited to come to Guelph for Central Pork Producers Conference during the first week in February and to provide pork chops for lunch. By this time, an investigation had shown that the initial cost plus sales tax (provincial and federal), plus duty and currency exchange would make the cost in Ontario prohibitive. However, the idea itself was valuable. As a practical engineer and chairman of the Board, Blake Snobelen was persuaded by his colleagues to design a machine that would perform the same job. By early summer, it was ready.

The decision was to concentrate on the promotion of inch thick pork chops, a chop that would not dry out in cooking and would present a really attractive flavour. A major step in this direction was the so called "Great Pork Chop Munch" set for the first week of August at Toronto's Casa Loma. In attendance were about 150 leaders from restaurant and home economist groups, broad representation from the press, packing house executives and producer leaders. A Casa Loma chef grilled inch thick pork chops for the dinner that was served. Included on the programme were the Hon. William Stewart, Ontario Minister of Agriculture, Doug Williams, Chairman of the Ontario Food Council, and Eric Alderson, President of the Canadian Swine Council.

It was a success, because a few weeks later the new barbecue machine was installed in the Foods Building at the Canadian National Exhibition where a popular demand developed with the crowds coming faster than they could be served. At the time of the International Ploughing Match, the barbecue machine again was in operation as the centre of the producer presentation. In between the two events there had been a few occasions where the machine was also in use, particularly at the Norfolk Fair in Simcoe, Ontario. In all sixteen thousand inch thick pork chops were sold, sufficient to whet the public appetite for more. In addition, more and more county associations were conducting their own barbecues. The Perth and Lincoln local associations led the field as they built their own equipment. At the end of the year it was decided that improvements could be made in the barbecue machine and back it went to the Snobelen shop to be torn down. From the rebuilding, two machines emerged for use in the 1971 season, one to be available on a subsidized basis for use at various events across the province. Mr. Fred Wicks, a retired farmer and former Secretary of the Federation of Agriculture in York County, was engaged to take charge of the mobile barbecue machine.

Radio and television paid advertising was used in the city press in co-operation with promotion being carried out by the supermarkets to promote increased purchases of pork products.

For several years, resolutions had been presented at provincial meetings calling for a change in name that would substitute the word "pork" for that of "hog". The thought back of the proposal was that the use of the name pork would tend to promote the sale of the product. Two or three times annual meetings rejected the suggestion. At the 1970 annual meeting the question only came before the meeting after about sixty percent of the delegates had left for home. This resulted in the passage of a motion tabling the question until the next provincial meeting when the question could be presented to a full complement of delegates. This was done at the 1970 semi-annual meeting when a distinct majority endorsed the change of name. It was agreed, however, that it would be good business to use up letter heads, etcetera, bearing the old name before the change should go into effect. Thus, in May 1971, the Ontario Hog Producers' Marketing Board became the Ontario Pork Producers' Marketing Board.

CHAPTER XIV

EPILOGUE

By R. Jerry Bluhm, P. Ag.

The history of the Board and the Association in the seventies cannot be told as an "eye-witness" account in this journal. Mr. Bishop retired as a director of the Ontario Hog Producers' Marketing Board in 1961, but remained as a director of the Association until December 1970, when the functions of the Association were merged with those of the Board. In 1970-73, he again served a term as director of the Board, but attended his last meeting in this capacity on April 25th, 1972. For this reason, the story in this last chapter is a factual recording of the Board's operations, perhaps lacking somewhat in the colour and detail that these eventful years deserve.

The Seventies: Reorganization

On December 1st, 1970, the Board began operations on its reorganization basis. It was proposed that the province be divided into four areas or zones, North, South, Central and East. The North Area was to include six counties (Bruce, Grey, Huron, Perth, Waterloo and Wellington) and, during the base period, the 11,009 producers in these counties marketed 1,224,045 hogs. The Central Area included ten counties (Dufferin, Durham, Halton, Northumberland, Ontario, Peel, Peterborough, Simcoe, Victoria and York) and its 4,837 producers marketed 529,569 hogs. The South Area included twelve counties (Brant, Elgin, Essex, Haldimand, Kent, Lambton, Lincoln, Middlesex, Norfolk, Oxford, Welland and Wentworth) with 7,494 producers who marketed 909,564 hogs. The East Area with fourteen counties (Carleton, Dundas, Frontenac, Glengarry, Grenville, Hastings, Lanark, Leeds, Lennox and Addington, Prescott, Prince Edward, Renfrew, Russell and Stormont) had 1,672 producers marketing 152,118 hogs.

Representation on the Provincial Board was based on the statistics of producer numbers and hog marketings. The North Area was to elect 110 producer members to the Area Pork Producers' Council and these councilmen then elected six members to the Board. The South Area was allotted 77 councilmen and four Board members; the Central Area 48 councilmen and three Board members and the East Area, 15 councilmen and two Board members. These figures were revised subsequently according to the changes in the basic statistics but the size of the Board has remained at fifteen.

The councilmen were designated as the Council for each area and they were the only producers privileged to vote at provincial meetings. Councilmen were to be elected at annual county meetings for a three year period on a staggered basis to provide for some continuity on the Councils and on the Board. The county associations continued their operations, electing officers and county directors according to their own constitutions.

As of December 1st, 1970, the re-organization came into being. All the incumbent directors of both the Marketing Board and the Association retained their office. Provision was set out in the regulations that the directors from the North Area would hold office until March 31st, 1971; those from the East and Central until 1972; and those from the South Area until 1973. This rotation would continue on a three year basis.

The re-organized Board was faced with the responsibilities and the duties concerning all matters previously handled by both the Marketing Board and the Association. The solution which avoided the need for the Board to be in session an undue number of days per month was the formation of a number of standing committees to handle a major portion of the necessary details. In addition to its regular duties, the Executive Committee was designated as the Finance Committee and the other three standing committees were designated as: Sales and Yards, Promotion and Education. The Sales and Yards Committee, as its name indicated, was given the main responsibilities for the mechanics of marketing. The Promotion Committee was given the responsibility for the ever expanding program of promoting pork products. Finally, the area of the Education Committee was that of relations between the Board and producers, including – the "Market Place"; educational promotion in the technical field; relationships with the County Associations; and other educational studies as delegated by the Marketing Board.

From the start, the new format showed every sign of working well. Chairman of the Board, Blake Snobelen, set standards, both in parliamentary procedure and business methods, for the handling of Board business and the delegating and proper channelling of various matters through the appropriate committees.

At the time of the 1971 annual meeting, two new members joined the Marketing Board. In the North Area, James McGregor of Huron County came on the Board for the first time and gave additional representation to the younger generation of commercial hog producers. In a by-election in the South Area to fill the vacancy created by the resignation of Brian Ellsworth to take the position of Secretary-Manager of the Ontario Egg and Fowl Marketing Board, Willard Bilderback was elected. It has already been mentioned that Mr. Bilderback had moved from the U.S.A. to Canada and had already been quite active in producer activities. Bilderback had left the home farm in Indiana in 1939 and had gained a great variety of experience in the general field of engineering – in the aircraft industry and later in housing construction.

The Education Committee, early that year, embarked on an ambitious program to achieve better co-ordination between the extension work carried out by the Ontario Department of Agriculture and the technical education efforts of the County Associations. Through district workshops and co-operative programs, much progress was made, forming a firm basis for future correlation of effort in this field.

However, progress in the promotion program was hindered by the resignation of John Badger, who, for many years, had been directing this phase of the Marketing Board efforts. Mr. Badger left to accept an appointment giving him the franchise for the distribution of scientific books from Britain in the United States. He retained his other publishing interests in Toronto but could not continue his public relations functions with the Pork Producers' Marketing Board. In mid-summer of 1971, the pork promotion account was taken over by Mr. Jack Wilcox, an experienced public relations expert who brought a great flair and imagination to the position.

The Pork Insurance Program (P.I.P.)

During the greater part of 1971, the hog industry of North America was plagued with prices far below the cost of production. The average weighted price, per hundredweight, was only $25.49 – the lowest in a decade. In the late spring, the members of the three committees: Executive, Education and Promotion, all developed the idea that there would be great merit in the development of some kind of a price insurance program. Later the concept became labelled "stabilization". For some time, various aspects of such a program had been discussed by County Associations and had been the subject of resolutions at provincial meetings – for instance, a proposal to reduce the marketing weights of carcasses in times of surplus production. A proposal for the price insurance program was endorsed, in principle, at the semi-annual meeting in September.

The plan that was finally presented to the producers in the early winter of 1971-72 contained many details: the levels for deductions, the levels for payment and other conditions. Examples were given with certain carcass weights being used in the calculations. For instance, it showed an example where the deductions might be made at the rate of one percent when hogs reached a price of thirty-two dollars per cwt., and that payments might be made when prices were under twenty-six dollars; with a carcass weight of 150 lbs.

Unfortunately, many producers took the examples as rigid lines to be followed. This misunderstanding resulted in opposition to certain aspects used in the examples. At county annual meetings some producers in almost every area said they did not like this or that and therefore were opposed to the whole package. A majority of the counties gave approval to the principle but many of the larger producing counties were opposed and instructed their councilmen to cast negative votes at the 1972 annual meeting. In the provincial vote on the question, a narrow margin of six votes gave approval to the price insurance program or perhaps more correctly what might be called a price stabilization program.

The combination of a heavy volume of hog marketings in 1970 and 1971; the disastrously low prices; and a general dissatisfaction with the federal support program brought about the proposal for this insurance program. Its major objectives were summarized as:

1. To ensure producer returns at such a level that his investment has a measure of protection in times of critically low prices and thus avoid the economic loss common to the industry, e. g. entry and exit due to unstable returns.
2. To alter market supplies promptly by reducing average carcass weight during periods of over-supply and depressed prices.
3. To encourage improvement in quality by giving preference to a higher grade index.
4. To discourage the "inner" and "outer".
5. To institute a type of supply management which would not cause interference with free competition in the market place or would not prejudice our position in export markets.

Following the vote, the Marketing Board decided that there was not enough positive support for this plan and it was not implemented. However, they issued a statement proposing continued discussion with the Federal Government through the medium of the Canadian Pork Council and with other provinces to develop a stabilization program that would command popular support.

The Ontario Pork Institute

During the years that producers were striving to build up an efficient and equitable plan for marketing, there were people in all aspects of the industry who supported the concept of co-operation and liaison for a mutual exchange of ideas and solutions to their common problems. The first forum for this purpose was the Ontario Swine Improvement Council, organized in September, 1962, with Professor George Raithby, of the Ontario Agricultural College, as its first Chairman.

The main objective of this organization was to act as the medium for the exchange of information and the promotion of understanding among all its members, having the common concern of a better swine and pork industry in Ontario and to enlist the support of all in the promotion of programs beneficial to the industry. Its liaison function was perhaps the most important. An increased status for the industry was established by the Council's organization of annual Swine Conferences. These were area producer meetings, sponsored by the Council, the Pork Producers' Association, O.M.A.F., the University of Guelph, and the Colleges of Agricultural Technology at Kemptville and Ridgetown. Their programs were designed to inform producers about current problems and developments in all facets of the industry.

In June, 1969, the organization changed its name to the Ontario Pork Council, widened the scope of its constitution and broadened its membership. An even wider interest in this type of liaison led to the formation, in 1966, of the Canadian Swine Council (later the Canadian Pork Council). The prime example of the benefit derived from this industry-wide, country-wide organization was the development and final agreement on a new grading system.

In 1971, when Mr. Wilcox took over the direction of promotional efforts for the Pork Producers' Marketing Board, he established the "Ontario Pork Institute", as an agency to handle these functions. Soon it became apparent that it would be most logical to amend the constitution of the Ontario Pork Industry Council and combine its efforts with those of the Institute. This was done at the 1972 annual meeting, and a constitution was set up with three basic objectives:

1. To provide a medium of exchange among all groups having an interest in a better pork industry in Ontario.
2. To enlist the support of all groups interested in the pork industry in the development of programs beneficial to the industry.
3. To implement the market promotion program of the O.P.P.M.B.

The membership of the Ontario Pork Institute (22) consisted of representatives from eleven different groups and its manager was Mr. Wilcox, in his capacity as the supervisor of the O.P.P.M.B. promotion program. As well as its involvement in promotion, publicity and advertising, the Institute continued its role in organizing and supporting the Regional Swine Conferences, the Ontario Barrow Show and the Pork Hostess Competition.

However, after the organizational changes in the O.P.P.M.B., resulting from the recommendations of a survey carried out by Huntley Professional and Educational Services Inc., the promotional functions were taken over directly by the Board. The new set-up included a "Consumers' Communication Division" and the responsibilities for pork advertising and promotion were put under its wing. As for the Insitute's liaison function, it had fostered this aspect so successfully that the various segments of the industry now were communicating readily and regularly to deal with any matters requiring attention.

Thus the role of the Ontario Pork Institute had declined; in early 1976, it was formally disbanded; and the residual funds of the Institute were turned over to the O.P.P.M.B. to establish annual scholarships for students in the various agricultural diploma courses. Subsequently the Board supplemented the funds and provided two annual bursaries for students in the agricultural diploma courses at Ridgetown, Centralia, Guelph, Kemptville and New Liskeard.

Mr. Willard Bilderback, the Director from Middlesex County was the 1975 Chairman of the Ontario Pork Institute and his support and enthusiasm for this "final" project was reinforced by a personal financial contribution to the bursary fund.

The Seventies: New Faces

Re-organization of the Board structure brought about staff changes. Mr. Dayre Peer, who had been Comptroller and Office Manager for many years became General Manager of the Operating Division of the Board. Earlier J. R. Kohler had held such a position but after his retirement in 1969, the management function was carried out by a committee of three people: Dayre Peer, Robert Gray and R. D. Kohler (Jake's son).

Mr. Gray was succeeded as Sales Manager on his retirement in late 1969 by Jim Rollings. Bob Kohler functioned as Yards Manager until January 1973, when, after sixteen years of service to the Board and the Association in many capacities, he joined J. Wilcox and the Ontario Pork Institute. Later, after the Promotion Department of the Board was established, Bob re-joined the Board briefly to co-ordinate public relations and promotion at the county associaton level. Early in 1976, he accepted the position of Registrar for Peel County and again left the Board.

The appointment of Mr. Peer as General Manager in 1975 was the result of a recommendation by the consultant firm of Huntley Professional and

Educational Services Inc., who had been commissioned to review the entire management structure. Another major staff change occurred late in 1975 when James Boynton, Executive Secretary to the Board, accepted the challenge of revitalizing the Ontario Commodity Council and took over its management. Later in 1976 he was appointed a member of the Federal "Farm Products Marketing Council." His replacement was R. Jerry Bluhm, an O.A.C. graduate of 1942, with a long and varied career in Canadian Agribusiness.

As the business operations of the Board expanded, the accounting procedures kept pace. Settlements for the hogs marketed, which were originally processed by hand now were computerized. In 1970 a sophisticated system involving modern computer techniques was set up and until 1973 the Board utilized such facilities on a shared basis. However, in 1973 the Board bought an IBM System/360 data processing installation, established a complete computer department and hired Mr. Ken McKenzie, (who had previously programmed the operation) to manage the operation.

Frequent mention has been made about the Promotion Department of the Board. This was formally organized as the Consumer Communications Department in 1975 and Mr. John Howell was engaged to administer a comprehensive promotion program.

The 1972 Board of fifteen directors included only one new face. Howard Malcolm, a veteran of many years of service in the Durham County Association, was elected from the Central Area. Mr. Malcolm had attended the very first organizational meeting in 1941 and was a delegate to most of the provincial meetings in the intervening years.

The sixteen man Board of Directors for the Ontario Pork Producers' Marketing Board for 1972-73 was composed of:

Murray Aberle, Waterloo (N)	Peter McDonald, Oxford (S)
Eric Alderson, York (C)	George Mannerow, Grey (N)
Willard Bilderback, Middlesex (S)	Howard Malcolm, Durham (C)
Carl Clayton, Lennox & Addington (E)	Fred Noble, Wellington (N)
Clare Curtin, Victoria (C)	Blake Snobelen, Kent (S)
Sid Fraleigh, Lambton (S)	Ken Thompson, Grenville (E)
George Lupton, Perth (N)	Keith Weeden, Bruce (N)
James McGregor, Huron (N)	Wilfred Bishop (S)

Blake Snobelen continued as Chairman of the Board with Keith Weeden as Vice-Chairman. The same group of directors served as the Board for the Ontario Hog Producers' Association with Keith Weeden as President and Sid Fraleigh as Vice-President.

The Standing Committees continued to expand their activities. To better describe its function, the "Promotion and Education Committee" changed its name to the "Communications Committee" in 1974. The terms of reference for this Committee were defined as:

1. Communications between the Board and County Associations including publications.
2. County projects and approval of financial assistance on promotional work at county level.
3. Schedule of payments – county grants and delegates expenses.
4. Seminars – councilmen and directors.

The Seminars – Training sessions to familiarize new personnel on county association directorates with the fundamentals of meeting procedures, Board organization and communication techniques were a popular and effective activity of this committee during the early 1970s. Some of the participants, who got their initial training in leadership at these sessions later became directors on the Provincial Board. One of these was Mrs. Marion Myers, the first female director of any Ontario producer marketing board.

In March, 1973, Keith Weeden succeeded Blake Snobelen as Chairman of the Board, which saw directors Bishop and McDonald replaced by Warren Stein from Oxford County and Murray Clark from Kent County. Mr. Carl Clayton was Vice-Chairman of the Board, and for the Association the executive was Mr. Weeden as President and Mr. Lupton as Vice-President.

The following year, Mr. Bishop was re-elected as Chairman, and Mr. Howard Malcolm assuming the position of Vice-Chairman and Mr. Eric Alderson taking over as Vice-President of the Association. The Board remained the same except that Douglas Farrell and Adrian Vos replaced Carl Clayton and James McGregor.

In 1975, three new directors appeared: Cedric Harrop replaced Fred Noble; Clare Curtin was succeeded by Tom Smith; and Mrs. Marion Myers replaced Ken Thompson. The Chairman was Mr. Sid Fraleigh, with Mr. Howard Malcolm remaining as Vice-Chairman.

In 1976 Mr. Willard Bilderback returned to his native U.S.A. and his place on the directorate was taken by Mr. Lloyd Smit from Elgin County. The only other change was that Mr. Wally Matte from North Niagara replaced Murray Clark.

The Seventies: A Final Word

In 1941, a few Ontario hog producers had the idea that they should have an organization that could speak for them in the same fashion as the group representing the milk producers. No one had any idea what it should be called, how it should be financed, or what programs it should promote. The principle of commodity marketing boards was still relatively untried and unaccepted. Indeed, the concept of putting marketing authority in the hands of the producers was not entirely acceptable to the farmers themselves!

Many farm leaders participated in the development of the Marketing Board both through service on elected bodies and in meetings and consultations. By trial and error many services were established. There were constant struggles to gain producer acceptance and government consent for the use of Board authority. Often the efforts established precedents and made the way easier for the formation of boards for other agricultural commodities.

As is the case in many evolutionary movements, circumstances, times and places changed and the emphasis upon immediate goals changed too. The initial goals had been to establish a representative and authoritative organization which would be able to give leadership to Ontario hog producers. Then the organization had to forge the tools necessary to carry out its marketing function – country assembly yards, office facilities and accounting procedures for handling producer settlements, efficient sales techniques, active and well financed county associations, and over-all, a smoothly working marketing board.

The history of these thirty-five years is the continuing story of the growth of a dedicated movement, that has matured into a vigorous organization that is capable of facing up to problems both old and new and eager to meet all challenges with an ever sound and progressive outlook. This structure, built on the firm foundations of faith and equality with its story of constructive achievements, its history of courageous pioneering and its proven record of effectiveness now stands on the threshold of a new vista – in which it can provide further leadership to the pork producers of Ontario, to their colleagues in other provinces and indeed, to all of the farming community in Canada.

APPENDIX

Membership in Ontario Hog Producers' Organizations
1941-1976

List of the Organizations

1941 — A committee was formed on March 21st called: *Commercial Hog Producers' Committee*:

Chairman: Chas. W. McInnis, Iroquois

Members: Harry N. Scott, Norwich
R. A. Templer, Burford
A. D. Wilson, Chatham
J. C. Weaver, Owen Sound
C. B. Boynton, Gormley
Stan Joss, Belleville
Chas. Milton, Princeton
V. S. Milburn, Toronto

On April 21st, 1941, this committee was re-organized:

Chairman:	Chas. W. McInnis	
Vice-Chairman:	A. D. Wilson	
Secretary-Treasurer:	V. S. Milburn	
Members:	W. L. Bishop	A. D. Wilson
	W. W. Weber	R. A. Templer
	Harry Hewitt	Chas. Milton
	Chas. McInnis	V. S. Milburn
	C. P. McAllister	

1942 — This committee continued and in 1942 its directorate was:

Chairman:	C. W. McInnis
Vice-Chairman:	A. D. Wilson
Secretary-Treasurer:	V. S. Milburn
Field-Secretary:	W. L. Bishop

1943 — Ontario Hog Producers' Association formed.

1946 — Ontario Hog Producers' Marketing Board formed.

1955 — Ontario Hog Producers' Co-Operative Marketing Agency formed.

Ontario Hog Producers' Association

Year	President	Vice-President	Secretary
1943	C. W. McInnis	A. D. Wilson	W. L. Bishop
1944	C. W. McInnis	W. W. Weber	W. L. Bishop
1945	C. W. McInnis	Chas. Milton	W. E. Tummon
1946	C. W. McInnis	Chas. Milton	W. E. Tummon
1947	C. W. McInnis	Alva Rintoul	W. E. Tummon
1948	C. W. McInnis	Alva Rintoul	W. E. Tummon
1949	C. W. McInnis	Alva Rintoul	W. E. Tummon
1950	C. W. McInnis	Alva Rintoul	W. E. Tummon
1951	C. W. McInnis	Alva Rintoul	W. G. Johnson
1952	C. W. McInnis	Alva Rintoul	W. G. Johnson
1953	C. W. McInnis	Alva Rintoul	W. G. Johnson
1954	C. W. McInnis	Alva Rintoul	N. G. McLeod
1955	C. W. McInnis	Alva Rintoul	N. G. McLeod (1)
1956	C. W. McInnis	Alva Rintoul	E. F. Marritt
1957	C. W. McInnis	Alva Rintoul	C. J. Boynton
1958	C. W. McInnis	Clayton Frey	C. J. Boynton
1959	C. W. McInnis	Clayton Frey	C. J. Boynton
1960	C. W. McInnis	Clayton Frey	C. J. Boynton
1961	B. Steers	W. L. Bishop	C. J. Boynton
1962	B. Steers	W. L. Bishop	C. J. Boynton
1963	B. Steers	H. Huctwith	C. J. Boynton
1964	B. Steers	H. Huctwith	C. J. Boynton
1965	B. Steers	H. Huctwith	C. J. Boynton
1966	B. Steers	H. Huctwith	C. J. Boynton
1967	B. Steers	F. Crowe	C. J. Boynton
1968	F. Crowe	B. Ellsworth	C. J. Boynton
1969	F. Crowe	B. Ellsworth	C. J. Boynton
1970	F. Crowe	K. Weeden	C. J. Boynton
1971	F. Crowe	K. Weeden	C. J. Boynton
1972	K. Weeden	S. Fraleigh	C. J. Boynton
1973	K. Weeden	G. Lupton	C. J. Boynton
1974	K. Weeden	E. Alderson	C. J. Boynton
1975	K. Weeden	G. Lupton	C. J. Boynton
1976	M. Aberle	E. Alderson	R. J. Bluhm

Notes: (1) Died November 1955: Replaced by H. Arbuckle on December 2nd, 1955; by E. F. Marritt on December 30th, 1955.

Ontario Pork Producers' Marketing Board

Year	Chairman	Vice-Chairman	Secretary
1946	N. G. McLeod	Geo. Johnson	W. E. Tummon
1947	N. G. McLeod	Geo. Johnson	W. E. Tummon
1948	N. G. McLeod	Geo. Johnson	W. E. Tummon
1949	N. G. McLeod	Geo. Johnson	W. E. Tummon
1950	N. G. McLeod	Geo. Johnson	W. E. Tummon
1951	N. G. McLeod	F. C. Newton	W. G. Johnson
1952	N. G. McLeod	F. C. Newton	W. G. Johnson
1953	N. G. McLeod	F. C. Newton	W. G. Johnson
1954	E. Aiken	F. C. Newton	N. G. McLeod
1955	E. Aiken	F. C. Newton	N. G. McLeod
1956	E. Aiken	C. Frey	E. F. Marritt
1957	E. Aiken	C. Frey	C. J. Boynton
1958	E. Aiken	C. Frey	C. J. Boynton
1959	E. Aiken	C. Frey	C. J. Boynton
1960	E. Aiken	W. L. Bishop	C. J. Boynton
1961	E. Aiken	B. Steers	C. J. Boynton
1962	E. Aiken	L. Dickieson	C. J. Boynton
1963	L. Dickieson	C. V. Curtin	C. J. Boynton
1964	L. Dickieson	C. V. Curtin	C. J. Boynton
1965	L. Dickieson	C. V. Curtin	C. J. Boynton
1966	L. Dickieson	C. V. Curtin	C. J. Boynton
1967	C. V. Curtin	B. Snobelen	C. J. Boynton
1968	C. V. Curtin	B. Snobelen	C. J. Boynton
1969	C. V. Curtin	B. Snobelen	C. J. Boynton
1970	B. Snobelen	S. Fraleigh	C. J. Boynton
1971	B. Snobelen	K. Weeden	C. J. Boynton
1972	K. Weeden	C. Clayton	C. J. Boynton
1973	K. Weeden	C. Clayton	C. J. Boynton
1974	K. Weeden	H. Malcolm	C. J. Boynton
1975	S. Fraleigh	H. Malcolm	C. J. Boynton
1976	S. Fraleigh	H. Malcolm	R. J. Bluhm

Note: In 1946, Chas. Milton was Treasurer; from 1947 on, the offices of Secretary and Treasurer were combined.

Ontario Hog Producers' Co-Operative Marketing Agency

Year	President	Vice-President	General Manager
1955	C. W. McInnis	E. Aiken	J. R. Kohler
1956	C. W. McInnis	E. Aiken	J. R. Kohler
1957	C. W. McInnis	A. Rintoul	J. R. Kohler
1958	C. W. McInnis	A. Rintoul	J. R. Kohler
1959	C. W. McInnis	A. Rintoul	J. R. Kohler
1960	C. W. McInnis	L. Dickieson	J. R. Kohler
1961	C. W. McInnis	C. Curtin	J. R. Kohler

Notes: (1) J. R. Kohler was General-Manager and Treasurer.

(2) Secretary: 1955 — N. G. McLeod
                 1955 — H. Arbuckle
                 1955-57 — E. F. Marritt
                 1957-61 — C. J. Boynton

(3) Co-operative merged with Board, December 2nd, 1961, but retained its own Board of Directors until 1964; Executive was same as that of the Association.

Directors of the Ontario Hog Producers' Association

Name		Years Served
Aberle, Murray	Elmira	1969 — 1976 *
Aiken, Eldred	Allenford	1951 — 1967
Alderson, Eric	Aurora	1969 — 1976 *
Barnett, John	St. Marys	1961
Becker, Melvin	Ayr	1955 — 1960
Bilderback, Willard	Putnam	1972 — 1975
Bishop, Wilfred	Norwich	1943 — 1971
Carroll, Eugene	Dunrobin	1968 — 1971
Clark, Murray	Thamesville	1973 — 1975
Clayton, Carl	Napanee	1970 — 1973
Crone, Fred	Warsaw	1962 — 1971
Curtin, Clare	Lindsay	1958 — 1974
Dickieson, Lance	Ariss	1955 — 1968
Ellsworth, Brian	Ridgeway	1965 — 1971

Directors of the Ontario Hog Producers' Association

Name		*Years Served*
Farrell, Douglas	Roslin	1974 — 1976 *
Fraleigh, Sid	Forest	1967 — 1976 *
Frey, Clayton	Sarnia	1945 — 1960
Geisel, Clayton	Elmira	1967 — 1968
Harrop, Cedric	Guelph	1975 — 1976 *
Huctwith, Howard	Forest	1961 — 1966
Johnson, George	Owen Sound	1945 — 1951
Lannin, Darwin	Mitchell	1969 — 1971
Lupton, George	Stratford	1970 — 1976*
Magwood, Wesley	Hanover	1955 — 1960
Malcolm, Howard	Janetville	1972 — 1976*
Mannerow, George	Chesley	1962 — 1976*
Matte, Wally	St. Ann's	1976 *
Milligan, Chas. A.	Halloway	1955 — 1958
Milton, Charles	Princeton	1943 — 1946
MacDonald, J. L.		1943 — 1944
McCague, Heber	Gormley	1946 — 1947
McDonald, Peter	Bright	1970 — 1972
McGregor, James	Kippen	1972 — 1973
McInnis, Charles	Iroquois	1943 — 1960
McLeod, Norman	Galt	1945 — 1955
Myers, Marion	Dalkeith	1975 — 1976*
Newton, Charles	Barrie	1948 — 1955
Noble, Fred	Palmerston	1972 — 1974
Pollock, George	Berwick	1947 — 1948
Pringle, Thomas	Shallow Lake	1961 — 1962
Rintoul, Alva	Carlton Place	1945 — 1960
Robson, Thomas	Denfield	1945

Directors of the Ontario Hog Producers' Association

Name		Years Served
Scott, R. J.		1943 — 1944
Sills, Roy	Halloway	1959 — 1961
Smith, Tom	Utopia	1975 — 1976*
Smit, Lloyd	St. Thomas	1976 *
Snobelen, Blake	Thamesville	1970 — 1972
Steers, Ben	Bradford	1956 — 1968
Stein, Warren	Woodstock	1973 — 1976*
Stobbs, Cecil	Leamington	1945
Thompson, Kenneth	Kemptville	1961 — 1967, 1972
Tummon, W. E.	Foxboro	1944 — 1957
Vos, Adrian	Blyth	1974 — 1976*
Warner, Alfred	Bayfield	1962 — 1966
Weber, Wellington W.		1943 — 1944
Weeden, Keith	Paisley	1968 — 1976*
Wilkinson, George	Alliston	1943 — 1945
Wilson, A. D.	Chatham	1943
Young, Mac	Thamesford	1961 — 1964

*Still in office in 1976

Directors of the Ontario Pork Producers' Marketing Board

Name		Years Served
Aberle, Murray	Elmira	1971 — 1976*
Aiken, Eldred	Allenford	1951 — 1968
Alderson, Eric	Aurora	1971 — 1976*
Barnett, John	St. Marys	1961 — 1963
Becker, Melvin	Ayr	1955 — 1960
Bilderback, Willard	Putnam	1971 — 1975
Bishop, Wilfred	Norwich	1945 — 1960, 1971
Broughton, Thomas	Oakville	1967 — 1971
Carroll, Eugene	Dunrobin	1971
Clark, Murray	Thamesville	1973 — 1975
Clayton, Carl	Napanee	1969 — 1973
Conlin, Joseph	Clandeboye	1964 — 1967
Crocker, Emerson	Aylmer	1961 — 1963
Crowe, Fred	Warsaw	1961 — 1964, 1971
Curtin, Clare	Lindsay	1958 — 1974
Dickieson, Lance	Ariss	1955 — 1969
Elliott, Milton	Tweed	1965 — 1968
Ellsworth, Brian	Ridgeway	1965 — 1970
Farrell, Douglas	Roslin	1974 — 1976*
Fraleigh, Sid	Forest	1968 — 1976*
Frey, Clayton	Sarnia	1945 — 1960
Geisel, Clayton	Elmira	1965 — 1970
Harrop, Cedric	Guelph	1975 — 1976*
Huctwith, Howard	Forest	1964 — 1966
Johnson, George	Owen Sound	1945 — 1951
Kaufman, Vernon	Woodstock	1961 — 1963
Lupton, George	Stratford	1963 — 1976*
Magwood, Wesley	Hanover	1955 — 1960
Malcolm, Howard	Janetville	1972 — 1976*
Mannerow, George	Chesley	1962 — 1976*

182

Directors of the Ontario Pork Producers'
Marketing Board

Name		*Years Served*
Matte, Wally	St. Ann's	1976 *
Milligan, Chas. A.	Halloway	1955 — 1958
Milton, Charles	Princeton	1946
McCague, Heber	Gormley	1946 — 1947
McDonald, Peter	Bright	1964 — 1972
McGregor, James	Kippen	1971 — 1973
McInnis, Charles	Iroquois	1955 — 1960
McTavish, Ross	Shakespeare	1961 — 1962
McLeod, Norman	Galt	1945 — 1955
Myers, Marion	Dalkeith	1975 — 1976*
Newton, Charles	Barrie	1948 — 1955
Noble, Fred	Palmerston	1970 — 1974
Pollock, George	Berwick	1947 — 1948
Pringle, Thomas	Shallow Lake	1961 — 1962
Rintoul, Alva	Carleton Place	1945 — 1946
		1949 — 1960
Robson, Thomas	Denfield	1945
Schweitzer, Gordon	Petersburg	1961 — 1964
Sills, Roy	Halloway	1959 — 1960
Smit, Lloyd	St. Thomas	1976 *
Smith, Thomas	Utopia	1975 — 1976*
Snobelen, Blake	Thamesville	1961 — 1972
Steers, Ben	Bradford	1956 — 1967
Stein, Warren	Woodstock	1973 — 1976*
Stobbs, Cecil	Leamington	1945
Thompson, Kenneth	Kemptville	1961 — 1964
		1968 — 1974
Tummon, W. E.	Foxboro	1945 — 1957
Vos, Adrian	Blyth	1974 — 1976*
Warner, Alfred	Bayfield	1961 — 1964
		1968 — 1970
Weeden, Keith	Paisley	1969 — 1976
Wilkinson, George	Alliston	1945
Willow, Glen	Toledo	1965 — 1967

Directors of the Ontario Hog Producers'
Co-Operative Marketing Agency

Name		*Years Served*
Aiken, Eldred	Allenford	1955 — 1964
Barnett, John	St. Marys	1961
Becker, Melvin	Ayr	1955 — 1960
Bishop, Wilfred	Norwich	1955 — 1960
Crocker, Emerson	Aylmer	1962, 1964
Crowe, Fred	Warsaw	1962 — 1964
Curtin, Clare	Lindsay	1958 — 1964
Dickieson, Lance	Ariss	1955 — 1964
Enos, Erford	Ancaster	1961 — 1964
Frey, Clayton	Sarnia	1955 — 1960
Huctwith, Howard	Forest	1961, 1963
Magwood, Wesley	Hanover	1955 — 1960
Mannerow, George	Chesley	1962 — 1964
McInnis, Charles	Iroquois	1955 — 1960
McLeod, Norman	Galt	1955
Milligan, Charles A.	Halloway	1955 — 1958
Newton, Charles	Barrie	1955
Pringle, Thomas	Shallow Lake	1961 — 1962
Rintoul, Alva	Carleton Place	1955 — 1960
Sills, Roy	Halloway	1959 — 1961
Steers, Ben	Bradford	1956 — 1964
Thompson, Kenneth	Kemptville	1961 — 1964
Tummon, W. E.	Foxboro	1955 — 1957
Warner, Alfred	Bayfield	1962 — 1964
Young, Mac	Thamesford	1961 — 1964